RPA Solution Architect's Han

Design modern and custom RPA solutions for digital innovation

Sachin Sahgal

BIRMINGHAM—MUMBAI

RPA Solution Architect's Handbook

Group Product Manager: Alok Dhuri

Senior Editor: Kinnari Chohan

Technical Editor: Maran Fernandes

Copy Editor: Safis Editing

Project Coordinator: Manisha Singh

Proofreader: Safis Editing

Indexer: Manju Arasan

Production Designer: Shyam Sundar Korumilli

Development Relations Marketing Executives: Deepak Kumar and Mayank Singh

Business Development Executive: Puneet Kaur

First published: June 2023

Production reference: 1300523

Published by Packt Publishing Ltd.
Livery Place
35 Livery Street
Birmingham
B3 2PB, UK.

ISBN 978-1-80324-960-5

www.packtpub.com

To my dear father, Mr. Satish:

Your unwavering support, belief in my abilities, and encouragement have driven my pursuit of knowledge and passion for technology. This book is a tribute to your love and guidance.

To my beloved mother, Mrs. Uma:

Your boundless love, nurturing spirit, and unwavering faith in me have shaped who I am. This book is dedicated to you, in gratitude for your sacrifices and belief in my dreams.

To my loving wife, Monica:

Your support, understanding, and belief in my dreams have anchored my journey. This book is dedicated to you, my partner and inspiration.

To my cherished child, Shivali:

You are the light of my life. This book is dedicated to you, as a reminder of the importance of education, exploration, and embracing passion.

With heartfelt gratitude,

Sachin

Contributors

About the author

Sachin Sahgal is a visionary Solution Architect and esteemed Director of Intelligent Automation with over 20 years of invaluable experience in the dynamic IT industry. His expertise lies in leveraging cutting-edge technologies to optimize business processes and drive organizations towards unparalleled success. Sachin has mastered the art of Business Process Analysis, Business Process Automation (BPA), Robotics Process Automation (RPA), and Intelligent Process Automation (IPA). As a preeminent Solution Architect, he plays a pivotal role in pre-sales consultations, showcasing his uncanny ability to assemble compelling proof of concepts (POCs), address client requests for proposals (RFPs), and deliver captivating technical demos that highlight the immense potential of his solutions. Sachin has forged a formidable reputation as a trailblazer in RPA, with a track record of successful COE setups and RPA solution deliveries on platforms like Blue Prism, UIPath, and WorkFusion. His involvement in global RFPs for automation and cognitive solutions, coupled with his expertise in process review, proposal creation, ROI realization, and implementation planning, reflects his unwavering dedication to excellence. Specializing in industry-leading technologies and RPA tools, such as Blue Prism, UIPath, OpenSpan, Automate BPA, WorkFusion, NICE RPA, Machine Learning, and Deep Learning, Sachin stays at the forefront of technological advancements. His commitment to staying ahead of the curve ensures the continuous delivery of groundbreaking solutions that drive innovation and catalyze success.

I would like to express my heartfelt gratitude to my parents, wife, and child for their unwavering support and trust in me throughout the writing of this book, making my dream come true.

About the reviewers

Narendra Upadhya is a Techno Functional expert and Automation Evangelist with 20+ years of experience in Retail Banking, Digital Transformation, and Intelligent Automation. He possesses rich domain proficiency in Retail Bank operations, including Assets and Liability, Deposits, Payments, Mortgage loans, and Compliance. Narendra is a CBAP® certified Business Analyst Professional and excels in identifying Intelligent Automation use cases, ROI analysis, and providing roadmap for organizations to embark on their Automation Journey and establish Automation Centre of Excellence. Additionally, he holds certifications in 'AMFI - Association of Mutual Funds in India' and 'JAIIB - Junior Associate of Indian Institute of Bankers'. Narendra's unique blend of Retail Banking domain expertise and IT knowledge has enabled him to successfully identify and implement Automation solutions (RPA, AI/ML) for various banking organizations. He has also contributed to solving industry-wide challenges in the Wealth Management domain, particularly in Compliance areas such as AML alerts and Fraud detection, through the implementation of Automation solutions (AI/ML). Narendra is a CSM® certified ScrumMaster® and has extensive experience in Agile and Waterfall project management methodologies. He has led and executed multiple Automation projects, helping clients achieve significant ROI. With his vast experience, Narendra is passionate about guiding and mentoring the next generation of talent, assisting them in exploring the realm of possibilities and achieving their career goals. Outside of work, Narendra enjoys Indian Classical Music and plays the Tabla, an Indian percussion instrument. He resides in Charlotte, NC, USA, with his wife and two lovely daughters.

Luca Valente is a trusted advisor specializing in Intelligent Process Automation, with a strong commitment to assisting organizations in shaping and executing their automation vision and strategy. With a remarkable career spanning over 30 years in information technology, Luca has gained extensive international experience across Europe and North America. Renowned for his strategic mindset, technical expertise, and unwavering passion for innovation, he excels in revolutionizing work methodologies by harnessing the power of technology advancements. Luca is deeply dedicated to driving positive change through technology-driven solutions and fostering seamless collaboration between human and digital workforces.

Table of Contents

3

Part 2: Being Techno/Functional

4

5

6

Need for Documentation and Working with SIT/UAT Scripts   87

7

RPA Development Phases   99

8

Customer Obsession in the RPA Journey   119

Part 3: Tool Agnostic Approach

9

10

11

12

RPA as a Service (RPAaaS)   171

13

Finding the Best Solution   183

Part 4: Best Practices

14

Design Best Practices   197

15

Data, Security, and Logs   215

16

Key Performance Indicators (KPIs)   231

17

Reporting, Analytics, Efficiency, and Efficacy   245

Preface

Welcome to this comprehensive guide on becoming an RPA Solution Architect!

In this book, we will provide you with step-by-step explanations of essential concepts and the skills required to excel in this role. Through practical implementation and easy-to-understand examples, we will take you on a journey of designing, defining, and executing RPA processes, covering key considerations, techniques, and strategies based on real-life scenarios.

RPA Solution Architects hold a crucial position in the automation journey and initiatives within organizations. They bear multiple responsibilities, ensuring that RPA implementations and solutions effectively fulfill the purpose of automation when deployed in production environments. If you are seeking a playbook to architect well-designed and scalable RPA systems, then this book is tailor-made for you.

To start, we will explore the different roles, responsibilities, and interactions between cross-functional teams involved in RPA projects. You will gain a solid understanding of the pillars of good design, including stability, maintainability, scalability, and resilience. We will guide you in developing crucial documents such as process design documents, solution design documents, SIT/UAT scripts, and wireframes.

Throughout the book, we will emphasize the importance of designing reusable components to achieve faster, more cost-effective, and improved RPA implementations. You will learn the best practices for module decoupling, handling garbage collection, and managing exceptions. Furthermore, we will delve into topics such as privacy, security, reporting automated processes, analytics, and proactive measures for maintaining healthy bots.

By the time you reach the end of this book, you will have gained the confidence to apply the skills and traits discussed within these pages, empowering you to advance your career as an accomplished RPA Solution Architect. Whether you are just starting out or are looking to enhance your existing expertise, this book will serve as your invaluable companion throughout your journey.

So let's dive in and unlock the secrets of becoming an exceptional RPA Solution Architect!

Who this book is for

Whether you are an RPA Developer, RPA Sr. Developer, RPA Analyst, or an RPA Solution Architect looking to excel in your field, this book has been crafted with you in mind. It is designed to cater to a diverse range of professionals who are either aspiring to become an RPA Solution Architect or have recently embraced this role and seek to enhance their expertise.

While basic familiarity with RPA documentation such as SDD and PDD, as well as hands-on experience with one or more RPA tools, can be advantageous, they are not mandatory prerequisites. This book aims to provide valuable insights and practical knowledge to all readers, regardless of their existing level of familiarity with RPA concepts.

What this book covers

Chapter 1, Why Do We Need a Solution Architect? introduces the reader to the role of SA.

Chapter 2, A Case Study of a Bank Client, is a case study of a fictitious Banking client which will be referenced throughout the book. It'll help you to put things into context. In this chapter, we will learn about the scope, how to perform opportunity assessment, define the team structure, RACI, and learn how to do the T-shirt sizing of the projects.

Chapter 3, Extracurricular Activities, discusses the other responsibilities and activities in which SA gets involved and are not related directly to the role.

Chapter 4, Studying the Lay of the Land, talks about the interaction and communication between Solution Architect and the other cross-functional teams.

Chapter 5, Designing Framework for Consistency and Resiliency, will present the concept of design and develop the framework for the client based on the information knowledge gathered in the previous chapters.

Chapter 6, Need for Documentation and Working with SIT/UAT Scripts, talks about the need for documentation, how to develop PDD, SDD, project plan, non-functional requirements, and SIT/UAT scripts.

Chapter 7, Development Phases in RPA, is about the development phases, how-to guide the team, manage the team, how to do a POC, how to design a wireframe, code review, and integration testing.

Chapter 8, Customer Obsession in RPA Journey, talks about the customer-centric approach and how to keep the customer engaged throughout the lifecycle of RPA implementation.

Chapter 9, Hyperautomation:What is the Future of RPA? discusses hyper automation and how to design it.

Chapter 10, How to Make Automation Intelligent? is about intelligent automation, use cases, and teaches how IA helps in increasing the footprint of RPA.

Chapter 11, Reusable Components, talks about the concept of reusable components, how to design them, and how they help in faster, cheaper, and better RPA implementation.

Chapter 12, RPA as a Service (RPAaaS), discusses RPAaaS, its use cases, and its architecture.

Chapter 13, Finding the Best Solution, teaches how to find the best solution from a list of viable solutions.

Chapter 14, Design Best Practices, talks about the best practices which are tried and tested by the author and can prove to be helpful to you as well in a real-life scenario.

Chapter 15, Data, Security, and Logs, is about data privacy, data security, process, and environment security, and logs. It shows how to manage the data requirements, its security, and non-functional requirements related to data and security.

Chapter 16, *Key Performance Indicators*, discusses the key performance indicators and the metrics around RPA implementations.

Chapter 17, *Reporting, Analytics, Efficiency, and Efficacy*, talks about the need for reporting and analytics for RPA implementations. We will also discuss the health of the bots, and how we can monitor and take proactive and preventive actions to keep the bots healthy and make them resilient.

To get the most out of this book

As you embark on this transformative journey through the pages of this book, it is paramount to approach it with an open mind and an insatiable thirst for knowledge. To fully leverage its potential, I encourage you to actively engage with the content, immersing yourself in the presented concepts. Take the time to grasp the foundational principles of RPA and familiarize yourself with the key components of solution architecture. Embrace the real-world examples and case studies provided, as they hold invaluable insights and practical applications. Furthermore, I urge you to venture beyond these pages. Delve into the vast resources available online, connect with RPA communities, and actively participate in discussions. Remember, achieving proficiency as an RPA solution architect necessitates ongoing learning and adaptability in the face of an ever-evolving landscape. So, grab a pen, make notes, and relish this enlightening journey through the captivating realm of RPA solution architecture.

Download the color images

We also provide a PDF file that has color images of the screenshots and diagrams used in this book. You can download it here: `https://packt.link/MhYQY`.

Conventions used

There are a number of text conventions used throughout this book.

Bold: Indicates a new term, an important word, or words that you see onscreen. For instance, words in menus or dialog boxes appear in **bold**. Here is an example: "Select **System info** from the **Administration** panel."

> **Tips or important notes**
> Appear like this.

Get in touch

Feedback from our readers is always welcome.

General feedback: If you have questions about any aspect of this book, email us at customercare@packtpub.com and mention the book title in the subject of your message.

Errata: Although we have taken every care to ensure the accuracy of our content, mistakes do happen. If you have found a mistake in this book, we would be grateful if you would report this to us. Please visit www.packtpub.com/support/errata and fill in the form.

Piracy: If you come across any illegal copies of our works in any form on the internet, we would be grateful if you would provide us with the location address or website name. Please contact us at copyright@packt.com with a link to the material.

If you are interested in becoming an author: If there is a topic that you have expertise in and you are interested in either writing or contributing to a book, please visit authors.packtpub.com.

Share Your Thoughts

Once you've read *RPA Solution Architect's Handbook*, we'd love to hear your thoughts! Scan the QR code below to go straight to the Amazon review page for this book and share your feedback.

https://packt.link/r/1803249609

Your review is important to us and the tech community and will help us make sure we're delivering excellent quality content.

Download a free PDF copy of this book

Thanks for purchasing this book!

Do you like to read on the go but are unable to carry your print books everywhere? Is your eBook purchase not compatible with the device of your choice?

Don't worry, now with every Packt book you get a DRM-free PDF version of that book at no cost.

Read anywhere, any place, on any device. Search, copy, and paste code from your favorite technical books directly into your application.

The perks don't stop there, you can get exclusive access to discounts, newsletters, and great free content in your inbox daily

Follow these simple steps to get the benefits:

1. Scan the QR code or visit the link below

https://packt.link/free-ebook/9781803249605

2. Submit your proof of purchase

3. That's it! We'll send your free PDF and other benefits to your email directly

Part 1:
Role of a Solution Architect

In this part of the book, we will enlighten you on the significance of a Solution Architect (SA) and unveil the coveted trade secrets that make them a highly sought-after asset. Prepare to delve into the following chapters:

1

Why Do We Need a Solution Architect?

In the modern age of industrialization, every industry is divided into segments, sectors, and **lines of business** (**LOBs**). Each of these divisions is then subdivided into roles. These roles are assigned responsibilities that become the core functions of that role. The IT industry is no different. It is also divided into LOBs, and those LOBs have functions and roles assigned to them. One of the roles is of a **solution architect** (**SA**). This is a generic role with subcategories such as enterprise SA or SA for a software tool or application.

It is very important to understand why an SA is needed in a project. This will help in establishing the credibility of the role as well as understanding the value this role brings to the table. An SA is like the glue that keeps the team together and brings integrity to the team. People debate whether they need an SA or not, and this chapter will focus on resolving all those doubts. You can be an aspiring developer who wants to become an SA or a project manager putting together a team for a project— all can benefit from the knowledge of why an SA is important and how their contribution leads to successful project delivery.

The agenda of this chapter will cover the following main topics:

- Understanding the importance of the SA role
- Bridging the gap
- Being a guardian angel, influencer, and enforcer
- SAs as solution owners
- SAs and the multiple hats they wear

So, let's dive right in!

Understanding the importance of the SA role

Robotic process automation (**RPA**) is also nowadays one of the mainstream functions of IT. So, as with other IT functions, RPA also has to have an SA as a role. But the question arises: *Do we need an SA?* This question has a straightforward answer, and that is: *Yes!* What are the valid reasons for having an SA as a role? How would we justify this role? To answer this question, we need to understand the responsibilities of an SA.

An SA is a person who is a problem solver and specializes in identifying processes that are good candidates for RPA. This person knows the ins and outs of the underlying technology, its strengths and weaknesses, and how to overcome them. An SA for RPA has extensive knowledge about the core function and automation and is a master in finding solutions, be they technical or non-technical. They understand the other IT functions and how to amalgamate them to find a viable solution for a problem. An SA is known as *a jack of all trades and a master of solution design*. They can be a master of other traits, such as programming, networking, infrastructure, and so on.

Having an SA on your team will give you the peace of mind to find the *best* solution and not the *easiest* solution for the problem. A good SA will approach a problem with integrity, customer focus, and frugality. They also possess some ethical and moral responsibilities. Knowing that your SA will do what is best for the processes, people, and company makes this role invaluable. An SA is also responsible for evaluating the potential of an RPA project, its limitations, and its efficacy. If something can be automated, that doesn't mean it should be. Based on this principle, an SA can weed out processes that seem to be a good fit but are not a good fit.

For example, let's assume you have a team working on an RPA project. There is no SA available, and the responsibility to find the best solution and technology is the responsibility of the developers. As developers are also tasked to deliver the code on time, they tend to get biased in selecting a solution that is easy and fast to develop. An easy solution is not always the best solution and is prone to introducing future issues. To avoid this, the responsibility of selecting the technology and the best solution should be decoupled and should be given to an SA. They also bring along thought leadership, which is needed to bring people, processes, and technology together.

An SA will do regress research and will try to find the best solution. They will evaluate the solutions based on future scalability, manageability, and maintainability. A proper evaluation should be done as to whether an SA is required or not based on the team's capability and experience in design, development, and delivery. However, note that an SA can be a costly affair. Their cost can add to the budget, but not having an SA engaged in the initial stage can be costly in the long run. You need a person who can challenge the status quo. They question the team and provide guidance with respect to design principles and development standards, and can avoid cutting corners. In relation to what we discussed about the importance of the SA role, let us now look into the various ways in which an SA can bridge the gap and how they are able to help the team and project to succeed.

Bridging the gap

Now that we have established the importance of having an SA in your team, let's talk about one of the most important functions an SA plays in the life cycle of an RPA journey—bridging the gap.

You might be thinking, what does *bridging the gap* mean? The phrase is self-explanatory, but to give it some context, we will use a scenario as an example.

Let's say you are an SA and have been invited onto an introductory call by the client. The client has their **subject-matter expert** (**SME**) walk you through the current process, for which they want you to develop a solution. After listening to the SME for 15-20 minutes, you realize that there will be a need for a mechanism to read the PDF files used in the process as they are scanned images' PDFs. Currently, as humans are doing the process manually, they don't feel the need for any other technology other than just looking at the PDF and extracting the information.

In this scenario, there is a gap that you have identified, and you might have already started thinking about how to approach this problem. In your mind, you know that you will need **optical character recognition** (**OCR**) to solve the problem. You were about to spill the beans when you were interrupted by the **vice president** (**VP**) of IT. He said, *Just so you know, we try to solve a problem not tactically, but more strategically.* What he meant was for you to think of a solution that is not only used for RPA but something that can also be used as an enterprise-wide solution such as OCR, which can be leveraged in other applications and solutions as well. It can also become a service that can be called in future automation as well.

After you understood what the VP meant, you realized that the *gap* has increased, and you now have to come out of the RPA box and think like an integrator who will *bridge the gap*. In this scenario, you have the job of not only coming up with a viable solution but also bringing all the necessary teams together to turn that viable concept into a real functional solution implemented in production. This is what is not written in the job description, and neither will anyone tell you that it is your responsibility. But it is assumed that you already know what needs to be done as you are the SA.

Though it seems and looks like it is fairly simple, the task has multiple action items. You need to design the solution and do a **proof of concept** (**POC**). Then, you need to identify all the processes, people, and technology you will need to make this solution a reality. After your POC is approved, you will have to identify all those teams that are needed for this mini-project of yours.

This brings us to a very important point, and that is: **an SA should possess knowledge of not only programming and technology but also networks, security, infrastructure, and industry standards**. Having this knowledge will help you define the infrastructure needed for the solutions—for example, *What kind of security should be in place? What kind of infrastructure is needed?*; so on and so forth.

That is why I can't emphasize enough that an SA should be a jack of all trades. An SA should be up to date with the current technologies and should have enough knowledge to have a serious discussion with the other teams so that they can understand the requirements and recommend the right course of action. It also helps to know the client technology stack so that you can easily and efficiently design the solution based on what is already available in-house rather than go on a shopping spree.

Frugality should be one of the strongest traits of an SA. You, as an SA, are hired to do the job using the tools and technologies available. Anyone can google and say that *XYZ vendor* has a product that we are looking for and that we can go and buy off the shelf. Well, that costs a lot of money, and everyone knows that there is always a readily available product on the market. But you are hired so that they don't have to invest in something new and still end up owning it. So, always try to find a solution that is economical. It's not that SAs don't use or suggest self-solutions, but that is only when there is a dire need for it for a faster **go-to-market** (**GTM**) strategy and budget is not a constraint. We will talk about this in detail in the *Design principles* section of *Chapter 5, Designing a Framework for Consistency and Resiliency*.

Being a guardian angel, influencer, and enforcer

When it comes to the responsibilities of a project or program, a project manager comes to mind. Similarly, when we are working on a project that has a lot of unknowns and we need someone we can trust, then an SA comes to mind. RPA SAs are no different. They are just like a new flavor of the same brand of candy that you like and have been eating and loving your entire life. Now that we have established how important the role of an SA is for any project, and in this book's context for RPA projects, let's also understand the few hidden talents that SAs should possess to increase their role's efficacy.

As we progress in the RPA project, we kind of realize that two specific roles have the responsibility and are held accountable for the successful delivery of the project. The first is the project manager and the second is the SA. The former takes care of all the logistics and runs the project as per time and budget. The latter is responsible for designing and implementing a robust solution. For a robust design, an SA should act as an *influencer* and an *enforcer*.

To understand this better, let me present you with a scenario. An existing client approached you and asked for a meeting. In the meeting, he showed his interest in RPA and requested you do an introductory presentation to the CEO and CIO of the company. While you were walking them through the presentation and explaining how RPA works, you were asked a question by the CTO: *Tell me how you will help us in the RPA tool selection*. This is where you become an *influencer*. Your role is now to help the client, who has little knowledge about the different tools in the market and doesn't know which criteria should be used for a tool selection. Being an influencer is using your knowledge and experience in different RPA tools to help the client reach a decision. Your input, suggestions, and recommendations are what the client is looking for, and that is how an SA becomes an influencer. The moral of this scenario is that **an SA should at least be an expert in two or more RPA tools**.

Now that, based on your recommendation, the tool of choice has been selected and implemented, your role switches to that of an *enforcer*. Let's try to understand the enforcer part through another scenario. When working on an RPA project, an SA works with many different teams. Among all these, the development team is the most important one that will help your dream come true. The SA, being the guide, has the responsibility to explain to the developers what needs to be done and how to approach a problem. The SA's strategy should be to teach developers how to approach a problem and not to provide a readymade solution. If you give a man a fish, you feed him for a day. If you teach a man to fish, you feed him for a lifetime. This is why we need an enforcer who can put a guide rail of standards, processes, and procedures to the developers so that only the approved solution gets developed and deployed. The enforcer makes sure that the guidelines are met and followed.

This brings a question to mind as to why an SA has to do that. Well, for the simple reason that an SA is designated to find the best solution and not the easiest solution. The SA needs to keep in mind **scalability, maintainability, sustainability, and usability**. To keep the development in check and maintain consistency and quality, the SA becomes an enforcer of rules, best practices, and coding standards. These standards come from various sources—some are from the client, some are from RPA vendors, and some are from their own experience.

While developers are well equipped to manage any trick situation, sometimes they get tangled in office politics. This is when an SA has to switch to their *guardian angel* hat and come to the rescue. The development team does not always report to the SA, but they are still responsible for their actions in the project. As SA is held responsible—they also have to defend the team when needed. This is not always practiced but is a good way to build trust in the team and helps keep its morale up. A healthy team can work miracles. Keeping this in mind as a mantra, every SA should be ready to speak on their team's behalf. SAs are more senior than developers and have more industry experience. That helps them to articulate things better and present them in a simplified manner. This also helps to prevent a crisis.

That being said, SAs are not called guardian angels just for defending the developers but also are of great help if the team is short of hands or needs an extra set of eyes to review the code and provide suggestions. This is when the code is broken, and no one has any clue why it is not working. The SA, as stated earlier, has knowledge of not only development but also other functions of IT, and they can easily decouple themselves from the problem and step back and try to gauze it holistically. This helps them to identify issues that others might have not even thought of. Also of note is the fact that they have seen so many similar issues and problems in their life that they can quite easily put their finger on the real issue.

When it comes to being a guardian angel, influencer, or enforcer, the SA has to be completely involved in the day-to-day activities of any given project. There are many scenarios where you as SA might have to work in parallel on multiple projects, and when you are stretched thin, you can't be any of the three. So, keep yourself up to date with your projects and have a daily connection with your team so that you get all information firsthand.

SAs as solution owners

As the name itself suggests, SAs have ownership of their solution. It's their creation. They designed it and they will be the ones who will have the final say. This has its own pros and cons. A solution is generally based on a quick POC. As the POC is not detailed enough, there might be challenges that are faced by the developer in the later stages of development. This is when the SA is called and asked for an alternative way to get the specific task done. Owning the solution means that no one else can make any changes to it unless it is reviewed and approved by the SA—their blessing is needed. That doesn't mean recommendations are not welcome. The SA should practice a collaborative approach to recommendations and work toward the greater good.

Ownership comes with a lot of glory and fame. Your name is registered in all the documents as an SA, and everyone knows that you were the key to success. But don't get too excited—the road to fame always goes through a tough path. Let me walk you through a scenario where you are working on finding a solution that you did not design earlier, just to give you a glimpse of what kinds of curveballs you can face while designing a solution.

You have been asked to design an RPA solution where the process involves thousands of Excel sheets. These sheets have many different templates, and those templates are used by customer care and other teams. These Excel templates are stored on a network drive accessible to all teams from many different geographical locations. As we know, once an Excel sheet is open, it gets locked, so there are multiple versions of the same sheet being created by each user. This flaw in the process is due to a limitation in Excel and the fact that the existing process was designed 15 years ago; it never went through digital transformation. You have been asked to automate this process so that bots and humans can work in conjunction with each other.

You start thinking of various viable solutions, but then you realize that those solutions are more time-consuming and need more investment and effort. You keep scratching ideas and you end up nowhere. Then, you get the idea of splitting the problem into small achievable goals. You go to a whiteboard and draw the existing process and then gaze at it for a few minutes. You immediately realize that this process has two main clients to cater to—one is humans and the other is bots. Even if you are the SA responsible for automation, this doesn't mean you need to solve all problems and issues pertaining to the process. SAs have to work within the scope of the project. The expectation is to design a solution that can be scaled, managed, reused, and does not disrupt the existing process. You decide that before the automation, you will simplify it from a bot's perspective. You design a workflow that extracts the Excel template into an XML file. This is called decoupling. Once you do that, the human side of the process and the bot can co-exist.

But the question is: why would you go to such lengths to get this done? The answer is that you are the **solution owner**. You are responsible for designing and owning that till it is deployed to production and even after that. Having the mindset of an owner will take you to those uncharted territories of your mental creativity and unlock them. As the SA, you won't think about why you should do this, but you *know* that *you are the only one who has to do it*.

Keeping the mindset of an owner always gives you the anchor that will keep you going on at times when you think going forward is impossible. The owner is also responsible for any decision, changes, and outcomes of the solution. Be always ready to own them as well and know that it is inevitable. This is a great responsibility and comes with its own challenges, but then you are the one who will be basking in the glory of success once your solution gets to see production. Now, you have already realized that you are not the person who is going to put your solution into production. You have many teams involved in this life cycle.

As an owner, it is your responsibility to see that the solution you designed and the solution that is getting deployed in production are the same. For this reason, you have to be involved in the day-to-day operations of development, testing, **user acceptance testing** (**UAT**), and deployment phases. You can't lose your focus as there will be questions, comments, suggestions, and cutting corners to get the job done. Owning the solution doesn't mean only owning a diagram on a piece of paper but owning it from an implementation perspective as well. If the team has challenges, then you should know how to help resolve them. Guiding the team in the entire development phase is also your responsibility, or else you shouldn't be surprised if the end product is different from what you initially designed.

At times, you will face some situations where developers are frustrated to know you designed a solution the way you did, even when there are easier solutions to the given problem. Well, always keep in mind you have designed it that way as it is one of the best ways to do it rather than it being the easiest way, and thinking in that way makes you an SA. Not only developers but other teams might also crib for the same reasons, and you have to defend your solution like your baby—that is what I call ownership.

When I say defend, that doesn't mean you have to say *it is my way or the highway*, but always be prepared with rational reasoning and an explanation of why you did what you did. Having the pros and cons or a comparison metric always makes a difference and helps people understand. When you have to defend or explain yourself, talk with facts and figures—just saying that you are the SA and you can do whatever you want doesn't work and will just be rude. As I mentioned earlier, SAs have to work with many teams, and having the right attitude is the key to having synergy.

Now, let's talk about some of the challenges aspiring SAs and new upcoming SAs might face. They still tend to be in the persona of their earlier role, and as they might have not faced these types of situations, it is tough to react in the right way. The best thing to do when you go to a meeting where your design is going to be questioned is to be prepared and have all the facts ready to discuss. Now, as we discussed earlier, having the right mindset and attitude helps in confronting this kind of situation. If you made a mistake, own it. Trying to rationalize a mistake is like adding fuel to the fire. It also tarnishes your credibility as an SA. It goes without saying that the more knowledgeable you are, the humbler you become. Ownership is not only for the name and fame but also for your mistakes. A humble acceptance makes you a better SA and helps build a rapport with others.

To summarize, an SA is the owner of the solution, but at the same time, has to get feedback and blessings from other teams and stakeholders to get the design approved. They have to be patient and humble and have an open mind to suggestions.

SAs and the multiple hats they wear

In the IT industry, there are a few roles that, when defined and written on paper, are very different when compared to reality. An RPA SA's role is no different. During the entire life cycle, an SA has to play many different roles. These roles are like switching hats as they have to switch them multiple times in a day or week. For example, an SA will wear a consultant hat in the initial stages of the project where they are talking to the business. They help the client identify the right process or help them select the right RPA tool or vendor, or maybe just help them understand what RPA all is about. This might be the role they played in one of the meetings, and on the same day, they again have to switch their hat from a consultant hat to an SA hat when talking to the development team or having a technical discussion with the CIO's team. This clearly shows that an SA should be a master of switching profile and tone as per the situation, project phase, and requirements. Similarly, while talking to the development team, an SA has to be very technical and should be able to talk in a language that the developers can understand. For example, just saying that getting the data from queues and converting it into an Excel report is not detailed enough. An SA would have to tell the team to extract the data from queues in a tabular format and maybe store it in a dataset or collection. Use that to format the data and arrange the columns as per the report template agreed upon earlier. Then, write the data to an Excel file that has a specified file naming convention.

Let's now deep dive and find out more about the multiple hats an SA has to switch between phases or situations so that it can give us a clear picture and highlight some focus areas.

Being a consultant

When you get engaged in the early stages of an RPA project or program, you are expected to talk in layman's terms or in business terms. The reason is that you will most likely be talking to a business or non-technical group that is more interested in learning about the technology and how it is applied to different LOBs rather than the technical aspects of it. They want to hear from you about your experiences with other clients. Do not talk in your regular technical language—as they say, **know your client** (**KYC**)! Knowing your client and audience always helps in tailoring your conversation, which then makes more sense to them rather than becoming a boring conversation. This doesn't mean that you have to drop all your knowledge, but play it by ear. Listen to what is being asked and who is asking the question. Tailor your answer accordingly—this gives you a better response and a fruitful conversation. Always try to use examples in your talking points. Prepare some PowerPoint slides that you can walk them through, as a picture is worth a thousand words. During your conversation, you might get a few technical questions, so being prepared is the key.

In the next stage, you will be given a process that has already been selected and vetted to be a viable candidate for automation. This stage is more of an assessment of the process.

Being a business analyst

You will most likely be accompanied by a **business analyst** (**BA**) who may or may not have experience working on RPA projects but knows how to talk to SMEs and gather requirements. If you are lucky enough to be accompanied by a BA who is seasoned in RPA projects, then you can sit back and relax at this stage and just be in listen-only mode. But if that is not the case, then you have to change your hat and wear a BA hat. This is where it becomes tricky. You need to go against your technical thought process and think like a BA. Asking the right questions to the SME is a trick of the trade. Having an experienced BA in RPA is a blessing. Knowing your BA's skill set and background helps you be prepared for these situations where you have to step up to *bridge the gap*.

BAs can definitely break the ice, but then extracting the right information from the SME is the key. Also, time is of the essence in this phase. You get very limited time from the SME. They are very rare, and their time is precious. You can't ask for their time whenever you feel you need them. So, asking the right question is the key to the success of this phase. Some questions you might want to ask are as follows:

- What is their team's size?

- How much time does it take for them to complete the process?

- Can they show you how they do the process, and can you record it? This is called a *time and motion study*, which is a very crucial step in finding all the small steps to a mouse-click level. This will help you find the **average handling time** (**AHT**) of the process.

- What is the daily, weekly, and monthly volume of the transaction?

- Is there any peak time during the year?

- Which **service-level agreements** (**SLAs**) do they have to follow?

- Last but not least, what are the pain points for the process?

This is not an exhaustive list, but just gives you an idea of how you have to get involved and play the role of BA when you are not accompanied by an experienced one. We will revisit this topic in detail in the process design document in *Chapter 6, Need for Documentation and Working with SIT/UAT Scripts* .

It's not only your job to get the **functional requirements** (**FRs**) but also to find out the **non-FRs** (**NFRs**). There might be a few things that might have been bothering the SMEs for a long time, and you need to convey the message that you are here to at least try to solve them while trying to automate the process. This is called a strategic approach toward the RPA project that has greater success not only in the near future but for years to come.

Being an SA

This is your primary role. This is a hat that you wear all the time. Once you are done with the other temporary hat, you go back to wearing the SA hat. Remember that you are and will always be an SA and will be addressed with the same name, but the expectations from you will be much more than an SA. You are expected to be a magician who can perform many tricks. I sometimes fail to understand why everyone thinks that SAs will have the solution not only for technical but also for functional and operational challenges.

For instance, you are in a meeting and the project manager is figuring out the change management activities, and they look at you and ask, *What do you think?* Well, you are not an expert in change management activities, but still, they are directing that question to you as they have a firm belief that you can either tell them exactly what to do or at least will share a few stories from your past experience. Though these situations are sometimes confusing and you might ask why this type of question keeps coming to an SA, they have great significance. Now, I am going to reveal a secret that will help you prepare for an SA interview.

This type of question is asked of you because the project manager has been briefed about you as well. You are not only the one who reviews and understands the strengths and weaknesses of the team members; other team members also do the same. Remember how you went on and on about all the different roles that you played—and let me remind you, that was the reason you were chosen for the SA's position. So, technically, you brought this upon yourself!

An SA is an important position that we already understood, but it also comes with responsibilities. These are responsibilities that you signed up for when you took over this project. They are moral and ethical responsibilities. You pledge that you will adhere to the policies and procedures of the client. You might also have to undergo a few pieces of training before or during onboarding. Take those responsibilities seriously. They can be as follows:

- Don't send any emails to your personal or employer email.
- No documents should be shared outside the client's domain.
- Do not use a **virtual private network** (**VPN**) from unauthorized machines.

Not complying with these policies can end badly for you, your team, and your company. So, try to show leadership and *lead by example* by following these policies and procedures and encouraging your team to do the same.

Being a developer

Everyone knows you are an SA. No one expects you to develop unless it is evident. But again, it is expected of you to roll up your sleeves and get your hands dirty when the team needs you. Don't shy away and say it's not your job or that you didn't sign up for this. You can't even get away with saying you don't know how to. This is a very common situation that will come up multiple times during the project life cycle.

Let's visualize this through a scenario. You are working on a complex project. You have designed a solution that uses technologies that your developer is not familiar with. It is not a new technology; it is just that your developer has never worked on it. Now, you have two options: one, do it yourself, and second, teach and guide the developer to get it developed. The choice of option depends on many factors. Do you have time to spend doing it yourself? Can you guide the developer, and then they can pick it up? What are your developer's background and experience? You are the best judge and can answer most of these questions by having a conversation with the developer and analyzing the situation. This is also one of those teaching moments when you help in grooming and developing talent.

You analyze the situation and decide to take this on yourself and get your name assigned as a developer. You have switched your hat again from SA to the developer. You took the responsibility to get that piece of code or module written and at the same time teach the developer how to do it so that in the future, they are ready for this type of work. This is another example where an SA *bridges the gap*. You develop the code and then do a **knowledge transfer** (**KT**). This step is very important, both for the continuation of the code maintenance and for you to switch your hat back to an SA.

Likewise, you have to change your role to a developer when you have to do a POC. Though the scope of a POC is very small and has time constraints, there are still development activities that you need to perform. A POC is a key step in proving the technical feasibility of the solution and proof of value. This step is generally performed in the initial phases of the project when you don't have a developer or a team at your disposal. You have to do the heavy lifting and spin the POC. This is inevitable, and your chances of getting a developer at this point are pretty slim. The expectation is also that you are capable of developing a functional POC on your own—after all, you were once a developer yourself. **This again ties to the answer you gave during your interview when asked that if a situation arises and you have to develop, are you comfortable doing it, and you answered: Yes!**

An SA is also known for being a developer's developer. The developer always looks to you to get an answer to their queries, fix and review their code, and help them overcome any impediments. You are again their savior and *guardian angel*. This is why when a **responsible, accountable, consulted, and informed** (**RACI**) chart is prepared, your name comes under responsible and accountable for all development activities during situations where you are racing against time and either development is not yet completed or **system integration testing** (**SIT**) has unearthed a lot of bugs that need attention before the code can be considered ready for UAT. These are the phases an SA should keep an eye on, and they should be ready to roll up their sleeves and get their hands dirty.

Being a delivery facilitator

When it comes to the smooth delivery of a project, there are always challenges. There are so many moving parts that it sometimes gets challenging. Having a set of eyes to achieve the ultimate goal is always appreciated. For this reason, it is considered an *all-hands-on-deck* kind of situation as everyone is considered to participate and take it to the victory line. An SA, being a senior resource, has a lot of say and can sometimes help in making critical decisions in a time of need. They are the ones who are involved in the day-to-day activities and have a more holistic view of the project, though SAs are not responsible for the delivery, as that would be the responsibility of the delivery manager and the project manager.

That being said, an SA can be of great help in making quick decisions. Let's see a scenario where an SA helps in making some decisions that can become a big impediment in the delivery process. When it comes to full-life cycle projects such as RPA projects, there are a lot of requirements that are functional in nature. These can be requirements from the SME, info security, or any other team from the client side. So, you are working on a project and everything is going great, and suddenly, one day, you receive a meeting request from the client to discuss some new changes that came up recently. You join the call, and after setting the stage, the client tells everyone that there is a new mandate from the corporate that they are moving away from the traditional file storage system that was used to be the network drives to cloud-based storage.

Clients further explain that there is an enterprise-wide solution from Microsoft Office 365 that gives you the opportunity to store your files in a Microsoft Teams folder structure, which makes it more convenient for collaboration with humans. Now, because the bot you are developing will have to use the same location because maintaining two different file locations is not cost-effective and cumbersome, the process needs to be modified. The client asks what you and others on the call think, and you decide to take it offline and come back to them in a couple of days.

Now, this is a very common scenario, where we see that the existing process is being modernized by banking on the current RPA opportunity. As we can see, it is the future of all other upcoming projects you might have to work on, so avoiding this is not an option. You try to run some numbers based on the new requirements and the effort it will take from your team and the client's team to come up with a game plan.

As you can see, the SA has to step up and help in even making a decision in this critical situation as they are the one who has that holistic view of all that is currently going on in the project from the timeline, delivery, resources, and other perspectives. A decision has to be made quickly and should also be within the budget and timeline. There might be a little wiggle room for you to ask for a few extra days for development and accommodate the requirements. Things such as this always fall on SAs' shoulders, though we can argue that the project manager could have pushed it back based on the scope and given that we have already advanced in the development phase. It is always advisable to try your best to accommodate things that are not in the *good-to-have* category but can be a deal-breaker. Clients also know what they can live with and what is inevitable. As we can see, this is an enterprise-wide change, and 99% of the time, these can't be pushed back. A more realistic solution would be to come up with a solution and let the client know what it will take to accommodate this new requirement and help them make a decision.

You need to present a solution that is feasible based on the timeline, budget, and delivery. Always try to evaluate these ad hoc requests based on good-to-have versus a deal-breaker or showstopper. These scenarios are some of the nuances you might face during the entire delivery of the project, and they can arise in any phase of the project. This is how an SA becomes a facilitator in decision-making and the smooth delivery of the project.

Summary

To summarize, an SA is one of the most important roles in an RPA project. We saw how an SA can be helpful for not only bringing integrity to the team but also bridging technical and functional gaps in the team. Other than their primary role and responsibility, they have to take on extra responsibility to make sure that the end goal is achieved. Only results matter—keeping that attitude, the SA helps the developer overcome technical impediments and at the same time helps the team as a guardian angel, influencer, and enforcer of best practices. They also keep the team moving forward in the right direction by guiding them and keeping them focused. They are the owners of the solution so as to make sure that it gets implemented to its utmost extent. They help in filling other people's shoes, such as being a consultant, developer, and delivery facilitator. This gives us a clear picture of what it takes to be an SA. An SA has to possess many skills so that they can be used as a trump card whenever needed.

Having an SA on the team gives peace of mind and helps make sure that the project goes smoothly. This is why SA selection should be exhaustive.

In the next chapter, we will talk about a case study of a banking organization, which will be our reference point and help build a story for future scenarios. This will also help to visualize an end-to-end RPA engagement unclear for understanding the length and breadth of an RPA project.

Questions

1. Why do you think the SA role is important?
2. How does an SA bridge gaps?
3. Is an SA involved in any decision-making?
4. Which other roles might an SA need to play?
5. What does ownership mean for an SA?

Case Study of a Banking Client

In the previous chapter, we discussed the role of SA, its importance in the industry, and its responsibilities. Now, I plan to take you for a deeper dive into the day-to-day activities of an RPA SA and familiarize you with what it takes to become an RPA SA, the tricks of the trade, and more. In this chapter, we'll visualize a lot of scenarios. To do that, we need to assume a lot of things and paint a picture in our minds of a fictitious organization. Remembering all that information and being able to correlate with it can be challenging. I want you to focus on things that are more important, such as finding gaps and building a roadmap for becoming a successful RPA SA. For this reason, in this chapter, we are going to visualize a case study of a banking client. The reason I chose this domain and industry is that its processes are the most complex and error prone.

This chapter will cover the following points:

- Introducing the scenario
- Synopsis of the case study
- Finding RPA opportunities
- Learning more about the team structure
- T-shirt sizing—sizing the project

Let's get into it!

Introducing the scenario

You are a seasoned RPA SA and have been working in this role for a multinational IT company for several years. Your recent project has almost ended, and you are invited to join a quick internal call. You join the call, and the facilitator tells everyone on the call that your company has won a multi-year contract with its existing client, Bank of Plutus. This call is to talk about engagement, logistics, and strategies. You know that you have been called to this meeting to listen to the vision and goals that the bank's management has discussed and shared with the account team and ask questions—if any.

You have always dreamed of working for a large bank, and you are thrilled to know that your dream is manifesting. With all that enthusiasm and zeal, your mind is swamped with a bunch of questions, such as the following:

- What stage are the clients currently at?

- Have they already started their journey, and do they want help to take it forward?

- Have they already selected an RPA tool?

- Have they curated a list of processes?

- Which operating model are they planning to use?

- What is their implementation strategy?

You refrain from asking all these questions in the meeting and instead ask a quick question:

Excuse me—hi, this is Sam. I am an RPA SA and would like to ask a few questions.

There is a 5-second silence and then someone replies: *Hey, Sam, of course—I will arrange a separate technical call for you to ask all your questions to the RPA core team that the bank is putting together.*

And then, they go on with other discussions, such as who will be a part of the executive committee, the engagement manager, and the account manager, and then about escalation protocols, governance model, and so on.

Though you wanted to hear all of that, you were more focused on preparing a list of questions that you want to ask in the first meeting with the client's core team.

Synopsis of the case study

Bank of Plutus is one of the largest banks on Pluto. Bank of Plutus has headquarters in New York and branches all over the US. It is popularly known as the bankers' bank. It has several **lines of business** (**LOBs**). The LOBs have their **subject-matter experts** (**SMEs**) scattered all over the US and in different time zones. It is always helpful to know about the client's business. Having domain knowledge helps you articulate the requirements meticulously. It is not a hard requirement for being an SA as the ultimate goal should be to become an SA who is tool- and domain-agnostic. To achieve this, you have to be knowledgeable about at least two or three RPA tools and domains. Knowing about the business, its processes, and how they differ from each other helps you form a holistic view of solution design.

Bank of Plutus is no different, and as we can tell, it is from the banking and finance domain. This domain has some of the most cumbersome and mundane processes—processes that do not add any value to the human resources performing that process. It is most likely that human talent is getting wasted. This is the type of process we are looking to automate. They are boring, mundane, and cumbersome but stable, standard, and rule-based processes.

Some of the LOBs and processes that are most suitable for automation are mentioned next.

The LOBs for the consumer and retail segments are as follows:

- Retail banking
- Lending and mortgage
- Cards (debit and credit)
- **Know your client** (**KYC**)
- **Anti-money laundering** (**AML**)
- Account maintenance

The LOBs for the private banking segment are as follows:

- Trade finance
- Account servicing
- Trade execution

The LOBs for the enterprise services segment are as follows:

- Sourcing
- HR services
- IT and infrastructure
- Auditing

These are some of the banking segments and LOBs that can benefit from RPA. Now, let's review some of the engagement details. The following details are also a part of the **statement of work** (**SOW**), which is an official document signed and agreed upon by the client and the **service provider** (**SP**).

Engagement details

Your company won a multi-year contract with the Bank of Plutus for the implementation of the RPA program. The bank has requested help in the following areas:

- Educating businesses and LOBs about RPA
- Identifying use cases and processes that are the best fit for RPA
- Designing, developing, deploying, and maintaining RPA projects
- Setting up a **Center of Excellence** (**COE**)
- Setting up a governance model
- Setting up a support model for RPA

This is a multi-year engagement, and for your company to be successful, there has to be a team of highly skilled and cross-trained IT professionals. There will be two teams: one from the client side and one from your own company. Let's see what a typical team looks like for an engagement of this size.

A client's team has the following teams/personnel:

- **Executives or stakeholders**: These are the higher-ups. They are mostly interested in seeing the value this new technology is going to deliver in the next 5 years.

- **Sponsor**: This role is responsible for running the program and funding the program.

- **Program manager**: This role is responsible for setting up a **project management office** (**PMO**) for RPA. The PMO can be inherited from the corporate team or can be designed as per the company's culture.

- **Enterprise architect**: This role is responsible for setting up the governance for RPA project infrastructure guidelines and best practices related to data security and access applications.

- **SMEs**: They are considered the gurus of their processes. They are called upon to educate and give you a crash course on the process. Whatever they have learned and experienced over the years will be shoved into your brain in a couple of hours. They are one of the keys to a successful and smooth RPA implementation. Always try to build a good rapport with them, and thank me later. They are the ones who will tell you about the pain points, and they are the ones who will be using your automation. They are going to certify if your process is adding any value, and you know which group tracks the value—executives.

- **Information security**: This group is responsible for setting the guide rails for the entire team so that they don't end up in a data or security breach. They provide consultation on data security, data retention policies, and which data should be classified and declassified.

Now, let's take a look at your team:

- **Engagement manager**: This role is responsible for the overall delivery and management of the client's expectations. This will also be the highest level of escalation for any issues that might arise during the program's execution.

- **Scrum master or project manager**: This role depends on which project methodology the client has in house, or what they prefer. The most common is the Agile methodology of project management. A hybrid version of the Waterfall and Agile methodologies works best in complex project delivery.

- **RPA SA**: This is what you aspire to and is your reason for reading this book: so that one day you can become one. This role is also the owner of a **solution design document** (**SDD**) or **development specification document** (**DSD**).

- **Business analyst** (**BA**): This role is responsible for gathering all **functional requirements** (**FRs**) and **non-FRs** (**NFRs**). This role is the owner of the **process design document** (**PDD**), which is the key document for the successful delivery of the RPA process.

- **Senior developer**: This role is like your squad leader. This role has seen and attended a lot of solution design reviews, has contributed to a few, and has extensive development experience. This is one of the roles that has read this book and is on the path to becoming an SA.

- **Developer**: This role is self-explanatory. This role is responsible for all development activities and delivering clean, structured, and well-formatted code.

- **Quality analyst or tester**: This role is responsible for writing test scripts, executing the test scripts, and reporting bugs or process flow issues.

This concludes the team structure. Knowing the team structure, skill sets, and role helps with the delegation of work and resource utilization. This also helps with project execution and timely delivery.

Vision and strategy

Every business that is successful has always started with a vision and then worked on making that vision come true. For a vision to come true, you need to have a strategy, and that is what we are going to understand from our client's perspective.

Vision and mission: what you understood after reading a 120-page document is that your client is focused on increasing efficiency, reducing the cost of operation, eliminating compliance issues, and boosting their employees' morale. This is also known as a **return on investment** (**ROI**). All this needs to be achieved in the next 5 years with the help of this new technology known as RPA. This definitely gels with what RPA is known for. It can help increase efficiency because, technically, a bot can run 24x7 with 100% accuracy. When you deploy a bot that costs 1/10 of the cost of human resources, the operating cost will be reduced drastically. When it comes to issues such as compliance and mandates, a streamlined and error-free system is needed that can run for months without breaking.

RPA provides that kind of commitment, given that it is designed and executed within the limits of a controlled environment. Obviously, when you have taken away all the mundane and repetitive work from humans and deployed them to more challenging work, the morale of the employees will boost automatically. Firstly, they will feel that their employer respects their talent and wants them to grow rather than become a machine. Secondly, it fosters job satisfaction among employees and reduces staff turnover.

Now we've discussed what the vision and mission are and how we achieve them, what should our strategy be so that we can have an action plan for each of those visions and missions? First and foremost, you shouldn't use a tactical approach to automation. For example, let's assume that you have been asked to automate a process, and the pain point is that the client is under pressure to fix a compliance issue. One of their loan origination processes uses a database that contains the addresses of their clients and customers. As this database is not updated, some of the mandatory communications sent to those addresses are not received. It is mandatory that these communications are received by the customer as per the **Internal Revenue Service** (**IRS**).

Now, if you have to take a tactical approach, you will try to design a solution to immediately fix the issue by getting the database updated. But a strategical approach suggests that when you are trying to resolve the issue at hand, always look at the process holistically and try to find other areas of improvement that can be accommodated at the same time. It is also advised to have a strategic approach as that will help to ensure that the automation is sustainable, maintainable, and scalable. This will streamline the process and make it future-safe. We will talk more about this in *Chapter 5*, *Designing a Framework for Consistency and Resiliency*.

Finding RPA opportunities

To run an organization, you need the two most important things—people and processes. Without these, no organization can function properly. A process is made by the people, for the people, and from the people. This makes them best buddies. But sometimes, processes do get boring. No one wants to work on a boring process, but just because we think a process is unexciting does not mean we simply replace it with an exciting or fun process. We look for other ways to get the work done and not have to deal with boredom. There is a solution to this pandemic-like problem—it is called automation. Automation helps you get away from a boring process and move the people who were working on or managing that process repeatedly to more exciting work.

Now, the question is, how can we identify what is boring? The process is not going to tell us anything. It is the people who work on those processes that will. This gives us a starting point, which is to do some interviews with people and groups. The first rule of successful automation is *finding the right opportunity*. No matter how much you invest in development and do a good job, if your automation is not used by anyone or has no ROI, then it is a failure.

Let's see how we can find the right opportunity for RPA projects. Finding an opportunity is like finding a needle in a haystack. It has some characteristics that'll help you identify it, but you should know what you are looking for to find it, or else you will end up guessing. Sometimes, the client might have already identified a few opportunities and processes for you to look at, but it is not the case for us. A list of characteristics that should be considered while identifying opportunities is provided, as follows:

- **Pain areas**: These are the most important characteristics of a good opportunity. There can be pain areas within the process or the people. Both can give birth to an opportunity for automation. Let's understand this through an example. You met an old colleague who works in the Appeals and Grievances department, and they looked very frustrated. During your conversation, they told you that their boss has asked them to increase the efficiency and efficacy of their grievance process by 20% in the next few months. They further mentioned that it is so challenging to do that, and they have tried doing it in the past, but it has never worked. You asked more about why their efforts failed, and they said that is due to the broken process. The appeals and grievances process is very cumbersome, repetitive, and lengthy. It is also time-consuming and mundane. Good and knowledgeable people don't want to work on this process. Your old colleague is forced to use new hires who have less experience and thus end up making a lot of mistakes, which reduces efficiency. This is a classic example of a broken process that is old and boring but at the same time is an important process for the organization. This can be a part of your opportunity assessment.

Now, let's see a scenario where an automation opportunity arises from people. You are in the cafeteria and are greeted by a voice. You turn around and see Mike. Mike is an old veteran in the company. He has been with the company for the last 30 years. He tells you that he is retiring in the next few days. You congratulate him and say: *But you are the only one left who knows that program in the mainframe. Are you getting a replacement, or what is the guidance from management?* Mike tells you that he is here to talk to you about that as well as it seems like no one is ready to learn that old language and there is no one on the market who is willing to work on that legacy technology. Mike tells you that management wants to automate his work so that he can retire peacefully and his legacy can be continued. This is the type of opportunity that arises when there is a lack of human resources, especially for old, outdated, and legacy technologies.

- **Compliance**: Every business, whether it is big or small, has to adhere to government rules and regulations. To be compliant, businesses have to spend money on people, processes, and technology. There are times when this can become one of the key areas of focus because non-compliance can lead to monetary fines and even become a threat to the business. It is also a no-brainer for the client to immediately let the team know that they are facing challenges with being compliant, and that opens an opportunity for automation.

- **Efficacy and efficiency**: Processes that are heavily dependent on human resources and are manually intensive are very error prone. Having errors in processes increases rework and decreases efficiency. Decreased efficiency is costly, and that opens an opportunity for automation. Automation can bring the consistency and efficacy needed for the process.

- **Repurpose the talent**: Sometimes, your talent pools are underutilized or are stuck working on processes that are mundane and are not worth your highly talented human resources spending time on. To get your resources redeployed to more critical processes, you have to use technology. For these types of situations, automation again becomes your go-to strategy and helps to solve the problem.

- **Capacity planning**: Scaling a resource pool is always a challenging, time-consuming, and costly affair. A bot can be leveraged in areas where the process is well defined and can be automated. This is one of those opportunities that can become an asset to the company. For example, if the business need is to hire temporary resources for specific work at a specific time of the year, then bots can fill that position without going through the painful and cumbersome process of hiring and can be easily discarded or repurposed when the peak workload ends. Hiring human resources also comes with a cost, and RPA can help by having a piece of code that can do the job. When you need to deploy a pool of resources that are temporary in nature, bots can be a great solution. Once a process is automated, it can be copied on multiple **virtual desktop infrastructures** (**VDIs**) or machines that can work in parallel to give you the same capacity that you might have been building using human resources in the past.

- **Replacement for human resources**: When it comes to cost-cutting, automation is one of the tools used by management. It is a bit controversial and is always considered a threat to the jobs done by humans. There are people who believe that humans can be completely replaced by bots. That is a myth and a fallacy, though, because in practicality, bots can complement humans by freeing them from doing mundane work and giving them the opportunity to move to more value-added work.

As we now understand where the opportunities may exist, let's see how the team is structured for this use case.

Learning more about the team structure

Every project needs a team. It goes without saying that a great person can make a difference, but a team can work miracles. To work that miracle, there has to be a highly functional team. For this use case, we will build a team that will be cross-functional and modular.

A list of roles within the team is set out here:

- Project manager or Scrum master
- SA
- BA
- Senior developer
- Developer
- Quality analyst

Now that we know what the team looks like, let's set some roles and responsibilities for each role. The industry standard for formalizing the roles and responsibilities of a team is called the RACI matrix. **RACI** stands for **responsible, accountable, consulted, and informed**. Segregation of responsibilities is the key to a highly functional team. We don't want conflict and concerns arising from confusion as to who does what and who needs to be kept in the loop in a conversation between the team and the client. An example of RACI is given here for your reference:

	Project Management	**Infrastructure**	**Development**	**SIT**	**UAT**
PM or SM	R,A	I	C	A	A
SA	I	R,A	R,A	C	I
BA	I	I	I	C	I
Sr. Developer	I	C	R	C	I
Developer	I	C	R	C	I
QA	I	I	I	R	A

Figure 2.1 – RACI matrix

The team looks great, but one of the requirements from the client was that they have the goal of achieving a certain amount of automation in production by the end of the year, and for that reason, they need to have a modular team structure. Modular teams are like small pods that only have only team members who have to invest 100% of their time in a single project. To visualize what the teams look like, let's review the following screenshot:

Project Manager or Scrum Master				
SA				
Pod1	Pod2	Pod3	Pod4	Podx
BA	BA	BA	BA	...
Sr. Developer	Sr. Developer	Sr. Developer	Sr. Developer	...
Developer	Developer	Developer	Developer	
QA	QA	QA	QA	...

Figure 2.2 – Modular team

As we can see from the preceding table, two roles—project manager and SA—are stretched across all the pods, and then we have modular teams of BA, Sr. Developer, Developer, and QA each focusing on a single process at a time. This gives you a team structure that is highly functional and super productive and can churn out automation at a fast pace. It also provides centralized governance for the project manager and SA to keep an eye on all projects and apply the learning from one project to another. It also helps in filling resourcing gaps because a team can collaborate internally and the team members can help each other in times of need. This structure does have an initial investment, but as the client had a set goal of achieving a certain amount of automation by the end of the year, this will be the best team structure.

Team structure depends on what we are trying to achieve and what our **go-to-market** (**GTM**) strategy is. In this case study, the client had a goal that was defined by the leadership, and to achieve it, we needed a modular team structure. But this is not the silver bullet for defining a team. Teams can be structured in many different ways, and it all boils down to one thing: what is our goal? Do we want to take it slow and scale or do we want to go with a big bang?

Team composition also depends on how much bandwidth each team member has and how many projects they can focus on in parallel. We need to keep in mind the skills each member has and how much guidance they will need to function properly. Client in-house processes also dictate team composition. We need to account for the time and manpower it takes to keep up with the FRs of the PMO and other formalities that the team has to accommodate apart from its regular activities.

We are now ready to take over some of the projects, but before we do that, we need to define a framework to determine the required effort for a project. Effort estimation is a complex and time-consuming process, but a high-level estimate is needed to facilitate a decision. Estimates can be in man-hours or can be defined as **Small** (**S**), **Medium** (**M**), **Large** (**L**), and **Extra Large** (**XL**). As we are not providing an exact estimate but more of a guesstimate, we will go with what is called T-shirt sizing. This is a technique to quickly provide a high-level effort estimate in weeks or months that can later be expanded and converted into man-hours. During the initial phases of a project, this technique is more realistic than investing time in going through the exercise of finding an estimate. Let's discuss the process of T-shirt sizing and see what that will look like for this case study.

T-shirt sizing – sizing the project

A T-shirt sizing or estimation model is defined based on previous experience, general components used for automation, and technologies. Microsoft Excel has proven to be a great tool for designing this kind of estimation model. Let's define a model for our current client.

The first step in defining an estimation model is to list all the general components and categorize them into buckets. Each component will be given a high-level effort estimate. Keep in mind that this is not an estimate for a complete project but only for the development phase.

The following screenshot shows an example development effort estimation model that can be used for sizing an RPA project:

Development effort estimation sheet				
Application		**Type**	**Complexity**	**Effort in man hours**
	Application 1	Web	Medium	40
	Application 2	Desktop	Low	20
	Application x ….	Web	High	
UI components				
	Number of screens	75		40
	Text fields	150		60
	Mouse clicks	250		20
	….			
Technologies				
	Optical character recog	Yes		20
	API / Web services	Yes		30
	Custom development	No		
	Mainframe	Yes		20
	Citrix	No		
	Structured data	Yes		20
	Unstructured data	No		
	….			
Total				270

Figure 2.3 – Development effort estimation sample sheet

Let's review the effort sheet and some of its components. We have to divide the process into components, such as applications, UI components, and technologies. Then, these categories can be subdivided or extended based on the client's technology stack and as we know more about their technology ecosystem. This gives a base to keep adding items to expand the effort estimation sheet. For this case study, we will use the template shown in *Figure 2.3*. As we can see, this template can give you a quick guesstimate. Always keep in mind that this is just a high-level estimate to give an idea of whether the project size is S, M, L, or XL.

The total we get from the development effort estimation sheet can then be converted into days or weeks. It depends on the individual, but for me, weeks work best. Let's do the math:

Total man-hours = 270

Typical working hours per day = 8

# of days = 270/8 = 33.75 days

# of weeks = 41.25 / 5 (working days) = 6.75 weeks

Based on this, we can see that it will take roughly 6-7 weeks to get the development done. This estimate was based on initial knowledge of the process and not based on a deep dive.

Now, let's see how we can use this estimate to formalize T-shirt sizing. To do that, we will take into consideration the team structure and the pace at which we need to churn out the automation processes. If we consider the pod team structure, each team has two developers, and one of them is a senior developer. Considering their skills and experience, we can say that the development resources will work at equal capacity, giving us an estimate of around 3-4 weeks. Based on our experience, 4-5 weeks of development falls into the small project category. Based on this, let's define our T-shirt sizing, which will look something like this here:

T-Shirt Sizing				
	Small	Medium	Large	X-Large
Applications	1 - 2	2 - 3	3 - 5	5+
Total Duration in Weeks	4-6	6-8	9-12	13+

Figure 2.4 – T-shirt sizing

Once we have defined the T-shirt sizing metrics, it becomes easy to provide a ballpark estimate and tweak it based on the requirements and information we gather for that process.

Summary

To summarize, this chapter focuses on providing a case study for future chapters so that we can build a complete picture of scenarios and correlate them. It also helps in understanding the concepts and the flow of an RPA project. We also saw the engagement details that act as building blocks of our thought process while designing and developing the process. This helps in understanding the objective and the goals from the client's perspective. Engagement details help us to visualize the team structure that we can expect from the client, as well as our internal team. It helps in building a holistic view of the types of resources and what kind of help we can expect from them.

Next, we observed how opportunities are identified and the key areas that can be considered when identifying opportunities. We also looked at the different kinds of team structures and formalized a team based on the requirements given by the client for this case study.

Finally, we saw how a development effort estimation model can be designed for each client, which can facilitate defining T-shirt sizing. This is key for providing quick high-level effort estimates, which in turn can be helpful for decision-making.

In the next chapter, we will see how an SA contributes to the other functions of an organization. The SA role is very vast and does not stop at the end of a project. SAs sometimes need to participate in pre-sales, talent development, building a talent pool, and contributing to the COE. These can be considered extracurricular activities of an SA.

Questions

1. What are the key components that can be considered for an estimation model?

2. What are the key factors that can be the basis for defining an estimation model?

3. What are the different types of team structures that we studied in this chapter?

4. What are the key areas or scenarios that can be considered for finding opportunities?

5. What are the different sizes used in T-shirt sizing?

Extracurricular Activities

In the previous chapter, we discussed the case study of a bank client and focused on building an imaginary story to put our learning into perspective. This chapter will continue to talk about the SA and its roles and responsibilities. As we discussed in the first chapter, the role of an SA is so vast and open-ended that it is tough to list all the tasks and activities that an SA does. That is why, in this chapter, I'll introduce you to some of the extracurricular activities that an SA ends up doing that are considered an account- or practice-level contribution. These activities are not project-based but are more of an SA's contribution towards the overall growth of the account or practice.

The agenda of this chapter will cover the following points:

- Contribution to presales activities
- Attending Orals and client presentations
- Building talent pools
- Coaching and mentoring
- The Center Of Excellence

By the end of the chapter, you will know the other activities that an SA performs within the organization. Having this knowledge will help in understanding the SA's role holistically and will help in your preparation for a job interview.

Let's get into it.

Contribution to presales activities

SAs' responsibilities are divided into two groups: **business as usual** (**BAU**) and ad hoc contribution requests. BAU activities are defined and listed in the job description and are related to the given project. These activities generate revenue for the company and are called *billable activities*. It can also be said that these are the primary activities of an SA.

Then comes activities that are ad hoc in nature and can be added to an SA's to-do list as and when required. These activities are not revenue-generating but will require a significant amount of the SA's time. You might wonder why an SA should invest their time in a non-revenue-generating activity. In a real-world scenario, contributing to a project is one part of an SA's role, while keeping a healthy project pipeline is the other part.

Imagine a scenario where you are almost at the delivery end of a project. The go-live date is set for the next week. Now, you can take a couple of days off to relax and get away from the hectic schedule you have been working on for the last few months, but what about after that? You need a pipeline of projects to continue to deliver and generate revenue for the company.

For this reason, sales and presales teams work continuously to generate new leads and reply to **requests for proposal (RFPs)** so that you and your team always have work. Let's see how an SA can contribute to these sales and presales activities.

Before we explore the nitty-gritty of the presales activities, let's understand what *presales* means. As the name suggests, it is a set of activities performed before a sale can be made. It is the stage of an RFP where the vendor (in this scenario, your company) will try to convince and prove to the client that they have the expertise, experience, and resources to complete the project within the given timeframe and budget. In this stage, different teams come together to understand the requirement provided by the client, which is usually very high level, and then propose a high-level solution backed by case studies and previous experience.

Here are a few common presales activities:

- A thorough review of the RFP
- Analyzing the client's technology stack
- Understanding the intent
- Analyzing the requirements
- Questionnaire for clearing doubts
- Preparation for Orals

Let's understand this using a scenario. You are an SA. You receive a meeting request with an agenda to review the RFP for a client. You attend the meeting and the account manager gives you an overview of what the RFP is all about and how they want each one of the team members to contribute. This is the starting point for you to contribute to presales activities. You have been identified as one of the key contributors, as the client has asked to implement RPA in their organization. As an SA and a person who has extensive knowledge of RPA, you need to lead the RFP reply. The reply is due in 5 days. This is an opportunity to understand what the RFP is requesting and ask questions related to the client. Some of the questions that you can ask are as follows:

- Is this a new client?

- Do we have an existing relationship with the client? If yes, how are we engaged?

- Who are the competitors?

- What is the RFP response format?

- Can you connect with someone already working for the client to get some insights?

- What is the engagement model we are going to follow?

- Will it be a fixed bid or a **time and materials** (**T&M**) project?

These initial questions will give you a better understanding and help you finalize your strategy for the RFP response.

Once you have some of your questions answered, the next step is to read the RFP thoroughly and prepare your questionnaire. This has to be exhaustive and not generic. Your questions should be focused on gathering the information that is not available publicly and is needed to formulate your RFP reply. It would be best to assume many things that are primarily based on your previous experience, as there are only one or two chances for you to get your questions answered. Keep in mind that the client has floated the RFP and has to go through a similar exercise with their alternative vendors. This sometimes is a bit frustrating for the client if you are not asking the right questions.

Now that your questionnaire is ready, the client might opt for a written reply or ask for a discovery call. Either way, be prepared and ask questions to get satisfactory answers. There might be some vague answers too as the client is also in the initial stages of their RPA journey, so make assumptions and list them in your RPF reply.

There will be scenarios where you might have to collaborate with other internal teams to finalize the questions. Let's assume that the requirement is to set up the RPA infrastructure on one of the cloud providers. You will need to talk to your cloud infrastructure team to add their questions to the list. Consolidation of all the questions will be the best strategy. There may be other teams that you want to get involved as well. So, the emphasis is on reading the RFP document thoroughly and identifying all the teams that might need to be involved. Missing out any team will end up with you making risky assumptions that might not end up in your favor.

So, coming back to the scenario, you attended the discovery meeting and got all your questions answered. The next step is to have internal discussions and formalize the strategy for the solution. As an SA, you might not be responsible for the pricing model and other logistics, but your responsibility is to give a high-level solution and approach. You also have to provide a rough estimate for resources and a timeline to put a dollar value on this proposal. Once you develop the solution and your approach is internally reviewed and approved, it gets added to the final deck or presentation. It depends on the organization's process for replying to the RFP and the format they want to send their proposal.

Once all this is finalized, you will submit your proposal and wait to hear from the client. You are called for a final meeting called **Orals** if your submission is selected. This is the most critical meeting; the client will scrutinize you and the team based on your proposal and ask all the questions they deem necessary for making a decision. So, be prepared for the meeting. Keep all the facts handy. Don't assume that a meeting with C-suites can't get technical. You will be the focus for all the technical questions, and most of the time, that becomes the pivot for decisions.

Now that we understand what goes into replying to an RFP, let's talk about Orals.

Orals

This is the meeting when the teams come face to face. Your squad will accompany you, and the client will be coming with theirs. This meeting will look like a regular meeting, but be cautious about what you say. Read the body language, as a lot of people will be judging you and the team based on how well-organized you are, how well you take questions, and how you address them or transfer them to your team members. A lot of planning and dress rehearsals need to be done for all this. Now, please don't get scared that you have to do it all. There will be other senior leadership members accompanying you, and they will help you prep. But they can only tell you the technique; the rest is all you. Anticipate some questions and prepare some answers and rehearse them. This is like an interview, and you should be ready to ace it.

Let's talk about what you can do to prep for this meeting. I am not a guru of Orals but based on my experience, I will give you some tips that worked for me in the past:

- **Organize your thoughts**: This is the key to answering all the questions. Organizing your thoughts will help you give precise and good answers while avoiding vague answers. Discuss your solution with the team and take feedback. Incorporate them in your answers so there is no confusion and the team is on the same page as you.

- **Form firm opinions and facts**: Double-check your facts and have a positive opinion when answering the questions. Don't use phrases such as *maybe* or *it depends*; rather, say *based on my previous experience, this is what I have seen and this was the outcome*. Clients like to hear answers based on your experience, which will set their confidence level to help them decide. This also showcases the thought process and experience you are bringing to the table. If you are not sure for some reason, then let them know that you are not sure and that you will get back to them and take notes. Answering the question for the sake of answering can backfire.

- **Death by PowerPoint**: This is a common saying in the industry, mostly used when there are a lot of slides and the audience gets bored and loses focus. Try to keep it short and straightforward. This doesn't mean dropping key facts or slides, but at the same time, you need to keep it as precise as possible. Study the slides and mug them up. Anyone can read the slides, but it helps to engage your audience when you are reciting, and it helps produce a greater and smoother conversation.

  Slides should be arranged in a way that shows you're telling the story. This is an art and can't be learned overnight; you need to practice telling stories. Don't spend much time on the facts known to the client; instead, focus on the approach, the solution, why you chose that solution, timeline, the cost of implementation, and the outcome.

- **Time yourself**: When reciting, you might lose track of time, resulting in an incomplete presentation. Make sure you have a time specified for each slide and stick to that. Don't go overboard, and make sure you keep some buffer time to answer any follow-up questions. If you feel the conversation drifting, put it in the parking lot to revisit it in the Q&A section.

- **Take notes**: It is almost inevitable to forget critical points, so keep some notes for each slide you will cover and stick to the narrative. You might have other team members cover a few slides. Rehearse with them for a smooth transition, so it doesn't feel awkward during the meeting. When you practice, your team will know when it is their time to speak and will be well prepared. If you see a question when you need to jump in, then announce that you are willing to answer and then take the question. Cutting someone off and then apologizing for it doesn't sound good.

- **Three golden rules**: Practice, practice, and practice. These are the golden rules for a smooth and successful presentation. Always keep a wow factor at the end, so you end with a bang!

Preparing for the Orals is not only the preparation that you have to do, but you also need a good storyline. To tell a good story, you need a storyline, and that is where your presentation (PPT, or PowerPoint, as some of you may call it) comes into the picture. It would be best to ensure that your slides or deck has a storyline and that you can deliver it seamlessly. Let's see how you can arrange your topics or agenda, so it helps you tell the story you wanted to tell:

- Introduction – who you are as a person and as a company.

- What to understand about the client, their nature of work, and their requirement.

- Explain your understanding of the client's requirement.

- Based on your understanding, what your proposed solution is.

- Why you chose that solution and explain its pros and cons.

- A few slides on a deep-dive into the solution and how it helps achieve the goal.

- Timeline for the implementation of the solution (you can provide options based on aggressive and standard timelines).

- A cost estimate based on the previous choice.

- Some case-studied dials into the same or similar type of solution implemented. This should be divided into a problem statement, the approach or solution, and its outcome.

- In real life, there are no superheroes. Don't be shy to talk about your challenges but at the same time, also explain how you overcame them. This gives the real-life persona to your storyline and helps the client gain confidence in what you are saying. They also get that you are realistic and can deal with challenges and impediments.

So, we have talked about what Orals are and how to prepare for them. We have also talked about how your presentation should be aligned to tell a story. Now, let's move on to the next activity in which an SA is heavily involved, which is building a talent pool.

Building a talent pool

In the IT industry, it is always *we* and never *I*. Dependency on an individual is not considered a sustainable model as you can't achieve much with an individual. It takes a team to move mountains. So, building a great team is paramount. When it comes to building teams and a talent pool, an SA has to contribute, as they are experienced and seasoned professionals and are the best resources for mentoring and guiding teams. It will also help to have a successor ready to take over the baton from the SA if they ever leave or retire from the company.

So, what is a talent pool?

A talent pool is a group of individuals who are cross-trained and can take up any kind of techno/functional job in the area of their expertise. In our scenario, it is RPA. A group of individuals who can consult, understand requirements, understand and design solutions, and get them approved and implemented will be considered as the talent pool for RPA projects. This group of individuals can come from many different backgrounds and will have different skill sets and expertise. You, as an SA, would have to cherry-pick the best of the breed and then groom them so they can go and face the RPA world. To do that, the first step is to build a group of individuals. That is called **recruitment**.

Recruitment is the key to having a highly functional and cross-trained team, and it all boils down to finding the right candidates and then getting them to join your team. Well, a lot of these steps are dependent on your organizational processes, but one critical step that you control is the interview. This is the funnel and filter step and helps in identifying the best candidate for the job. We all have gone through an interview sometime in our life but this time, it is a bit different. You will be switching seats and now becoming the interviewer and not the interviewee. Conducting an interview is an art and also reflects the attitude of the interviewer. Some of the key things to keep in mind before you conduct an interview are as follows:

- **Be unbiased**: Make sure that you are not going to favor or lean towards a specific type of candidate based on their religion, political or social preferences, background, or gender. Keep it strictly professional. You might have already gone through training programs about the company's culture and how they do not tolerate any kind of racism and harassment. This is one of the areas where you get to show that you understand that training and can implement what you have learned by not being biased.

- **Willingness to learn**: While interviewing, the candidate's focus should be on their willingness to learn new technologies. An interview should not only be focused on the skillset you are looking for but also on checking whether the candidate is fit for long-term engagements. The candidate should be open to learning and adapting to the company's culture.

- **Level and years of experience**: If you are interviewing a candidate for a senior role, then reviewing their past experience and tailoring questions around their experience will help in identifying whether the candidate is a good fit or not. Asking situational questions will give you an idea of how the candidate handles those situations and how will they react to a situation. Questions around thought processes and mitigation plans will help in shortlisting the candidates who are ready to be deployed to projects without much hand-holding. Also, it is a good practice to get through a couple of technical rounds so you can get others' opinions as well before making a decision and selecting a candidate.

- **Multi-tool experience**: It is pretty common for candidates to work on multiple tools and technologies. Having a candidate with multi-tool experience helps in a better understanding of the technology. It also helps with better resource utilization and cross-training.

- **Developer position candidates**: It is critical for the candidate to have a development background. It helps with better logical reasoning and is necessary for custom development. It can be either .NET or Java, but candidates with a development background will need less supervision and help you build on their existing knowledge. Mentoring a seasoned developer is always easier compared to a fresher. This doesn't mean that we should eliminate candidates who are freshers. They are good for entry-level developer jobs and will help you diversify your team and keep the costs in check.

Now, let's assume you have recruited some new candidates and they are ready to work on projects. Before they can face the real world, the emphasis should be on knowing them better. Know their strengths and weaknesses so there are no surprises in the future. It also helps in preparing a mentoring plan for them to go through so they are ready. This brings us to the next topic: coaching.

Coaching and mentoring

Everyone in life needs some guidance, coaching, and mentoring. We, as humans, are wired to learn from others since childhood. Our parents were our first coaches and next, our teachers. You need to play a similar role in your talent pool. Your team will get the opportunity to know you and your coworkers in coaching and mentoring sessions. Let's talk about how you can build a plan for your resources and work with them so they become the next you. It goes without saying that *sharing is caring*. The more you share your knowledge with them, the stronger they become in the face of any challenges. It also helps to make them aware of your style of work and how you want them to address a specific situation or scenario.

Let's take a scenario: your team is working on a project and hits a roadblock. What are the steps they should take to find a solution, and when should they reach out for help? This is something that depends on individuals and their capabilities. A candidate might be capable of finding a solution in hours, days, or weeks. You will have to set some rules for them so they work within those boundaries and do not get stuck figuring out what's next. They should know that you are there to help and they should come to you with their due diligence sooner rather than later. You can set some rules around the time they can spend finding a solution on their own and when to ask for help. Setting these rules helps in the smooth delivery of the projects. Mentoring not only means building plans and assigning training, but it should also be holistic to cover all aspects of coaching. Here are some of the rules you can follow to mentor and coach your team:

- **Building a plan**: Each individual is unique and will need a tailored mentoring plan. Designing a plan depends on knowing your team and their development needs better. Setting some **SMART (Specific, Measurable, Attainable, Relevant, and Time-based)** goals for your team will help them grow and learn in a timely fashion.

- **Building a culture**: It starts with you. Building a culture in an organization or a team will always start with the leader. You are the leader of your team and you need to have the vision and help others to see the same. You need to lead by example, and that means doing and letting others do the same. This will help build the culture. Feedback is one of the key ingredients for an individual's growth. Without feedback, no one can know what they did right and what went wrong. Having a feedback loop between the team members and yourself will help the team to focus on their shortcomings. The feedback should be constructive and should tell them what the feedback is about and, based on whether it is positive or negative, how to act on it. Improvement can't be triggered without feedback and it should be coming from all levels so it becomes what we call **360-degree feedback**.

- **Motivation**: Motivation comes in different forms. Every individual is motivated based on their personal preferences, what stage of life they are in, and their aspirations. This is one of the key factors that can push a person to achieve their limits and become a go-getter. Motivation also pushes you out of your comfort zone and when you are out of your comfort zone, your performance peaks, and you can perform at your highest potential.

- **Listen to your team members**: Listening is key to coaching. It will help you to read between the lines and identify the gaps your team members have. Based on this knowledge, an effective communication and growth plan can be built. One-on-one feedback and surveys are some of the great tools that can be leveraged. When the team members know they are being heard and their opinion matters, you will get some great ideas to build an idea and a highly functional team.

- **Knowledge sharing**: Knowledge-sharing sessions are a great way to share individual or project learning and cascade it with other team members. Learning from others gives the team a platform to collaborate and know each other. Developing a culture of sharing helps in eliminating monopolies in the team. It also helps in filling any resource gaps if any team member is off sick or on leave. Conducting knowledge-sharing sessions once or twice a month helps bring the team together.

- **Building confidence**: Team members should be confident in what they do. This is one of the essential parts of coaching. Acknowledging team members' achievements and telling stories about their success is a great way of boosting confidence. A confident team member can achieve goals easily as this will help them reach their potential. Public acknowledgment of a team's achievements has always proven to be a good technique as humans like to get praised and share their achievements. Sending out accolade emails and appreciation from clients and customers always helps in promoting a healthy culture and helps others to put in extra effort to achieve similar goals.

- **Setting short-term and long-term goals**: Setting goals for the team and pushing them to achieve those goals is a great way to keep the team focused and motivated. Timely and periodic announcement of the goals achieved by the team members helps other members to follow the same path. It also eliminates any confusion and ambiguity among members so they know what they are supposed to do to get to their desired goal.

- **Offering help**: It is human nature to try to figure out things on your own and not to ask for help. Offering help to your team members shows that you care for their success and are willing to help and invest your own time. Good coaching is not only setting goals but also helping to achieve them.

We discussed mentoring and coaching and their importance in having a highly functional team. The next activity in which an SA spends a lot of time is helping and contributing to setting up a **Center of Excellence (COE)**.

Contributing to a COE

A COE is a group or a team that is responsible for sharing best practices, setting up guidelines, sharing project knowledge, and providing governance, leadership, support, and training to specific groups. It is a centralized body and works in a shared capacity. In the RPA world, the COE plays a very important role in streamlining processes and providing guidance. An SA is responsible for helping with technical guidance and providing best practices for design, development, and deployment. The SA becomes an integral part of a COE and has to contribute to the overall growth of the COE by documenting the guidelines and procedures, which can then be used in various projects by the teams.

The COE is needed to bring consistency and discipline to an organization. It helps in setting up guiderails for the teams and helping them with a smooth delivery. Now, let's see how an RPA COE is structured. The following is a mockup of the COE for our banking client:

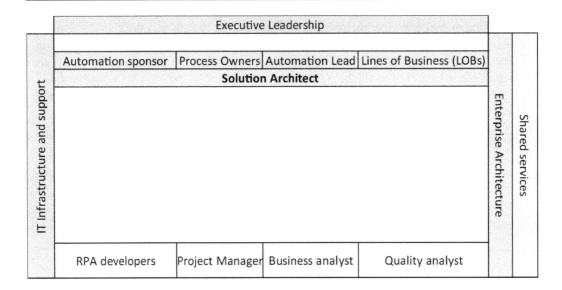

Figure 3.1 – RPA COE structure

As we can see, the topmost layer is **executive leadership**. They are responsible for setting up the mission, vision, and goal for the team members. This diagram is for illustration purposes and will need to be updated based on the client's organization. The next layer comprises the automation sponsor, processor owner, automation lead, and LOBs. These are the roles that individuals perform to maintain and manage the proper functioning of the COE:

- **Automation sponsor**: This role is responsible for communicating the overall status of the RPA program. This role also provides guidance toward the vision and goals of the RPA program. Funding and budget allocation are also managed by the automation sponsor. They are responsible for setting priorities and work distribution.

- **Processor owners**: Each LOB has process owners, who are responsible for managing and maintaining the process's stability, development, and changes. Process owners are senior SMEs who know the ins and outs of the process. They are responsible for providing the necessary resources for the knowledge transfer to the RPA team. They also provide guidance and help eliminate any impediments. They, in conjunction with their team, provide the requirements for the RPA project and set the success criteria for automation.

- **Automation lead**: This role is responsible for managing the entire suite of automation. All automation needs land on their desk and get filtered based on the mission, vision, and goals set by the executive team. This role acts as a liaison for the automation sponsor and champion and echoes the same vision and goals.

- **LOBs**: LOBs participating in the automation journey are responsible for bringing their processes to the committee and providing the business justification for their automation needs. They are also responsible for securing funds, if necessary.

- **Solution architect**: As discussed previously in this chapter, the SA is responsible for providing guidance for best practices for development, deployment, and helping in the smooth delivery of automation projects.

- **IT infrastructure and support**: This is an enterprise shared service that is used by all the automation for their VDI and server requirements. They also provide the infrastructure for network drives and shared folders as per project needs. They play a critical role in supporting automation and bot needs.

- **Enterprise architecture**: Every organization has a team known as the enterprise architecture team. They provide the necessary guidance and support with respect to the design and architecture norms followed at the enterprise level. They help the team to design a solution that is scalable and can be extended to integrate with the existing architecture.

- **Shared services**: These comprise many services that can be leveraged to inherit enterprise processes such as **project management office (PMO)**, quality assurance, governance, information security, and so on.

- **RPA developer, project manager, business analyst, and quality analyst**: These roles are contained within the automation team and are played by your team members or are shared between your resources and client resources. These are the roles that comprise the automation team.

Every project can escalate due to many unforeseen reasons. Having an escalation channel and process helps in removing the impediments in a timely manner. The bottom-up approach is used for any escalation, and the either the top-bottom or bottom-up is used for information flow.

Now that we understand how the COE is structured and how its operating model works, let's move on to see how the SA contributes to this organization.

Guide for best practices

The SA is the owner and the individual responsible for providing the best practices for the design, development, and implementation of automation projects. These guides are a set of rules based on the automation tools and technologies used by the organization. Some of the design best practices are listed as follows. This is not an exhaustive list but can be used as a starting point.

Designing and using a framework helps in a consistent design pattern. Here are a few best practices for designing:

- A modular design approach should be used.

- The focus should be on developing reusable components that can later be used for other projects. This saves time and money when the same applications are used in various automations.

- Data security should be considered when login credentials and other sensitive data are used in the project.

- The focus should be on finding waste and eliminating those activities based on Lean Six Sigma. This will help in streamlining the summation process and provide stability and resilience to the automation.

- Wherever possible, the focus should be on using technologies that are not complex to implement and should be easy to manage.

- Configuration files, global variables, assets, and other forms of common data storage should be used.

- Proper logging standards should be maintained throughout the process so that debugging is easy.

- Error handling should be used wherever necessary to make the process resilient and robust.

Listed next are a few development best practices:

- Hardcoding the values should be avoided so that the code is cleaner and easier to manage.

- The variables and naming conventions guide should be used to have consistency in the code. It also makes the code more readable.

- Project code should be organized in a folder structure based on the application and functionality.

- The process should be divided into small modules, which then should be divided into workflows. Each workflow should cover one functionality, which makes it easier to maintain and debug.

- Consideration should be made for memory consumption, and loading large datasets should be avoided in the memory. All automation software has its own memory limits. Knowing those limits and then working below those limits will eliminate any memory leaks or corruption issues.

- Logical blocks such as `IF-THEN-ELSE` and `LOOPS` should be concise and precise.

- Providing comments to each code block makes them more readable and easier to maintain.

- Avoid the nesting of workflows and flowcharts as they make the code complex.

- Subdividing the flows into subtasks or subprocesses helps in memory management.

- The use of garbage collection helps in freeing up memory and keeping it healthy.

- Adding the business requirements in comments will improve the readability of the code and also helps in mapping the requirement traceability matrix.

- Exception handling should be divided into business and system exceptions. Maintaining some code for known exceptions helps in reporting needs.

- Alerts and notification workflows should be used for the timely reporting of any exceptions.

- Global exception handling or exception bubbling are two of the techniques that can be used for robust implementation of exception handling.

- A retry mechanism should be used for resilience.

- Data formats and conversions should be done appropriately with consideration to different variations so that any data quality issues can be handled.

- Whenever you are automating any web- or desktop-based applications, the focus should be on using strong elements and selectors so that the bot does not get stuck. It is always advised to use properties that are non-textual in type.

And finally, these are the implementation best practices:

- **Calculating the number of bots**: It is always advisable to calculate or estimate the number of bots needed to support the process volume needs not only for current but also for near-future needs. For this, we should keep 10% of our bot's capacity free so that an increase or peak in demand can be handled without any extra effort or cost. This also makes the design and implementation more sustainable.

- **Request for hardware**: All organizations and clients are different, but requesting anything that involves approvals and has money attached to it takes time. So, hardware or **virtual desktop infrastructure** (**VDI**) requests should be made way ahead of time so you don't get in a lag situation due to the unavailability of VDIs. This doesn't only apply to production but also to the development and QA VDI requirements. Taking into consideration any network drives or shared folder access, any databases or data storage requirements should all be requested way ahead of time.

- **Testing**: When it comes to RPA, testing is the most important step for making your bot reliable, resilient, and robust. The more you test, the better your bot becomes. But it comes with its own challenges. Testing the VDI on which the bot will run, knowing the performance differences between production and non-production application environments, and other differences in performance will help you to tweak and tune your bot for optimal performance.

- **User acceptance test**: This is the stage when business users will test the output of your bot and will either provide you with defects or certify that the given requirements are implemented correctly.

- **Post-implementation support**: There should always be a warranty period or post-implementation support period for all the bots. This gives peace of mind to the client that they are not alone and there is someone to help them if they get stuck.

Having a guide is always helpful for the new team members and also helps the existing team members to be on the right track. It provides guidance for the team and sets boundaries for them. This brings us to the end of this chapter.

Summary

This chapter focused on some of the activities that mostly go unnoticed. Oftentimes, we don't know that an SA has to contribute to and invest in these activities as well. In this chapter, we saw that the SA has to work on presales activities to help in getting new business. They also have to invest their time in going and presenting their solutions in Orals, which is one of the most important parts of the presales activities. The SA's contribution does not end there; they also have to build a talent pool by recruiting the best candidates in the market.

Finding the right candidate and putting them through the selection process is time-consuming and needs a lot of patience. This step is the key to building a healthy team with few conflicts and little friction.

We also saw how the SA becomes a coach and mentor for their team so they can learn and grow. Building growth plans and training schedules are a great way to coach and mentor. Having an open conversation, sharing knowledge and information, and giving feedback are some of the industry-proven ways to help an individual achieve their full potential.

Lastly, we saw how an SA contributes to the COE, the different ways they can contribute, and how that helps in the operations of an RPA COE. In the next chapter, we'll see how an SA studies the client ecosystem of tools and technologies and makes themselves familiar with the lie of the land.

Questions

1. What are some of the techniques that an SA can use for coaching or mentoring?
2. How do you prepare for Orals?
3. What is the sequence of arranging your presentation to tell a story?
4. How can you learn the art of storytelling?
5. What are the presales steps mentioned in this chapter?
6. What are some of the best practices for RPA development?
7. What is the critical consideration before you start your RPA project?

Part 2:
Being Techno/Functional

In this part, we will provide an introduction to the fundamental nature of a Solution Architect (SA). We will discover how SAs effortlessly navigate the realms of both technical and functional aspects, adapting their expertise based on the intended audience. Brace yourself for the following chapters that lie ahead:

- *Chapter 4, Studying the Lay of the Land*
- *Chapter 5, Designing a Framework for Consistency and Resiliency*
- *Chapter 6, Need for Documentation and Working with SIT/UAT Scripts*
- *Chapter 7, Development Phases in RPA*
- *Chapter 8, Customer Obsession in RPA Journey*

Studying the Lay of the Land

In the previous chapter, we saw how a **Solution Architect** (**SA**) has responsibilities in the realm of projects and has to contribute to other account-level activities. This chapter will talk about how an SA prepares to adapt to the client's ecosystem by studying the client's corporate architecture. They need this to understand the *lay of the land*. Getting familiar with the type of shared services, departments, and business units will help an SA to incorporate them into the solution design. By nature, SAs are techno-functional. They need to know what policies and procedures they can inherit from the client's ecosystem so that there is a seamless integration of RPA services in the existing ecosystem.

This chapter will cover interaction and communication with the following:

- The project management team
- Business and process owners
- The information security team
- The infrastructure team
- The network and security team
- The production support team

Let's get into it!

Setting up the scenario

The role of an SA is very dynamic. An SA is not someone who sits behind the desk the whole day. They have to interact with many different teams. Effective human interaction is one of the key soft skills an SA should possess.

Let's try to visualize this using a scenario. You are assigned to a new project for a banking client. Today is the first day to report to the client's California office. You are at the reception, waiting for someone to sign you in from the client's RPA team. The moment you step into the client's office, that is the time you start your study of the *lay of the land*.

First, you meet your client manager who greets you at the reception, and you start your conversation so you can get to know them better. Now, I am not trying to give any communication advice but trying to emphasize how important it is for an SA to communicate effectively

Coming back to the scenario, after a bit of small talk, you should get to business and start asking questions such as the following:

- How do we kickstart the program?

- Who will be attending the meeting?

- Do we have a PM or scrum master assigned?

- What project management methodology are we trying to adapt for RPA projects?

These questions will give you the answers to build your knowledge and awareness of the client's ecosystem.

Let's assume that your client manager says that they use the **waterfall project management** model for all their projects. This will immediately give you the idea that you need to go the extra mile to help the client understand how the waterfall model is not best suited for RPA projects and how they can advance to adopt the Agile framework, which is a better choice. So, asking questions and knowing about the client always helps in avoiding last-minute surprises.

Now, as you have already provided your suggestion to the client manager, you would like to meet with their **project management office** (**PMO**) so that a decision can be made about which project management methodology to use. Let's see how the interaction with the PMO might go with the SA.

The project management team

The PMO or project management team is a group of experts in an organization governing the project management activities such as methodology selection, and defining templates to be used and artifacts to be produced during the project so that the project deliverables can be defined. They help in the awareness, training, and adaptation of any new methodologies or changes to the existing methodology. They play a crucial role in the success and closure of a project. By definition, a project is a set composed of activities that will deliver a service or product, or an outcome after a set defined timeframe. Based on the nature of the business and the project history, the PMO decides which project management methodology will work best for an organization.

Why is it important for an SA to know the PMO and their preferred methodology? It all boils down to the fact that *RPA projects are very short-lived*. This means that duration is the key to the methodology selection. Having the right project management methodology also helps in the timely delivery of the right outcome.

Waterfall project management is a linear approach to project management in which progress is tracked and measured sequentially through the completion of distinct phases. Each phase must be completed before the next phase can begin, and there is typically no overlap between phases. The phases of a waterfall project typically include initiation, planning, execution, testing, deployment, and maintenance. Waterfall project management is a traditional approach that has been widely used in various industries, but it may not be suitable for all types of projects. It is particularly well suited to projects with well-defined requirements and deliverables, where the scope of the project is fixed and there is little need for change. However, it can be inflexible in situations where requirements are uncertain or subject to change, and may not be the best choice for projects that require a high degree of collaboration and iteration. But, to give you an idea, the key difference between the waterfall and Agile methodology is that with the former, the end product is not seen by the business until the end of the project and it can be of any duration. With the latter, businesses get to see a partial completion of the product, and in the case of RPA, the bot helps in gaining confidence and also helps the implementation team and SA get early feedback. This early feedback also helps in shaping the bot in line with the requirements, and also gives better control to businesses to make small changes during the development phase. Giving the ability to modify, update, or add new requirements makes the Agile methodology a better choice. Also, businesses don't have to wait for the entire duration of the project to even see how the bot works. This answers the question of why an SA should know all about the methodology.

Now, let's talk about what would happen if an SA selected either of the methodologies and how a typical project plan would look based on these methodologies. Let's assume that, irrespective of the recommendation of the SA, the client wanted to use their existing project management methodology, which is the waterfall model. In this model, there are some standard phases, as listed here:

- Initiation
- Planning
- Analysis
- Design
- Development
- Implementation
- Production support or maintenance

The following figure shows a waterfall project management model, which looks somewhat like a staircase:

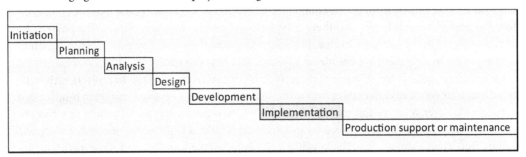

Figure 4.1 – Waterfall project management phases

The preceding phases are subdivided into activities and tasks, but for our understanding, we will study the phase level only. The waterfall model is known for its sequential approach, where the output or outcome of the previous phase becomes the input of the next phase. The same happens for the activities and tasks. Though there are ways to have parallel activities defined, that becomes a more complex model to follow.

As we know, the RPA project has a life span of 2 to 3 months, and having a complex model will not be sustainable for a small or micro project. For that reason, if we end up with this model, then the best approach would be to keep it simple. As we discussed earlier, the business has very limited visibility of the outcome and how the bot will look in production. They get to see something in action only post-development, and by that time, 80% of the project time has already been consumed. If there is rework required, or if the bot is not performing as expected or requirements are missed, then it becomes very challenging to accommodate those missed requirements. As the waterfall model follows a sequential approach, every phase has to be completely locked down and frozen in order to move to the next phase. This also becomes a problem, as the business has to come up with all the requirements upfront, which, most times, isn't possible as they have either not experienced how bots work or can't visualize what can be done to enhance the current process.

Now we understand the shortcomings of this model, but we still need to make it work. Nothing much can be done unless we reach the development stage, in which we get to develop and perform some unit testing. Only then will we know where we are heading. By that time, there is very little wiggle room left for improvements, and then the team ends up delivering a **minimal viable product (MVP)** bot. This also triggers a situation where the bot is not fully capable of covering the complete end-to-end process and needs a phase 2 to accommodate the missing or leftover requirements from phase 1.

To overcome these challenges, we turn toward a more flexible project management methodology, which is known as **Agile**. In this methodology, the business gets to see a working piece of the bot in the early stages and has better control over requirements. Let's understand all this using a scenario. So, assume that you were able to convince your customer that Agile is a better methodology for RPA projects and they were onboarded. Now, let's look at the phases of an Agile project management methodology:

- Plan
- Design
- Develop
- Test
- Feedback

Let's see what an Agile project management model will look like:

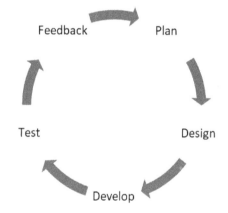

Figure 4.2 – Agile project management methodology

The preceding listed phases are connected in a loop and not executed sequentially. This looped approach is followed for each major requirement. Let's understand this using a scenario. You are tasked to implement an RPA process that involves two web-based applications and a desktop-based application. Data needs to be extracted from both of the web applications, and, post-transformation, needs to be keyed into the desktop application, which is the data's final destination. If we have to follow the Agile phased approach, we can break this process down into three separate logical chunks, called **iterations** or **sprints**. These are designed to execute all the phases as cycles, and at the end of each cycle, you get a partial working outcome or product – in our case, a partial bot that can execute the partial process. This clearly helps us in overcoming one of the issues we saw in the waterfall model: the business not having an early sneak peek at the bot and having less or no control over the changing requirements.

Now, with this new model, the business gets to see a partial working bot at the end of every sprint or cycle. They also have the flexibility to add or modify the requirements for the next sprint based on the outcome of the previous sprint. You will think this is a great model and every RPA project should use it to its fullest extent. Well, the answer is *no*. This model has its own flaws. Let's review a few of the important ones:

- **Not feasible for very short-duration projects such as RPA**: RPA projects are very short-lived. They tend to last for no more than 12 weeks. Within this small span, it is very unlikely to be able to run the full cycles of Agile. The challenges are with the time constraints from business and other teams. Also, as these projects are so small, the assignment of the resources poses another challenge.

- **Time commitment from business**: It is not feasible to get time commitment from the business and SMEs frequently in each iteration. They would request you to book their time once and get all the requirements at the same time. Calling for meetings in every sprint is time-consuming and more time is required to document, review, and approve the requirements.

- **Not enough time for documentation**: It is very common to misinterpret requirements, which can lead to totally unwanted outcomes. For this reason, it is highly recommended to document the requirements and process so they do not add confusion in the later stages. It is also necessary for future maintenance of the bots, as support teams will be referring to the project docs for their support needs.

- **Too much wiggle room for requirements to change**: We discussed that the business should have some control over the requirements but, at the same time, it needs to be capped. Introducing a stage for new and updated requirements will lead to unwanted project extensions and will defeat the purpose of completing and deploying the bot in such a short span of time. The **return on investment (ROI)** also depends on how soon you can deploy the bot in production so the business can start reaping benefits, which then contributes to the higher ROI.

- **Integration testing becomes challenging**: Integration and integration testing is the key to keep moving forward in any project. In the iterative model, each cycle will give you a partial working outcome that you need to integrate with the previous one to make sure that they work post-integration as well. Given the nature of the model that you keep changing, with new requirements being added, it becomes challenging to completely finalize and lock down the outcomes of previous complete cycles. For this reason, there should be a more controlled model that helps in overcoming these limitations.

This brings us to the next question: *is there a model that can work for RPA?* The answer is *yes!* Next, we are going to see how to design a *hybrid model* that can share the good traits of both the waterfall and Agile methodology and still maintain the time constraints of an RPA project.

Hybrid model

A **hybrid** model is a tailored model designed and based on one or more models to fit a specific need. In our case, we have reviewed two different project management models, and both have their own shortcomings. We need a model that can overcome these shortfalls and, at the same time, help us in achieving our goals in the given time. We are going to design the model based on both waterfall and Agile. Let's jump right into it.

The following figure shows what a hybrid model will look like. We have taken the best traits from both the previous models and tailored them so that they fit our RPA projects:

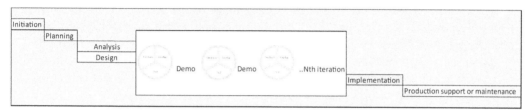

Figure 4.3 – Hybrid project management model

Now, let's review the model in detail. At first glance, we can see that the model starts with the same activities as the waterfall model for the first few phases. The question that might come to your mind is, *why is this, and how is going to help us in achieving our goal of a model that can overcome the previous two model's shortcomings?* Let's look at a few possible answers to the previous shortcomings:

- **Not feasible for very short-duration projects such as RPA**: If you remember from the waterfall model, we learned that some of the activities can be run in parallel, which will help in faster execution and reduction of time. In the hybrid model, we are trying to execute the analysis and design activities in parallel so that as soon as the partial requirement is ready, understood, documented, and signed, then it can be sent for prototyping or development. In the development cycle, you test and immediately get feedback by demoing the partial bot to the business.

- **Time commitment from business**: As your analysis, design, and development are all running in parallel, you are not limited by the business' availability and committed time to the projects as, in this scenario, you are not asking for extra time. The time commitment is still the same but an added advantage to the business is that they can now see the prototype in action and give you more realistic requirements. This also leads to process enhancements, as they can now visualize what can be done using RPA bots.

- **Not enough time for documentation**: Most of the projects that are executed using either the traditional/waterfall or Agile model tend to discount the documentation activity by either reducing it to a bare minimum or just creating a project plan in some project management tool such as Jira or Remedy. They believe that the project plan with activities will be enough to track the progress of the project and will also fulfill the documentation requirements. Well, it turns out that though you might end up saving time on the documentation, then you will eventually need more time explaining the process, its configuration, and requirements to the development team. So, the end result is still the same, not time-saving. With the hybrid model, you are running the parallel activities and thus not discounting or skipping any activity and, at the same time, keeping the same pace needed for delivering an RPA project in weeks.

- **Too much wiggle room for requirements to change**: Using the hybrid model, we are able to overcome the issue of too much wiggle room or not enough by presenting an opportunity to add, modify, or update the requirements between sprints or cycles. The business sees the bot running live and can then evaluate its previous requirements. This retains flexibility and, at the same time, puts a limit as to how much change can be introduced. How much change can be accepted depends on which iteration or cycle number the changes are being introduced at. If you are at the last cycle, then a major change will definitely push the timeline; the business is one of the stakeholders and will not want to do that unless something of dire need has been missed and, without it, this bot will be useless. As we saw, this model keeps everyone in check and lets you run the project in a controlled manner. This also helps us with the next issue, which is integration testing becoming challenging.

- **Integration testing becomes challenging**: The continuous feedback and adding and modifying the requirements help to keep the project moving forward. You get timely feedback and also reasonable new or modified requirements. This helps in keeping the integration and regression testing to a minimum.

In a hybrid model, the number of cycles or iterations depends on how many requirements can be accommodated in a cycle. A cycle or iteration length can be of a 1- or 2-week duration. The iteration length should be long enough to accommodate the requirements and at the same time, give enough time for the development team to work on them comfortably. The duration and length also depend on how many developers are working on those sprints or cycles or iterations.

Faster delivery

We saw the structure of the hybrid model and its advantages over the other two models. The hybrid model not only helps overcome the challenges of the other models but also helps in reducing the overall delivery timeline. In the hybrid model, we can run the activities in parallel and don't have to wait for the completion of the analysis and design activity to get them to development. This helps in a chain of events called **continuous design and continuous development (CD/CD)**. This helps in publishing the outcome and getting feedback in less time, thus reducing the overall timeline and giving faster delivery. This is how SA engages with the PMO and project management teams and helps with smooth delivery.

Now, let's move on to the next team, known as the information security team.

The information security team

Every process that is automated is an existing well-established process. As the process is already in use, it is already connected with data sources and other types of information that can be the bread and butter of the organization. Having a bot controlling those aspects on which the livelihood of the company is dependent directly or indirectly is a bit scary. How do we overcome this fear? We can do what humans do to cater to this problem – that is, follow the process and guidelines to get the automation certified. Now, there are many ways to engage the **information security team**. But the best and the most recommended way is to get them engaged early in the project so they have a clear view of the intent, process, and automation all together to help you better.

The first and foremost thing to do is to ask the information security team to share their process and guidelines so you and your team can study them and get familiarized with them. The reason it is important to know these things is they can come in handy not only in development but also in designing the process as well. Let's understand this with a scenario.

You met with the client automation manager and were asked to review the first process that the client is targeting to automate first. After reviewing the process, you noticed that the process involves a lot of data extraction from mainframe systems that have very important client data stored in them. You also noticed that the process involves extracting data in the form of ad hoc reports, which are then sanitized and declassified manually to avoid any data breaches. You also noticed that the process ends by sending an encrypted file to a remote FTP server for a client's vendor to process the data. Now, with all these steps involved in the manual processes, you wanted to know the right thing to do. You know that you will end up maintaining the same sanitization and declassification steps but there are a lot of questions. You want your client manager to set up a meeting with the information security team to brief them about the project and get some guidance.

You get a meeting with the information security team and their department head joins as they are keen to understand how RPA will handle all these existing data security requirements. The conversation started with you giving an overview of what RPA is and what your role is in this program. After listening to you for a few minutes, you get the feeling that they now understand, and it is a good time to ask questions. Before you even begin, the department head starts stating that they (as the organization) have lots of data security and information security protocols and procedures. These protocols are divided into three broader categories: industry, region, and organization. Now, it gets more interesting as you have been enlightened with the fact that the organization not only has a lot of policies but also that you have to adhere to the industry- and region-based regulations. Let's understand these information security policies in detail.

Industry-based policies

These are policies that are effective or applied to a specific industry such as healthcare, banking, manufacturing, life sciences, and so on. These policies are designed based on the nature of the business done by those industries. For example, healthcare-based organizations in the US have to meet certain requirements set by an organization, which are known as the **Health Insurance Portability and Accountability Act (HIPAA)**. This act labels a certain set of data pertaining to each individual as **protected health information (PHI)** and **personally identifiable information (PII)**. These are policies and procedures that are imposed by the government on these industries so that there is no data breach and information security is maintained. These policies help prevent healthcare fraud and ensure the safety of individuals' personal and health-related data. When it comes to manufacturing companies, they have to safeguard data coming out of their sensors, especially the data used for controlling heavy machinery. Regulations around how security needs to be maintained for devices and networks such as the **Internet of Things (IoT)** are governed by these industry-based policies. Data coming out of these sensors can make the company a target for being hacked for malicious intent. The next example is the life sciences industry, which is also governed by industry-based information security rules. This industry has to maintain and follow very strict rules related to electronic documents, their handling, authorization, signatures, and so on. Next comes region-based regulations.

Region-based regulations and policies

These are rules and regulations led by the local government bodies based on geographical location and region. These regulations are based on a specific state or city or based on adverse weather conditions. For example, regions prone to hurricanes and tornados have to maintain a directory of all individuals with their details and safeguard them based on the rules levied by the governing body. Next in line is the organization's policies.

Organizational policies

These are policies imposed by the individual organization based on their experience and the nature of work. For example, the state government can enforce a data retention policy for banks that spans 5 years, but your client, which itself is a bank, has extended it for another 2 years. So, in this case, there is a government mandate and then, on top of it, there is an organizational policy for data retention.

So, coming back to our scenario, you were given a crash course on data security and how the clients manage their information security by the department head. After hearing all the rules and regulations, one thing was clear: you will need to make data security your first priority. If not, even after a successful RPA implementation, if you miss any of the information security requirements, it will be considered a failure. Knowing all this, your next question was, *where can you find all these rules and regulations so you can get them converted as hard requirements for your projects?* The answer is to set up another meeting with the information security team's architect. This person will guide you on what needs to be done for this project and all future projects. Also, there is a confluence page that has all the general details on which artifacts are needed for approvals.

Now, you are thinking of another hoop to jump through in terms of securing approval from the architect for your design. You also got to know that you and the entire team have to go through data security training and present your certificate to get access to certain systems, which are the target for your automation project. Having this discussion, you get the idea that an SA not only has to accommodate the requirements of the project management team and business but also has to work with other teams, such as information security, to make the design and solution certified.

As we saw, there are some data retention and file retention policies that your *to-be* process has to cater to, so you will need to start thinking about how that can be managed and bring another very important team into the picture, known as the infrastructure team.

The infrastructure team

After the previous call with the information security team, you realized that you need a meeting with the **infrastructure team** to understand their policies and procedures for two main reasons: data storage and understanding how to acquire virtual machines for the bots. This team is responsible for all the infrastructure in the organization, whether it is a server, a virtual machine, or network storage. It is always advisable to meet this team way in advance to avoid any last-minute surprises, as these teams cater to the whole organization, and asking them to turn something around too quickly is like shooting yourself in the foot. When you meet with the team, have all the infrastructure requirements ready, including the requirements you gathered in the previous meeting with the information security teams. As these teams always work in conjunction, it is most likely that they already know a part of the requirements, which are more of a standard to any new project involving data and processes.

If you recall from our first chapter, I mentioned that an SA has to be knowledgeable about the different hardware requirements of the bot and should be able to come up with a bot sizing guide based on the processing capacity needed for the project. This is the stage where an SA uses their knowledge to provide a sizing guide to the team and then seeks guidance as to how it can be tailored based on the corporate directions. It doesn't matter whether the bot is on-premises or in the cloud – the sizing guide will work irrespectively. Let's see what standard bot hardware and software requirements look like:

Bot sizing guide	
Operating system	Windows 10
Memory	8 GB recommended
CPU	Standard CPU
HDD	C: ; D: drives
Network requirements	Connectivity to enterprise backbone

Figure 4.4 – Bot sizing guide

The preceding table clearly shows the standard bot sizing for any basic bot. This is a place to start and then modify based on the unique requirements of the process. The first line item talks about the operating system. All RPA tools, as of now, work best on the Windows OS. This can be any Windows 10 build based on the infrastructure team's standards. Make sure that this is not something that is custom-built and that it can be maintained on a regular basis, such as with OS patching and other OS maintenance requirements based on Microsoft's patch release schedule.

Next in line is the memory. This is one of the most important requirements. It is always recommended to review the RPA tool vendor's requirements and recommendations. It is advisable to have a minimum of 8 GB memory on a bot machine as, based on the OS version and bit (32 vs. 64), this can vary. Having low RAM can lead to memory leaks, crashes, and slow performance of the bot. The OS will reserve some of this memory, typically around 4 GB, and the rest is available for the RPA tool, bot, and other process-related needs.

The CPU or processor can be standard, whatever comes with the standard machine as per the infrastructure team. The focus should be on the type of work the bot is going to perform. If there is a need for more processing power for activities such as OCR, data extraction, large data manipulation, and parallel processing between multiple applications, then the number of CPUs can be upgraded. Keeping in mind that these upgrades will cost extra, a more educated decision should be made based on the process requirements. Having a multi-core CPU is also advisable for parallel processing and heavy data manipulation tasks.

The HDD can follow the standard template, but the focus should be to have at least two separate drives, such as C: and D: drives, so that the OS is kept separate from the bot storage needs. This will help with easy maintenance, and when machine crashes happen, the bot can be recovered and the OS can be restored without hampering any bot-related files or data.

Networking requirements should be specified in advance based on the process requirements, such as specific port access, SSL certificates, access to a specific subnet, access to shared drives, and the need for network storage. Having these listed helps in avoiding last-minute delays. These requirements need an ample amount of time from the infrastructure team to implement and should be discussed in advance.

The number of bot machines that will be needed for development and testing should also be added to the requirements to make sure that you get all that is needed to start the development on time. Initially, the VDI requirements are given for the development and testing as the production machines are calculated later based on many factors, which we will see in *Chapter 5, Designing a Framework for Consistency and Resiliency*.

Now we have defined the VDI or bot machine requirements, it's time to meet the infrastructure team and walk them through the requirements and get some feedback. This will help the infrastructure team evaluate any custom requirements and give an estimate as to how much time it will take for them to provide the requested VDI. This again ties back to the project plan, as you have to accommodate the time taken by the infrastructure team to at least give you the development VDI to get started.

Typically, infrastructure is managed either by an in-house team or by an external vendor. Extra time consideration should be given if it is managed by the external vendor as that might add more delays to the provisioning of the VDIs.

One size doesn't fit all

You will face this challenge when working on multiple projects. The challenge is that one bot machine configuration will not be suitable for all projects. For this reason, you will end up revisiting the configuration of your bot for every project. It also depends on what kind of bots are needed for the process. There are two types of bots used in RPA – namely, **attended** and **unattended**. Both of these types of bots will need specific requirements, which are again tied to the process. Attended bot requirements for two separate processes can also vary. That is the reason we say that *one size doesn't fit all the requirements*.

Attended bots

Attended bots are like a helper program installed on the machine of every individual who has the intention of using the bot to facilitate their daily work. It is an amalgamation of humans and bots working in conjunction with each other. In this mode, the human user will trigger the bot program on their own individual machine, and once the work is done, the bot gives the control back to the human. That is why the name is *attended*, as a human has to trigger and control the bot rather than the bot working in silos.

Some of the use cases for an attended bot can be in a call center where the user needs the bot to gather some data for the customer who is calling in. Another use case can be for customer care to set up a follow-up with the user for an issue that needs further investigation. These bots help with better customer satisfaction, as the customer care rep doesn't have to invest time and put the customer on hold while they go and research or gather data. While the bot can be initiated to do the heavy lifting, the customer rep can have a real conversation with the customer and keep them engaged and prevent them from hearing a boring hold tune.

With this type of bot, the requirements are more related to how the existing infrastructure, which is the user's machine, can be leveraged to install and maintain the bot program and other support software requirements. This does avoid the need for a new VDI but adds more work for the infrastructure team as the number of attended bots is mostly high. Assume you are developing an attended bot for a call center where there are hundreds of users. Each user will need this bot to be installed and integrated into their existing workstation.

Attended bots also save a lot of valuable time for the customer rep and increase the capacity of the call center by accommodating more call volumes compared to the existing call center process.

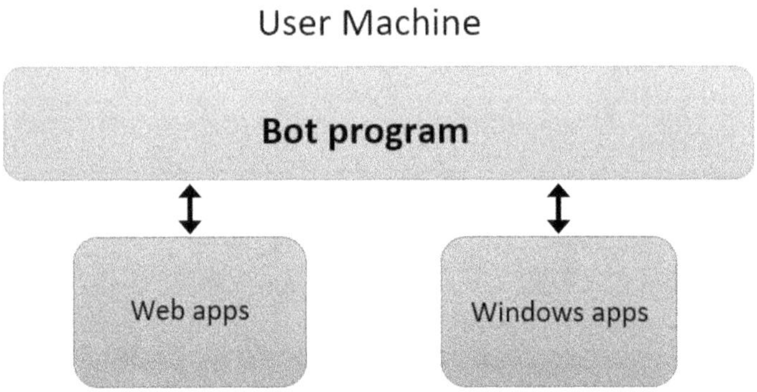

User Machine

Bot program

Web apps

Windows apps

Figure 4.5 – Attended bot architecture

The preceding diagram shows a high-level architecture where the bot program is executed on the user's machine itself and connects with the required web or Windows apps to get the job done.

Unattended bots

These bots are targeted for higher ROI processes. These can be implemented on VDIs, as we discussed earlier, and run on their own based on either a schedule or a trigger. These bots are intended to automate an end-to-end process or a partial process that doesn't need any human intervention. These are the preferred bots, as they are capable of doing a major chunk of the process without human intervention and help in achieving higher ROI. These bots can run 24/7 without any human intervention and are an integral part of RPA. They are also intended for long-running processes where a handoff is done between the bot and human for decision-making and back to the bot for completing the process. This is also called **human in the loop** (**HITL**). We will study this in more detail in *Chapter 9*, *What is the Future of RPA?*.

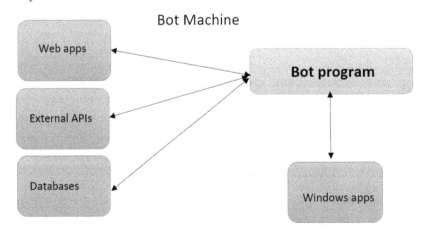

Figure 4.6 – Unattended bot architecture

The preceding diagram shows a high-level architecture where the bot has a dedicated machine allocated for the execution and connects with the required web apps, APIs, databases, or Windows apps to get the job done. An unattended bot can also be a resource hog based on the process and the task it is performing. At the same time, this can also lead to low usage of the bot machine if the process is not needed to run 24/7. It is a design decision that needs to be made based on the process requirements and **service-level agreements** (**SLAs**) defined for the process. Let's understand this through a scenario.

Assume you are designing a bot architecture where the requirement is to process huge volumes of incoming tickets and assign them to the respective team members before they start their daily jobs. Now, as we can see, there will be multiple bots needed to process the huge volume but the execution time for the process execution might only be 1 or 2 hours during the daytime. This makes the bot machine ideal for the rest of the day. Now, as per your design, this is a multi-bot architecture but at the same time it also leads to the utilization of bot machines for the rest of the day. Assuming you have deployed four VDIs that are used by the bot for only 2 hours a day, this leaves the bot unused for the remaining 22 hours. Now, the question that comes to you from the client manager is *how can we minimize this waste?* The answer is to use these bots for other processes once they are done processing the existing workload. This can be achieved by dynamically selecting the VDIs for parallel processing. Selecting the right process that can be executed parallelly and sequentially will help in minimizing resource wastage. We will study this in detail in *Chapter 5, Designing a Framework for Consistency and Resiliency*.

As we have now seen how an SA interacts with the infrastructure team, provides requirements related to the bot hardware, and manages expectations, let's move on to the next team on the list, which is the **networking and security team**.

The networking and security team

When you are working for a client whose key focus is data security and where and how the data is transmitted, then the networking and security team's involvement becomes inevitable. This team's key responsibility is to guide you concerning data handling, credentialing, and network-related requirements. Let's see the activities in which you will need help and guidance from this team. Some of the activities are listed here:

- **Static IP for the bot**: IP addresses are of two types: **static** and **dynamic**. As the name suggests, oftentimes, there is a requirement to have a static IP address for the bots. The reason is more security and better control over which machine is allowed to access what. Unless the bot machine is assigned a static IP address, it can't be whitelisted. Whitelisting means allowing access to some specific resources, services, or applications.

- **Secured data exchange between the bot machine and orchestrator**: Although perhaps not often, there may be requirements for an extra layer of security between the data that is transferred between the bot machine and the control center, also known as the **orchestrator**. This can be handled by deploying an SSL certificate, which will encrypt any data traffic between the bot and other machines and services. The default SSL port is 443, which can be changed as per the requirements.

- **Local data storage policies**: Bot machines are not used by humans so the only governance that happens on these machines is done using monitoring software. This can lead to leaks and data breaches. To avoid these scenarios, it is advised not to store any sensitive data on the bot itself. This is also enforced as a policy so all bot machines can adhere to this policy.

- **Use of a role-based access control (RBAC) model for the bot's access needs**: Every human resource has a role assigned and based on that, the access is decided for that resource. Similarly, having RBAC implemented for bots also helps in controlling the access needs and defining an audit track for the bots. This also makes sure that the bots only have access to those applications that are needed for the process, thus having a secured deployment strategy.

- **Access to a secondary storage site for data retention**: At times, organizations have the need to retain their data and documents for future reference as well as for external and internal audits. To adhere to these policies, the security teams' guidance should be taken for storage needs. These are special storage locations that also support periodic backups for any kind of disaster recovery needs.

- **Access to a secondary network domain for accessing legacy applications**: Many organizations still use old legacy systems, which have specific networking and hardware needs. Due to these specific requirements and limitations, these applications might use a secondary network that is separate from the primary enterprise network backbone. Bots might have to follow some specific policies to get access to these networks, and the security team can help in securing these accesses.

- **Policy regarding bot login IDs and password policies**: It is always advisable to refer to the accessibility guidelines published by the security teams specific to bot login policies. This is a good practice so that the design and architecture of your process can inherit the policies seamlessly. These policies generally cover the ID naming convention, password strength requirements, integration with the enterprise authentication platforms such as Active Directory, and so on.

- **Need for a virtual private network (VPN) for some of the bot operations**: Sometimes, the process you are automating ends up using a third-party application or website that might only work on a VPN. Special consideration should be given to these applications as automating the VPN clients are tricky and at times need some custom development.

- **Audit trail for bot operations**: This is one of the common requirements from the security teams when the process involved has monetary steps such as approving or reviewing monetary transactions. The team would like to know which bot machine worked on the transactions so that they can be traced back in situations of audit or errors. This is also a key consideration in a multi-bot architecture to make it transparent to the audit team and weed out a faulty machine or bot.

- **Log management and maintenance**: Mostly, all RPA vendors provide some level of logging out of the box. But there might be extra requirements for custom logging that are added by the security team. It also helps in troubleshooting and getting better insights into the process by analyzing the logs post-production. It can also help in finding improvement areas by analyzing the logs and metadata.

- **Regular vulnerability scans for bot machines**: Not all automation is straightforward. Sometimes, there is a need for custom development, and this can introduce loosely developed code, which, in turn, can introduce vulnerabilities. To avoid such issues, security teams perform scans using specialized software that is capable of capturing these loopholes. This can come as a requirement for a scan before the code is deployed to production for a sanity check.

- **OS patching requirements**: All major RPA vendor tools are based on Microsoft Windows operating systems. Microsoft keeps its OS safe from vulnerabilities by releasing security patches, enhancements, and add-ons. The security team might require you to make the bot available for a scheduled patching process that ends with a checkout. This is an add-on activity that is needed to keep the bot machine compliant.

- **Use of encrypted passwords and other sensitive information**: As security is the key concern for the security teams, they require the bots to use some type of secure way to use passwords. These can be passwords or sensitive data such as API keys and VPN tokens, which can be easily intercepted and extracted if a proper encryption mechanism is not implemented. Generally, this can be achieved by using a password vault or encrypted database for the safe storage of sensitive information used by the bots.

- **Sharing bot credentials between bot clusters**: Sometimes, it is easier to use a single login credential between a group of bots working on the same process in a multi-bot architecture. While it is convenient, it is not secure and highly discouraged as a practice. Each bot should get its own login credentials so that, during a breach, the damage can be confined. It also helps in business continuity; if for some reason any of the bot accounts is locked or has problems, then the others can perform the task without stopping work.

- **Policies regulating the use of bot machines**: RPA is no different than any other IT project. RPA also gets the same treatment in terms of the separation of machines, environments, and their use. Security teams implement the policy of machines used for their designated purpose. For example, a development machine should not be used as a production machine. Due to security and the segregation of roles applied to those machines and bot users, this can lead to a vulnerability.

- **Compliance assessment for bot access to sensitive data and applications**: This policy governs the review of the bot machine, architecture, and other configuration-related checks to make sure that the machine is compliant with the current policies as per the security team.

- **Use of two-factor authentication (2FA) or multi-factor authentication (MFA) for sensitive applications**: There can be situations where the bot needs to access applications that are secured using 2FA. Special consideration should be given during design and development, as these types of requirements are designed to be used by humans and might not work for bots. An alternative way should be approved by the security team or other options should be explored.

- **Strip down access based on the process needs and on a need-to-know basis**: This is a continuation of the other requirements of the use of RBAC for bots. Apart from using the role-based access requirements, teams might ask for an additional review of the roles assigned to the bots and strip it down to the only action bot that needs to be performed for the process. Oftentimes, RBAC is based on human access, and that might lead to extra privileges that the bot will not need.

As we can see from the preceding points, there is a lot that's needed to be discussed and inherited from the networking and security team. The next team on the list is the **production support team**.

The production support team

Every IT project needs post-implementation support. It is inevitable to not have a team, and RPA projects are no different. RPA projects also follow some of the same norms as other IT projects when it comes to supporting needs. Let's see how a support team is structured and how it plays an integral role in maintaining and managing the RPA bots.

Now, the question comes of why you should involve the support team in an RPA project. It is advisable to engage them around the UAT phase. The reason is that by that time, you will have a working product and the support team can start understanding the requirements for supporting the RPA project. Each project is unique and needs some specific support. Having that support team attend the daily meetings and hear about the issues and challenges you might be facing and how they are getting resolved firsthand will help them in providing better support. They will understand the working of the bot and what kind of issues may arise during support. They also get access to the development team to ask questions and resolve any doubts and queries. Support teams are your extended team who take over what you build and manage and maintain it. To do that effectively and efficiently, they need to know the ins and outs of the project and how it was developed.

Having them engaged in the early stage saves a lot of time and makes the transition smoother when the project is deployed in production. After the cutover, which is an activity to officially hand over the bots to the support team, they will be well equipped to handle any kind of issue and situation.

Team structure

The support team is structured in somewhat the same way as the development team; the only difference is that you will end up having a dedicated team to support multiple RPA projects and bots. Generally, the team structure is either flat or level-based. Let's review these structures in detail.

A **flat structure** entails a team capable of solving all kinds of issues and problems. They technically have the same skills as an RPA developer, know the RPA platforms, and know the working of the RPA infrastructure. These teams are cross-functional and can handle all the support needs for an RPA project. The team is structured so that any issue or ticket reported through the ticketing system can be triaged and worked on by these teams. The structure of the team looks somewhat as shown here:

Figure 4.7 – Flat RPA support team structure

Here are a few roles and responsibilities of support team members:

- **Team lead**: This role is responsible for estimating the RPA project support needs, resource assignment, allocation, capacity planning, triaging the tickets, and making sure that all the tickets are solved under a specified **SLA**.

- **RPA platform admin**: This role is responsible for managing the platform, especially the control room, command center, or orchestrator. The setup can be on-premises or in the cloud; this role is able to handle any type of setup. Some of the day-to-day activities of this role would include user access management, bot monitoring, bot health checks, running matrix reports, monitoring SLAs, managing configurations as per the project needs, upgrades, security patches, and license allocations.

- **RPA developer**: This role is very self-explanatory, as this is the same role we discussed in previous chapters. The role activities change slightly where the RPA developer in a support role is more responsible for fixing the bugs and not developing any functionality from scratch. This role also helps in developing any enhancements to the existing project that are not considered major add-ons.

- **RPA tester**: This role is responsible for testing the bug fixes and helps in **system integration testing** (**SIT**) and regression testing. **Regression testing** is one of the key steps when the project is already in production, as this type of testing makes sure that while adding new minor functionality or fixing bugs, the team has not broken any other functionality. As the developer has to touch the existing code, there can be human errors or they may be due to errors in the new code, which can lead to breaking the existing functionality.

We looked at the flat team structure; now let's see how a team is structured in a **level-based support structure**. The levels are defined based on the workload and the support needs. Sometimes, organizations try to either split these levels to do a specific activity or merge them based on the support needs. We will review the team structure, which will be split into three levels, as our model organization is a bank, and assuming that they have hundreds of RPA projects in production, that will need a three-level support architecture.

The following figure depicts a three-level support architecture that is suitable for medium or large organizations:

Level 1 or L1	TM1		TM2	TM3	TMx
Level 2 or L2	TM1			TM2	
Level 3 or L3	RPA vendor support				

Figure 4.8: Level-based support structure

As we can see, three different levels are defined in this support structure. Each of these levels plays a significant role in managing and maintaining the RPA support activities. Let's review them in detail:

- **Level 1 or L1**: They are the first line of support. All the tickets, requests, and inquiries land in their bucket. These support team members are responsible for monitoring the environments and bots for any immediate issues. For example, they will monitor the bots for timely execution, and ensure the bots are up and running, are healthy and don't show any issues with respect to their machine, are following the SLA as per the process needs. If they find any issue, they have a **standard operating procedure** (SOP) that they need to follow to resolve the issue. For example, if the bot machine is not responding or is in hung status, then the SOP would recommend restarting the machine and letting the process owner know that the machine showed signs of malfunction, and due to that reason, the decision was made to restart the machine. These team members might not be RPA developers but they know enough to keep the environments and systems in check. The number of these support personnel is greater compared to the L2 or L3 support members, as L1 mostly handles the day-to-day common issues that are more likely to happen. They are also responsible for keeping the bots running and making any configuration changes such as scheduled maintenance, password changes, and other routine activities.

- **Level 2 or L2**: They are the second line of support. These team members are responsible for handling issues that are out of the control of the L1 support team. They generally get engaged by the L1 support or in special requests from management. A ticket or issue reported to the L1 support is triaged and reviewed by the L1 support manager. Once they identify the need to engage the L2 support, the ticket is routed to the L2 team. The L2 team is more technically equipped with RPA knowledge and is technically comprised of RPA developers and **subject matter experts** (SMEs). These team members are responsible for resolving a ticket or request that is not resolved by following the standard SOP, such as a machine restart or other generic steps. This can be an issue with the existing code or an issue arising from a change introduced by the underlining applications of the project. These can be changes to any application screens or the addition of new functionality. Generally, these things are tracked by the RPA program manager or the process owner and are reported on time so they can make accommodations for these changes. But there can be some scenarios where there is not enough time or the application team has missed reporting and responding to errors, and that ends up in a broken bot situation. The L2 team doesn't follow any SOP and is freer to find a fix within the SLA. It can be code changes, configuration changes, or guidance to the application teams to keep them in the loop if they plan to make any changes. *It is always advisable to add RPA as an affected* *application when reviewing and performing an impact analysis of a change in an application that is used by the bots to avoid such a situation.*

- **Level 3 or L3**: This level is the last line of support and is the last resort for resolving any issue related to a bot. This support involves the vendor support team and is acquired under a support agreement with the RPA vendor when purchasing the licenses for the bots. This comes as an annual or multi-year contract where there can be different levels of engagement. Levels of engagement can be translated as how fast you want the vendor support team to respond to and solve an issue that arises in production. The shorter the response and resolution time, the higher the cost of support. Considerations should be given to the cost of not doing business for a few hours, or what we call downtime, compared to the cost of support. You might end up not using this service that often, but having this kind of support provides peace of mind that there is someone who can help in times of crisis. Clients who are relying on RPA in their mainstream processes and the financial process tend to purchase the platinum-level support from the vendor so as to avoid or minimize any downtime. L3 support is the expert from the vendor and can resolve any issue related to the RPA product. They have their own levels that can be engaged based on the need, which can go up to the core development and architects who designed and developed the product in the first place. Situations are very rare when the core team is involved as the L1 and L2 support from the vendor itself is capable of handling any issues given that the RPA product is pretty stable itself.

Now, let's review the support activities that each level can handle and are responsible for:

- **Level 1 or L1**:

  - RPA platform support including user access, bot configuration, license management, and other configuration needs

  - Bot monitoring, including health checks, resource utilization, uptime, and downtime

  - Support ticket and query resolution

  - Regular bot maintenance including the regular restart of bot machines, and checkout post-scheduled patching

- **Level 2 or L2**:

  - Bug fixes and issues that L1 support is not able to resolve

  - Minor enhancements to the existing bots

  - Bot updates due to changes in the underlining applications

- **Level 3 or L3**:

  - Major break fixes

  - The system is down and L2 is not able to resolve the issue

  - Custom development and functionality extension to the base product

Support teams not only provide support and maintenance activities but are also bound by specific SLAs for each process and bot. These SLAs are very stringent and also carry penalties if the issue is not resolved within the SLA timeframe. That is why support team personnel have to be very careful and knowledgeable to escalate the issue on time and not keep it pending and miss the SLA. The SLA is defined based on the business and process needs. It also depends on the impact of the issue. Broadly, there are incidents, problems, and service requests. Each of these categories has its respective SLAs. Incidents are mostly ad hoc issues and might happen intermittently. They are not widespread and might only affect a few individuals or users. A threshold is defined to determine when an incident becomes a widespread problem and has a major impact on the business. Problem tickets can further be subdivided into levels based on the impact of a system being down; then, it is considered a P1 or Problem 1 ticket. If there is functionality that is not available and a subgroup of users is affected, then it can be considered a P2 or Problem 2 ticket. There can be a problem that can be categorized as a P3 or Problem 3 ticket if only a specific team or small group of people is affected. This is all highly customizable and depends on the client and their preferences.

Service requests are tickets that are related to configuration changes, bug fixes, or minor enhancements. Again, the same rule applies to them as well and they are customizable based on the client's preferences. When we talk about types of tickets, there has to be a dedicated system that is used by the client for managing these tickets. It is advisable to get access to the ticketing system and make yourself familiar so that, if needed, it can be configured and customized according to the process needs. This brings us to the end of the chapter.

Summary

To summarize, in this chapter, we saw how an SA interacts with the different teams in a client's organization and how they have to inherit their processes to make the RPA project compliant and successful. The SA needs to manage all the requirements from these enterprise teams and bake them into the design and development so that the bot architecture is safe and secure. The SA needs to work with the project management team, information security team, infrastructure team, network and security team, and production support team for seamless implementation. There can be other teams as well that are involved in the process, and this depends on the client's ecosystem.

In the next chapter, we will see what frameworks are and how they can be implemented to make the RPA implementation consistent and seamless. We will also cover some of the design principles for RPA projects.

Questions

1. What is the role of the information security team in an RPA project?

2. How does the security and network team help in maintaining security?

3. What are the different types of project management methodologies that can be used for RPA? Which methodology is the best?

4. What is the purpose of demos in an RPA project?

5. How can data security be achieved in an RPA project?

6. What is the standard configuration for an RPA bot?

7. Why is it important to define SLAs?

8. What type of support structure can be seen in an RPA project?

9. When should the support team be engaged in an RPA project?

10. What are the responsibilities of the L1, L2, and L3 support levels?

Designing Framework for Consistency and Resiliency

In the previous chapter, we saw how a **solution architect** (**SA**) has to study the client's environment and make themselves familiar with the ecosystem. They also need to interact with various teams to understand and adhere to their processes and norms. This chapter will use all that knowledge you gathered previously to design a set of rules and procedures for designing, developing, testing, and deploying RPA projects. This set of rules and procedures is called the framework. This will become the base for all the projects implemented for the client.

Here is what will be covered in this chapter:

- Design principles
- Development standards
- Security standards
- Bot operating model
- Capacity planning

By the end of this chapter, you will know how to design a framework for your client based on their technology stack and internal service lines, such as information security, governance, data security, and project management.

Let's jump right into it.

What is a framework, and why is it essential in RPA projects?

A framework is a combination of rules, strategies, tools, techniques, and processes that helps in the speedy development of any software. As in RPA, we are developing bots, which are nothing but programs and scripts, so the same concept of software development applies. The framework helps lay a foundation for the development and structure of the whole development process. It helps speed up the development phase as the standard components for development and design are already decided as per the knowledge gathered by the SA.

The framework helps bring consistency, standard, reusability, and stability to all RPA projects. So, defining a framework in the early stages is important.

Let's understand this using a scenario. Assume that you are designing a process that needs technologies and techniques such as **optical character recognition** (**OCR**), **application programming interfaces** (**APIs**), connection to a third party, and data extraction from databases. When you start designing, you research each of these technologies and techniques and try to conclude what is best suited and will work for the current client.

For example, let's take the OCR engine – there are many tools and libraries available within the RPA tool, and there are paid and open source libraries on the market that can also be used and integrated with the RPA tool. Your first step is to formalize a strategy and find the best-suited OCR engine for the job. It would be best to keep in mind that the strategy should not be limited to the single project so that it can be used in the future as well. Based on the research, you conclude that **Google Tesseract** is the way to go.

Now, as you have invested a lot of time in researching and decision-making, this becomes the standard for all future RPA projects, unless there is a specific need for a project that can't be handled by your choice of OCR technology. There can be exceptional cases, but for most cases, you can still follow the defined guideline of using Google Tesseract for all OCR needs. This makes it easier for the development team to speed up development and, at the same time, save time in doing their own research and due diligence.

You have made a critical choice of what technology to use for OCR, which is added to the framework and becomes the default. This is going to benefit future projects; also, the code developed for previous projects can be ported and then becomes a reusable component. Imagine you don't introduce this framework, and each development team ends up doing their own research. What if they introduce different technologies for the same type of work? One group uses Microsoft's OCR engine, and the other uses Google Tesseract. Though both are free to use these technologies, in the later stages, it leads to a challenge for maintenance and support teams as now they have to be well versed in two different technologies.

If the same isolation continues for each of the technologies used in RPA projects, you will end up having a lot of technologies floating around and, eventually, you will end up needing to do a technology consolidation. It is better to have a structure and standard defined beforehand rather than investing time in consolidation in later stages, which is time consuming and costly.

Now we know what a framework is and why is it important to define one in the early stages of RPA programs. Let's now see what the components of an RPA framework are:

- **Programming language**: This is always defined by your choice of RPA tool and is either .NET or Java. Not much goes into this decision as it is tied to the tool selection, but it does open an opportunity to define the development standards based on the RPA tools' language.

- **OCR technology**: It is always advisable to do a thorough review of the OCR technologies available, their **out-of-the-box** (**OOTB**) features, and other integration possibilities. This would give you an understanding of what would fit best for both current and future use cases.

  For example, let's assume your current process involves invoice processing and the process needs to run OCR on forms and PDF documents. Reviewing the current process documents and doing a few proofs of concept will give you a good idea about the OCR technology you've chosen and its efficacy and efficiency. As OCR accuracy and efficiency are mostly based on document quality, you will get a good idea of how the technologies performed and which has the highest chances of success.

  Things to consider before shortlisting the technologies are accuracy, ease of use, maintainability, available support if it is open source, community support, inbuilt image correction, and support for color background and color text. This will help you narrow down the technology to use that will work most of the time, except for a few exceptions, and will become a part of your framework.

- **APIs**: APIs are nowadays the standard for integration and data exchange between applications. Having a framework for APIs can help save you from future complications. There are also security aspects that need to be considered while using an API.

  However, using APIs should not be your first consideration. Though they are an easy way to integrate with external components, at the same time, they defeat the whole purpose of RPA. RPA is used to automate what humans can do, and humans don't run API integrations. Humans perform UI-based actions, and that should be the first step to exploring. There can be situations where it's not possible to automate a step through a UI, and only then should the API route be explored. Now, this can become a rule for your framework so that developers don't just follow the easy route but the best-suited route for RPA.

  It also avoids the question of if APIs are the way to automate, then why is RPA needed? The answer to this is, you might also face a situation where your client has restricted the use of APIs, as it is costly and needs more maintenance than RPA projects. Having a plan that aligns with your client's norms and guidelines will help you in designing a universal framework.

  The goal should be to avoid APIs as much as possible and they should only be introduced when they are really needed – as a last resort.

- **Use of Microsoft Excel**: As an SA, you might have already realized that nearly all processes that qualify for RPA and automation are using Excel in some steps, if not all. Excel has become the go-to tool for all business needs, and SAs heavily depend on this tool. This doesn't mean that you should also design your automation using the same technology, only if it is really necessary.

  Let's understand this using an example. You are designing a process that has a trigger point – sending an Excel sheet as an attachment with a ticket number that needs to be processed in

ServiceNow, a ticket and workflow management tool. The process involves reading the attached Excel sheet and then processing all the tickets mentioned in the sheet. This approach seems straightforward as you can download the attached report and then work on that.

Though all RPA tools have great support for working with Excel – they've also realized Excel is a go-to tool for all businesses for data sharing and transfer needs—it has its own challenges. Not all operations can be performed without having Excel installed on the bot machine. It uses a lot of memory to run operations on large Excel files and it is not very efficient as it also possesses Excel corruption and other memory-related issues.

Now, the question is, is there a better and more effective way of using the data sent in Excel? The answer is yes. You can work on the same data by converting it into collections, data tables, or XML format. Why go to such lengths? To avoid Excel-related complications such as correction and memory issues and also to avoid license costs.

Assume you are designing a multi-bot architecture, and your process uses Excel. Each bot needs installation, maintenance, and a license for Microsoft Excel, which adds to the cost and maintenance.

Using a different approach and moving away from Excel for your bot processing will eliminate these challenges and make your design more robust. I know developers are not going to like this approach as there are extra steps that need to be implemented. But once they are accustomed to this approach, it can become a reusable component and easier to implement for future projects. This is again a key guideline and approach for your framework.

There might be situations where Excel can't be avoided, and that is OK, but the use of Excel as an easy way for automation should be avoided.

- **Alerts for sending notifications and system exceptions**: When it comes to automated and unattended systems, alerts and notifications are the best ways for you and businesses to get an insight into what the automation and bot are doing. Having a defined standard and embedding it in your framework will make it very easy to set the expectations of bot behavior. It might take a few iterations and discussions for you and the team to nail it, but once all the requirements are laid out and finalized regarding the alerts and notifications, that can become the norm and standard for all future RPA projects.

  This helps in building confidence in clients that all bots will follow a standard that is already agreed upon, and they don't have to revisit it for every project. Special requirements will just need to be added to the existing alerts and notifications section of the framework. This helps with faster development and is less time consuming, rather than every project going through the same discussion of how the alerts and notifications will be handled and who the intended recipients are.

  That said, let's see some of the common ways of sending alerts that will help businesses gain more confidence in bot operations and give great insight into the bot's operations. The first one is sending an alert that the bot has started the process. This is a great way to let the business know that the bot has started on time and that they can expect timely deliverables as per the process.

Next would be some kind of notification once a major part of the process is completed, such as steps in a specific application or a major task. This will keep track of the progress and, at the same time, give the insights that the business needs. This also eliminates the need for continuous monitoring of the process.

Needless to say, the framework should include a notification of any system exceptions that the bot can't handle. This can be application unavailability or any other exception that can result in bot failure and needs a manual override.

Sometimes a system exception is not a show stopper; in that situation, the alert is just informative so that the business can work in parallel on resolving the issue while the bot is progressing with the next steps. This ensures the bot continues to work instead of resulting in a total work stoppage.

On the other hand, there can be situations where the bot can't progress, as the failed step leads to a work stoppage, and nothing can be done by the bot. Again, sending an alert or notification will let the business plan for immediate remediation and will not result in a total loss of time and work. This is called manual override, where a human takes over in case of bot failure.

Last, if the bot is able to complete the process, then a report showing all the finished tasks—including the work that was left unfinished due to business exceptions—should be sent to the concerned parties for review. This will showcase a clear track of work that was done and what went wrong so it can be rectified for future bot runs. It also helps the business to get an insight into the process and find the reasons why the business exception occurred and how to avoid those in the future.

If needed, the same alert mechanism can be extended to send business exceptions in a consolidated form or on every occurrence based on the business's requirements. This will give the business an opportunity to resubmit the failed request for reprocessing to the bot.

- **Logs**: Logs are used as a mechanism to gain insight into and trace what the program, script, or software is doing. They help in having an audit track of what is happening behind the scenes. RPA projects are no different, and having a good logging habit leads to great insights and can build a base for great analytics over time. But all great things, building a log base included, need time and consistency. This can be managed by having this embedded into your framework. This will ensure that the developers write logs at the designated location in a given style. Encouraging developers to follow the framework and its components helps in developing good habits.

Logs also help in debugging any errors or issues that might occur at runtime. Though every RPA vendor provides some type of OOTB logging mechanism, they are mostly stored in the database and are very basic. Having a custom log component in the framework will help you get a 360-degree insight into the working and processing of the bot.

There is no such thing as *too much logging*. So, the focus should be on logging as much as we can. That said, there should also be a focus on not writing any sensitive data in the logs, as logs are written in plain text, which can be a vulnerability and lead to security risks.

Logs should follow a standard so that in a multi-bot architecture, they can be identified by some type of key – which can be the machine name, bot name, or IP address. Maintaining a history of logs is also a great way to build a database for future analytics.

Careful consideration should be given to the log retention policy of the company. Also, consider any process requirements. This brings us to another point, which is reporting.

- **Reporting**: Having their bots generate some standard reports can help businesses analyze their day-to-day workings. Reports can be built to showcase some of the metrics, which might be needed as a compliance for the process as an outcome.

  Now, as you have already added a good logging component to the framework, your reporting can be based on those logs and other sources, such as an RPA tool database. With these combined, you would be able to produce some great reports, which will end up being very useful for the business and your own review.

  As logs are mostly used by technical teams, a simplified version of that log can be included in the form of a report. It can be in whatever form is acceptable to the business. It will also make the business more confident, as they will know what has gone right and wrong on a daily basis. This is one of the strategies followed by technical teams to show the efficacy and efficiency of the bot to their clients.

  Without these components being made a integral part of the framework, developers might not focus on them, which will result in the loss of valuable data.

- **Security**: Security is sometimes neglected by developers when they have to make the delivery on a tight schedule. Having a framework that forces developers to adhere to security norms helps in keeping systems secure and avoiding any audit failures. These security norms can be in the form of code snippets, guidelines, or procedures to be followed.

  Security covers not only the data aspects but also the process of obtaining the bot credentials and how the bot credentials should be used throughout the process. The framework should define the use of only one bot ID per machine and no sharing should be allowed. It might look like an overarching requirement, but in the long run, these things come to the rescue.

  For example, if you are using the same ID for multiple bots, there can be scenarios where one ID is locked, and now not only one but all the bots with that ID will be down.

- **Data storage**: The framework should also include guidelines for the data storage and maintenance for each bot. Every bot should have two storage drives, where the *C:* drive can be used for the OS and the second *D:* drive can be used for bot operations and data needs. This helps in two ways:

  - First, if the bot machine crashes due to OS corruption or failure, the data on the *D:* drive will be safe. It will also be easier for the support team to restore the *C:* drive or OS drive by reinstalling the OS without worrying about losing any data.

  - Second, backups can be done for only the data drive, making it convenient and cost effective when you have to maintain backups for hundreds of bots.

Proper guidelines should be in place for data cleanup and deleting unnecessary data from these drives. It helps in keeping the drive clean and healthy while keeping the backup size small.

As you have seen, defining a framework is important for consistent, continuous, and seamless delivery. It also ensures developers adhere to proper enterprise processes throughout the lifetime of a project. Now, let's discuss our next topic, which is design principles.

Design principles

When it comes to designing a solution, whether it is for software, infrastructure, or anything else, having some ground rules and principles helps to give structure to your thoughts. It helps in transferring your thoughts and understanding to paper. The same thing applies to RPA as well. Having design principles and following them strictly will make sure that your design turns out to be robust and resilient. Let's see some of the common design principles used repeatedly in the RPA industry.

Modular design

Modular design means dividing your entire design into self-contained modules. It can be based on the functionality of an application or a series of steps that can give you a meaningful output.

Let's understand this using an example. Assume you are designing a solution where a couple of web applications are involved. These applications are used across the entire organization. Typically, all applications need some type of credentials to log in. Once you log in, you can navigate to your desired page or screen. There are a few ways you can design this automation. You could have a single module and have all the steps linked together in a series. Will it work? The answer is *yes*! Is it the right way? The answer is *no*. The reason we try to break this long chain of steps and make them modular is so that they can become reusable components. We try to make sure they can be used for future development if the same application is used as the underlying application. It also helps with maintaining the code base, as if there are any changes to the login module, you don't have to touch the rest of the code. It is also easier to navigate and debug issues if they arise due to any code errors.

Having a modular design helps with the easy maintenance and upgrade of the code. It also helps with integration testing and promotes a testing technique called **testing harness**.

Testing harness is a technique that arranges components into small processes to test separate functionalities when the modular design principle is used. For example, if you have separate modules for login and logoff, then any module related to the post-login steps can be plugged in between login and logoff modules to get them tested without running the complete chain of steps – which can be time consuming and unnecessary. It becomes like LEGO where each module can be rearranged to create a totally different outcome.

For this technique to work, each module should have an input and an output that work as connectors to connect the modules. The following figure shows the modular design for an application:

Login	Function 1	Function 2	Function n	Logoff

Figure 5.1 – Modular design

As we can see in the preceding figure, each function can be taken out of the sequence and still the process will continue to work – given that there is no interdependency between them. This is why great consideration should be made during the design of modules toward interdependency and steps that are tightly coupled to each other should be identified. Once you split the entire process into logical divisions, the design will become modular.

Multi-bot design

Whether or not the process needs a muti-bot architecture, it is advisable to leave room for future expansion and scalability. One way to achieve this is to use a multi-bot architecture in your design no matter the bot. By following this design principle, you will make sure that the bot is future-proofed by allowing increased capacity in the case of an increase in demand.

There can be situations when there is a temporary demand for increased capacity and then a ramp-down. If you have not thought about this in advance, your design will become a bottleneck. It is also not cost effective to revisit the automation for these capacity fluctuations.

Now, let's see how we can implement this through our framework. If you try to visualize this concept of multi-bot architecture, the main issue is how to manage the data feed that the bots use to perform parallel processing. You can design code and deploy to multiple VDIs, but the question is how do you feed data to each of the bots simultaneously? It also raises the question of how the data feed should be managed so that the bots don't overlap but access the same data feed for processing. For this reason, we implement **queues**.

Queues are an effective way of distributing the data feed to multiple bots simultaneously. They also have an inbuilt mechanism to lock the data feed already claimed by a bot, so others don't attempt to access the same feed and create *a deadlock*.

Implementing queues helps in designing a robust multi-bot architecture. Queues add resilience to the process – they have an inbuilt mechanism to retry any failed data item in the queue. There are also options to set priorities for a specific type of data item so that we can meet the business SLAs. The following figure shows the use of queues for parallel processing in a multi-bot architecture:

| Item 1 | Item 2 | Item 3 | Item 4 | Item 5 | Item 6 | Item 7 | Item 8 | Item 9 | Item … |

Queue

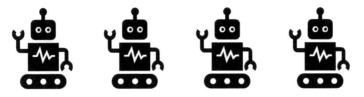

Figure 5.2 – A multi-bot architecture using queues

From the preceding diagram, it is clear that each bot accesses each item simultaneously and there is no conflict in accessing the items. Once a bot is done processing the item, it can move to the next available one in the queue. If you have noticed, the queue looks like a pipeline logically divided into blocks, which stores each item. In the figure, the first item is shown starting from the left side of the queue. This means that the first item that is added or inserted into the queue gets assigned and processed first. This is called **first in first out** (**FIFO**).

Similarly, if we want to process items that are added last first, then the bots will reverse the sequence of accessing the items, and that is called **last in first out** (**LIFO**). This way, a robust and resilient design can be implemented using queues.

Sometimes, there are scenarios where you have relationships between items or a scenario where one queue item will be considered as completely processed only when all the child items are processed. Let's understand this using the following diagram:

Parent Queue

Item 1	Item 2	Item 3	Item 4	Item 5	Item 6	Item 7	Item 8	Item 9	Item 10

Item A		Item B		Item C		Item D	

Child Queue

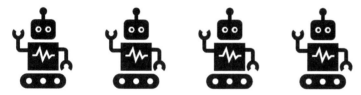

Figure 5.3 – Multi-bot multi-queue architecture

As you can see from the previous diagram, the bots access the parent queue items. Each parent queue item has a connected child queue. Each bot needs to complete all the child queue items in order to mark the parent queue items as completed.

Logic can be built to implement partial completion and retries and specify whether we want to have the queue processed in a LIFO or FIFO order. The next design principle is based on memory management. Let's see how we can implement it and make it a part of our framework.

Memory management

Every RPA vendor provides detailed documentation related to the maximum usage of memory allowed within the tool. The maximum memory allocated depends on the version of the application we are using for our bots. A 32-bit application architecture only allows for a maximum of 2 GB of memory and a 64-bit application can allow somewhere between 3.5 and 4 GB. Due to this limitation, we need to make some design considerations. A question that might come to mind is why is this important? The answer is there is a known error that the RPA tool will throw if it reaches the memory threshold, which is an *out-of-memory error*. It can come at any time while processing if proper attention is not given to each step and how much memory is getting consumed. While it is not possible to test the memory consumption at each step, we should focus on the steps that are processing data. The larger the data size getting buffered in memory, the greater the memory utilization will be.

There can be scenarios where a large chunk of data needs to be stored in memory for real-time processing, and that might lead to an out-of-memory error. To avoid this, we can make some design changes where we try to analyze the data we are processing and split it into chunks so that we can achieve real-time data processing and still can avoid the out-of-memory error.

Another way to avoid this error is to keep track of the data getting stored in memory and when data is not needed anymore, the memory should be created or reclaimed. By doing this throughout the process, we can make sure the memory is clean and healthy, and at the same time, a good amount is available for further processing. *The best way is to call the Garbage Collector, which is a function available in .NET Framework. It helps in clearing and reclaiming memory.*

Special consideration should be given to when to call the garbage collector as it can wipe out data in memory that you might need for future steps.

Now, let's discuss manual override. Let's understand what manual override is and why it is important to be included in the design as a design principle.

Manual override

When it comes to automation, we tend to believe that once something is automated, it will always work as expected. Well, that is a wrong assumption. There can be scenarios where the automation will fail for obvious reasons, which will trigger a need to run the process manually till the automation is fixed.

Also, there can be scenarios where the automation is time sensitive and will only run for a specified time or within a specified timeframe. What if there is a need to run it or trigger it outside the specified timeframe? For this reason, there should be a mechanism to trigger it manually. One of the ways is to log in to the command center or the orchestrator and trigger the automation.

But what if a business wants to trigger it without having to reach out for any help? For this reason, it is always advisable to have a trigger based on whatever mechanism the business agrees upon. It can be an email sent to the bot's email account or by dropping a file in a specified folder. This can be some extra work but it will add flexibility and robustness to the automation.

Now, let's talk about some development standards that as an SA you should lay down for the team to follow. These are the best practices and industry standards that bring structure, consistency, and ease of maintenance to the code base.

Development standards

One of the key responsibilities of an SA is to guide and equip the development team with best practices and industry standards for development. Code can be written in any form and structure and will still work, but having predefined standards and procedures helps in maintaining the code in the long run. It also helps in enhancing the performance of the automation.

Let's review some of the development best practices and industry standards for development:

- **Naming conventions**: In the development of any software, variables play a key role in storing and managing data within the code. Providing proper names and following a naming convention is key to having clean and readable code.

  Naming conventions can be lower camel case, such as *fullName*, or upper camel case, such as *FullName*. It depends on what to define as standard. This can further be standardized by giving structure to it, such as adding _ or $ characters to a variable.

  No matter what style you define as standard, the names of the variables should be meaningful. What that means is that the names should not be something such as *int a,b,c* or *string x,y,z*. This doesn't give any information about the variable and what value you are planning to store in it. Variable names should be self-explanatory.

- **Adding comments**: This is one of the fundamentals for writing meaningful, clean, and readable code. It is important to teach the new developers and even the seasoned ones. Though this is a very important step in writing code, it is very boring as well. Nowadays, there are automated libraries and packages available that can write basic comments for you as per your code. There is even software that uses **artificial intelligence** (**AI**) to predict comments as per your code and try to write them for you. Well, long story short, you need to make it mandatory for developers to write proper and meaningful comments wherever necessary. I would suggest even providing sample code with comments for developers to follow and adapt to the style. Providing developers with clear instructions and having a code review session will make the code structured and readable.

- **Removing orphan and junk code**: When it comes to development, it is not always straightforward. It is common for developers to experiment and follow trial-and-error techniques. So, a lot of code will have no meaning and would be commented on or just there for no reason. The same thing can happen with unused variables. While you are in development, it is OK to have that code there so you can refer to it when needed. But once the code review is done and finalized, it becomes the developer's responsibility to remove unnecessary code and declutter it. Removing this orphan code and variables helps in not only having clean code but also avoiding any memory leaks and unnecessary usage of resources. There are RPA tools that provide this functionality OOTB and help in identifying and removing junk and orphan code. Use of this functionality will make sure that the code base is not cluttered and is in good health.

- **Modular structure**: As we saw earlier in the chapter, modular design helps in keeping the development streamlined and also helps with the maintenance of the code base. Similarly, the same concept can be applied to development as well. Developers should be encouraged to follow modular design and use components and code snippets to develop. These components or code snippets can be arranged based on their function, such as a screen, a function, a scenario, web services, and APIs. We should also keep in mind the size of the code component. If it seems to be too big, then we should break it into parts so that it is readable and maintainable.

- **Hardcoding**: Hardcoding is a lazy style of coding. In this style, the variables are initialized in the code itself with the hardcoded values. There are a lot of challenges with this style and one of them is that the code becomes very static. It might run for a scenario, but if your bot runs on rules that change frequently, then this is definitely not the best style. In the developer community, it is not very popular, but while prototyping and creating POCs, developers might end up using this style as it is easier and less time consuming. SAs should define standards to discourage this style of coding. It should be replaced by the industry standard, which is the use of config files or databases. This way, you can achieve the dynamic switching of the variable data. Config files are most common as they can be defined as text, XML, JSON, or any other readable file format. You should pay attention to the data stored or written in these config files as the date is human readable and can lead to data security issues. It is advised to avoid storing sensitive data such as login credentials and API keys in config files.

- **Folder structure and local file path**: This is more of a housekeeping activity. Developers should be given proper instructions about how to arrange their code files. An example is in a folder structure. The following figure shows a folder structure of an RPA process:

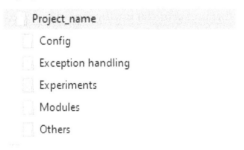

Figure 5.4 – Sample folder structure for an RPA project

As we can see, the folder structure is self-explanatory. A layperson can easily figure out which folder contains what type of code. This helps in maintaining and debugging the code. When it comes to the file path, consider using a relative path instead of an absolute path. Choosing a relative path helps in achieving robustness and avoiding hardcoding. It also ensures the code can work, irrespective of where it is deployed.

- **Value-based decisions**: As we know, RPA is all about rules-based processes. There are processes that are dependent on rules, which are based on values. For example, if the value of a specific field is less than or greater than a specific value, then it makes a decision or selection. These types of values should also be considered configuration values and moved to a config file or other locations where other dynamic values are stored. We do this so that if these values change in the future, then they can be easily changed without touching the code. If we end up making changes to the code, that will trigger the complete cycle of project management, which we can't afford and is also considered poor design.

- **Performance tuning**: All code needs to be fine-tuned after the basic functionality is deployed. Once the code is written and tested, it should be fine-tuned. The same needs to be done for RPA bot code. Tuning can be done by carefully reviewing the time it takes for the bot to complete the process. Time each step and review the code for hardcoded waits and unnecessary loops. These steps add to the total execution time. Replace them with intelligent waits, which are a concept in all RPA tools. Intelligent waits are based on conditions such as *element exists* or *wait for something to appear on the screen*. This is very important while dealing with network lag and all other kinds of slowness in an application. Intelligent waits can handle these time fluctuations and can save a lot of time compared to hard waits. Also, it is advisable to caliber the code based on the environment and the machine processing speed. Generally, a production machine is more powerful and has more processing power. We can use this to our advantage and tune the code to have better performance on specific hardware.

- **Error messages**: Most of the time, error handling is left to the default system messages, which are sometimes misleading or vague. This can lead to post-production problems as finding the root cause efficiently and fast depends on how well errors are defined. Custom error messages should be defined wherever needed so that they are intuitive and save time while debugging. It is always advisable to have a custom message defined in the *try-catch block*, which provides both default and custom error messages definition.

We've reviewed some of the development standards. Now, let's discuss some of the security standards that your bot should follow.

Security standards

Security is always paramount for the IT industry. It is inevitable to not define the standards that a bot should follow. To do this, there should be guidelines that developers can follow throughout the development process. This not only applies to development but also to design so there is no room for security breaches. Some of the ways we can achieve this are as follows:

- Predefining the bot access and evaluating it based on the actions it is going to perform will give you an idea of whether the bot has access it does not need, to avoid it from becoming a security issue. Having a **resource-based access control** (**RBAC**) design will make sure that the bot doesn't get any extra access. Also, baking the information security guideline into the framework will ensure it is implemented without fail.

- Do not hardcode any sensitive information, such as API keys and tokens, within the code. Rather, storing this sensitive information in a centralized database in an encrypted location will add extra protection to the bot code. Ensure periodic reviews of the code are carried out to keep it clean.

- Having a defined risk assessment strategy will make sure that we are following the rules and procedures.

- Have a healthy habit of not leaving sensitive data on the development machine. Developers should be trained and educated to not leave sensitive data open for prying eyes.

- Having a proper logging mechanism will also help ensure that the bot is doing what it is supposed to do. Periodically reviewing the logs and making sure that no suspicious activity is happening is the best way to avoid these security violations. If it is an attended bot, then implementing **two-factor authentication** (**2FA**) or **multi-factor authentication** (**MFA**) is advised.

We saw how the framework, development, and security standards help in structuring and building an integrated framework to provide optimal value and security to the development team and the RPA process. Now, let's review how a bot operating model helps in complementing the goals we are trying to achieve.

Bot operating model

An operating model is a collection of all the best practices pertaining to the vision and mission of the organization. It entails the organization design that best supports the delivery of RPA projects. It defines the strategy for governance and defines a pipeline for demand management. The delivery model, service model, people management, and technology selection are all defined and managed under the bot or RPA operating model. Let's review the sections of an operating model in detail:

- **Vision and mission**: Every RPA program should start with a vision and mission. The vision and mission should define the types of business benefits and clearly outline the strategy that should be followed by the RPA teams. This allows the teams to focus on the outcome and the **return on investment** (**ROI**) they will be getting from RPA projects.

- **Defining the organization structure**: This is crucial for the operation of the RPA program. RPA is not just about implementing a few projects. It needs a well-defined organization structure, which eventually becomes a machine that runs on its own. It requires its own governance and management. This brings us to the next topic of governance and having a pipeline of potential processes.

- **Governance and project pipeline**: The success of any project depends on how good the governance is. It is one of the most important functions of an organization to keep the system in check. Defining a governance model also helps in speedy decision-making and resolving conflict. While governance is important, maintaining a healthy pipeline is also important. If the pipeline is dry, the program comes to a halt, which can have an adverse effect on the entire vision and mission of the program.

- **Delivery strategy**: Having a strong delivery strategy and putting policies in place helps the team navigate challenges easily. There are always challenges in delivery as it is dependent on people and processes. If we don't have a well-defined strategy for managing people and processes, it can lead to failure and delays.

- **Service model**: Having a service model that defines how the RPA projects will be managed and reported as any other project is key. Not having these strategies in place can lead to bad decision-making. For example, if there are no suitable reports coming out of the system, then there will be no insight into how the process is working. This will lead to opportunities missed with respect to the optimizing and fine-tuning of the process.

- **People, processes, and technology**: Having a well-defined **responsible, accountable, consulted, and informed** (**RACI**) model for people will help you streamline their roles and responsibilities. This will ensure the smooth delivery of the process. Also, train people based on their competency and role to increase their efficiency. The appropriate selection of tools and technology plays a key role in the sustainability and future expansion of the program and platform. Wrong choices can lead to catastrophic failure and revenue losses.

This concludes our look at the bot or RPA operating model. Defining these components at the start of the program will make sure that the program has a strong base to battle any challenge. Now, let's understand how capacity planning for bots can help us in achieving optimum sustainability for future growth.

Bot capacity planning

You might have read frequently in many journals and management books that planning is the key to success. It can be any project – even if you are planning your vacation, you need to plan ahead of time to make it successful and less stressful. Similarly, a lot of planning goes into making sure that the bot we are trying to deploy in production has enough capacity to sustain any fluctuations in the load. We need to make sure it doesn't need immediate intervention.

Capacity planning of the bot starts well before we even start the design. It actually starts from the discovery and requirement phase itself. When we are trying to understand the existing or as-in process, the most important information for capacity planning is to know the daily, monthly, and yearly volume. Gathering information about the **manual average handling time** (**MAHT**) gives you an idea of how much time it takes for humans to complete a successful transaction. Sometimes, SMEs or individuals performing the task have no idea that this piece of information is also necessary or relevant. For this reason, it is always advisable to do a time and motion study in which you sit with the SME and ask them to perform the task as they do on a regular basis. Having a timer will help in timing each task and activity. This will provide a realistic picture rather than you asking a question and the SME providing a guestimate, which might not always be accurate.

It is also advisable to have multiple SMEs perform a similar task so you can calculate an average time that will be more realistic for calculating the MAHT. Let's review the components needed to calculate the capacity of a bot and the process of calculating the number of bots needed for an RPA process:

- **Volume**: As we have previously discussed, gathering information related to the volume is important for calculating the bot's capacity. Volume can be daily, weekly, monthly, or yearly. You should focus on finding out whether there is any need for a temporary increase in the processing capacity of the bots. For example, there can be processes that need more processing capacity during peak hours or during a specific month. Having such minute details can help you design an easily scalable solution.

- **MAHT**: This is another key metric that will become part of the ROI calculation. As we discussed earlier, these metrics can be derived by performing a time and motion study with the help of an SME, arriving at a number that is acceptable to all and will become the baseline for calculating the ROI or time saved by the automation.

- **Service-level agreements (SLAs)**: Sometimes, there are processes that are time sensitive and based on SLAs. Adding this metric to the calculation will help you avoid any miscalculation of the number of bots you need. It will also help in baking in some capacity from the start.

- **Bot sharing**: There can be scenarios where the same bot can run multiple processes, not necessarily in parallel but rather sequentially. This can save a lot of costs related to VDI, licensing, and so on.

- **Bot operating time**: This is the time during which the bot operates. It can be within business hours or any other timeframe.

Now, let's understand how the number of bots is calculated using an example. Let's assume that you have a process and, based on the preceding data points, you have gathered the following numbers:

- Volume per day = ~1,000.
- MAHT = 15 minutes.
- AHT of the bot = 2 minutes.
- SLA = 24 hours = 1,440 minutes.
- Bot operating hours = 24 hours = 1,440 minutes.
- Bot sharing is not feasible.
- Peak time = September to December every year. During this time, the volume doubles.

The formula for finding the number of bots needed is as follows:

Number of bots required = ((Daily volume * AHT)) / (Bot's operating hours)

= (Daily volume * AHT) / Bot's operating hours

= (1000 * 2) / 1440 = 1.4 bots will be needed to process the workload. As we can't allocate a partial bot, this number should be rounded off, which means we need two bots for this process. The remaining 0.6 capacity is still available for processing, which is good enough to handle some of the fluctuations. But, at the same time, it will not be enough for the peak time when the volume doubles. Let's use the same formula to derive the number of bots for peak hours.

(2000 * 2) / 1440 = 2.8, or 3, bots (after rounding off) will be needed to manage the increase in the volume. This clearly shows that we will have to add an extra bot for the peak time. It can help you plan and make a VDI ready with the bot code and only enable it when needed. This will also ensure that the license is not utilized when the bot is not in use.

This also proves that it is important to design a muti-bot architecture because you might start off having just a single bot, which will later become a bottleneck for scaling. Thinking ahead and taking strategic decisions makes an SA an excellent thought leader.

There can be many other scenarios where there are SLA implications, and you might need to consider that as a part of the calculation. When SLA is one of the factors for calculation, we should also try to find out whether the incoming volume is at the start of the business day or throughout the day. This will make our calculation more accurate and will help us avoid last-minute surprises.

So, how much bandwidth should be left baked into the bot's capacity initially? It depends on what number you get in your calculation. Anything between 15% and 30% is considered a good cushion for a sudden flux or increase in volume.

This brings us to the end of this chapter.

Summary

In this chapter, we saw how an SA has to define and design a framework that can then be used for the successful delivery of consistent RPA projects. Defining the framework also helps in giving a structure to all future RPA projects and also helps developers create reusable components that can then be used for speedy delivery.

In the next chapter, we will discuss the types of documents needed for an RPA project. We will also see how these documents play an important role in the development and delivery of the project.

Questions

1. What is the importance of a framework?
2. What components make up a framework?
3. Why is it important for an SA to lay down the development rules and guidelines?
4. What are the key considerations for security standards?
5. What is a bot operating model?
6. How do you calculate the number of bots needed for a project?
7. What are MAHT and AHT? What are the differences between them?
8. What are the different ways to find the MAHT?

Need for Documentation and Working with SIT/UAT Scripts

In the previous chapter, we saw how an RPA framework helps define and streamline the development process. Till now, we have gone through various aspects and how they play an important role in the life cycle of RPA projects. In this chapter, we will talk about the importance of documentation, the types of documents, and why they are important for an RPA project. To have a successful implementation of an RPA project, documentation is one of the key steps. Documentation starts at an early stage in the project. In this chapter, we will be reviewing the following types of documentation:

- Project plan

- Process design document

- Solution design document

- Nonfunctional requirements

- System integration and user acceptance test scripts

> **Note**
>
> Before we get into the documents and their structure, let's understand that every document can have different levels of detail. Defining what level of detail is good enough for the given RPA project is important to identify the time it will take to document the necessary steps. How much documentation is needed is always a topic of discussion on an RPA project. There are a few project management methodologies that believe that documentation is unnecessary and consumes a lot of valuable time. Though this is debatable, some type of documentation is needed for the current and future project maintenance activities. Let's now talk about the first document, the project plan.

Project plan

In the previous chapters, we discussed different types of project management methodologies. For this purpose, we will assume that a hybrid project management methodology is being used. Though the project plan is created by the project manager assigned to the RPA team, it is also the responsibility of the solution architect to understand the project plan and contribute to its development. It doesn't matter which project management methodology we are using, the project management phases should be very carefully crafted with input from the solution architect and the development team so that the project can be executed smoothly.

Let's see which sections within phases an solution architect has to focus on to build a complete and efficient project plan.

Initiation

While one might think that the initiation phase does not have any involvement from the solution architect, think again; that is absolutely untrue. In the initiation phase, while the regular project management activities are going on, the solution architect has to think ahead of time and plan for the next few phases and critical activities. Within the initiation phase, a solution architect plans for the access, hardware, and other resource requirements. As these activities take time, it is always advisable to work with the project manager and get these activities baked into the project plan. This will also ensure that a realistic timeline is developed based on the additional activities that need to be completed before the start of any specific phase.

Next comes the planning phase.

Planning

During the planning phase, the solution architect continues to focus on the activities initiated in the previous phase. This gives sufficient time to request the required access, hardware, and other resources. No specific activity gets added in the planning phase; it is more of a continuation of the activities that were commenced in the initiation phase. One thing to keep in mind is that RPA projects are very short-lived, and better planning leads to better execution. Planning is everything, and planning way ahead of time will always help a successful delivery.

Next comes the analysis phase.

Analysis

During the analysis phase, the solution architect works with the project manager and plans to request time from the **subject matter experts** (SMEs)and any extra time that they might need to help better understand the requirements. These are not activities but are more additional time and meeting requests that get facilitated during this phase with help from the project manager. While SMEs are available to help, we need to be cognizant of their time and utilize it wisely. During the analysis phase, the solution architect, with the help of a business analyst, understands and documents the requirements. The document that is used for this purpose is called a **process design document (PDD)**.

Design

The design phase is the most important phase for the success of the whole RPA project. While the requirements can be gathered and changed if the design gets completed and converted into the code, it becomes very cumbersome to make changes. For this reason, a lot of focus should be given to the design phase, and each and every step of the design should be documented. The document which is used for this purpose is called a **solution design document** or **solution definition document (SDD)**.

Development

The development phase is more weighted toward coding than documentation and you might think that this only has development or coding activities, but you might be surprised to know that the writing of test scripts, which is a kind of document, starts in the development phase. It is always advisable to start developing the **system integration test (SIT)** scripts in the early development phases so that none of the scenarios are missed, which is crucial for our study product. We'll talk about all these documents in detail in this chapter.

Implementation

The implementation phase focuses more on the deployment and delivery compared to any documentation activities. While it is more focused on the delivery, there should be a document that contains the implementation strategy and different configuration decisions taken during implementation. This can be combined with the SDD or maintained as a separate document.

Post-implementation

In the post-implementation phase, you will be handing over the RPA project to the RPA support team, and as part of the handover, you have to provide some kind of documentation. The document that is used during this handover is called the **runbook**. This document specifies scenarios and steps to handle and resolve those situations. This document also helps the production support team manage and maintain the RPA bot efficiently.

As we have seen, every phase of the project produces some kind of documentation used by the teams to effectively deliver the RPA project. Let's review each of these documents discussed earlier in detail.

Process design document

When we start the RPA project, the first step we perform is to try to understand the existing process by reading through the documentation available, process maps, and other artifacts related to that project.

Only after reviewing these documents and processes do we engage with the SMEs to understand any nuances within the process. Though this is an ideal scenario, most of the time it doesn't happen. In reality, we are directly introduced to the SMEs and given a walk-through of the process verbally. As you know, this is not a very efficient way of analyzing any process that is lengthier than 15 minutes. The question is: how do we overcome this challenge?

The best way to handle the situation is to create documents. This is where the PDD comes into the picture. Most of the time, a solution architect is accompanied by a business analyst to these meetings. A business analyst is considered an expert in understanding the process, retaining that knowledge, and documenting it well. Sometimes, due to a resource crunch, you might end up doing that on your own. Knowing the PDD and its structure always helps in stepping into a business analyst's shoes. A PDD can follow any template, there are RPA vendors who provide ready-made templates for you to start with. In reality, those templates are insufficient for fulfilling all the requirements that need to be documented for RPA projects. For that reason, we should try to come up with our own template, which can be an extension of the existing templates available from the RPA vendor. Let's now review some of the important sections in the PDD.

The AS-IS and TO-BE process

As we discussed earlier, the process we are reviewing for automation might not have proper documentation or artifacts available for us to use. That is why it is very important to transfer the knowledge you gained from the SMEs to a process map. This process map is called the AS-IS process map or diagram. This process map will help in baselining the original process and also helps in confirming your understanding of the process by getting it reviewed by the SMEs. Once the SME reviews and approves this AS-IS process, you can start designing the TO-BE process.

It is very important to analyze and review the existing process and use the Lean Six Sigma methodology to eliminate any wasted steps. This will help streamline the process for automation. This is one of the key steps the solution architect should focus on to have a strong base for automation. The common tools used for documenting the AS-IS and TO-BE process are Microsoft Visio, PowerPoint, or any other workflow design tool. The focus should be on designing these process maps in great detail so that all the small steps are covered. Sometimes, the TO-BE process is documented in the SDD. It does not matter where you document the process; the key is to have it documented somewhere so it can be referenced for current automation and future references.

When documenting the AS-IS process, the documentation should be accompanied by relevant screenshots and the identification of key areas on the screenshots which the bot will access. For example, a login page screen should clearly show the login ID, password, and the login button section. If any special handling is needed on the screen, then that should be clearly denoted by marking the screenshot or highlighting the area. The screenshot should also be followed by a brief description of the steps that the bot needs to follow. This will help the developer understand each text and click field on the respective screen.

Defining the in-scope and out-of-scope

In any project, defining the scope is a key step that helps set expectations for the project outcome. Similarly, in RPA projects, defining the scope becomes more crucial as RPA projects are short-lived, and not having a defined scope can lead to failures. In the PDD, there should be a section dedicated to the scope of the project, defining what is in scope and what is out of scope. Having the scope defined also helps in other project management and delivery activities. The scope can be defined based on the client's requirements, feasibility, and delivery timelines, or based on a **minimal viable product (MVP)**. The whole purpose of defining the scope and getting the document signed by the SMEs and business is to avoid confusion in the later stages of delivery.

Only defining what is in-scope is not sufficient, as there can be a lot of confusion and gray areas that need to be clarified, and that's why the out-of-scope section should also get equal focus and should be written clearly.

Business exception handling

Exception handling is one of the most important steps in any code or programming language. Exceptions are divided into two categories: business exceptions and system exceptions. The business exception section of the document maintains all the business exceptions that may arise during the bot execution. This section also talks about how the exceptions will be handled and what kind of notifications and alerts will be sent. This section keeps growing as the development happens, and more and more information is gathered around the process. But some business exceptions can be documented from the start, as these are the common exceptions that can be derived from the process. Sometimes the business exception section is subdivided into another section named *Known and unknown exceptions*.

System exception handling

In this section, all the known system exceptions are recorded. System exceptions can be anything generated from the application or the bot machine. This section also explains how each of these system exceptions will be handled and what kind of notifications and alerts will be sent to the respective teams.

While defining and documenting system exceptions, it is advisable to have a proper naming convention with some exception codes defined so that it is easier to refer to the exceptions in a production environment. Examples of exception templates are as follows:

Business exception				
Exception code	Exception Name	Description	Action	Notification
BE01	Excel template	No excel template found as attachment	Reject the request and move to the next request.	Send an email notifcation to abc@xyz.com
BE02	Wrong request	Request id missing	Reject the request and move to the next request.	Send an email notifcation to abc@xyz.com
BE03	Amount missing	Amount missing which is a required field	Reject the request and move to the next request. Add this to the final output report.	

System or Application exception				
Exception code	Exception Name	Description	Action	Notification
SE01	Application page	Application login page not displayed	Try 3 times with an interval of 1 minute.	Send an email alert to the support@application.com
SE02	Login failed	Login credentials expired	Try 3 times with an interval of 1 minute.	Send an email alert to the support@application.com
SE03	Browser not resp	Chrome browser not responding	Close the browser and try again. Try 3 times with an interval of 1 minute.	Send an email alert to the support@application.com

Figure 6.1 – Business and system or application exception

We have talked about the functional requirements and how to document them. The next important section is the nonfunctional requirements.

Nonfunctional requirements

Nonfunctional requirements are defined as requirements related to security, scalability, maintainability, and performance. Historically, it has been seen that nonfunctional requirements are gathered and documented separately in a document called a **nonfunctional requirements** (**NFR**) document. For RPA projects, it is recommended to have a section for NFRs to avoid the creation of multiple documents. It also helps consolidate all the requirements for the RPA project in one place. The NFR section can be subdivided into sections such as security, scalability, maintainability, and performance.

Reporting requirements

As we discussed earlier, reporting is one of the mechanisms to review the performance of the bot and also helps in providing governance. Every RPA project should follow a minimum requirement for reporting, which was discussed in the previous chapter. There can be extra reporting requirements that businesses might need and can be documented in this section. This section should also record the reporting format, the data, the matrix, and other requirements. This section should also include the delivery method for the reports.

I'm not providing any specific template for the PDD, as all the major vendors provide their own version that can be utilized for documenting the process. The template can be used as a base template and can be extended based on the client's requirements. Having a tailored version of the template always helps with streamlined documentation, which becomes the base for future development activities.

We talked about the project plan, PDD, and NFR document. The next document, which is considered the most important document in the whole project, is the SDD.

Solution design document

The SDD is the responsibility of the solution architect. The solution architect creates the document and maintains it. This document is a living document meaning that as the solution develops and matures, the documentation is also maintained accordingly. Now let's review some of the important sections of the SDD. As we saw, the PDD template is provided by the vendors; similarly, the SDD template is also available through these vendors. The first important section in an SDD is the approach section.

Solution approach

In this section, the solution architect describes the high-level solution and the approach taken to arrive at that solution. This gives the reader a clear view of why the solution was selected and how it will be designed and implemented. This section creates a segway to the next section, the architecture diagram. This section also includes the design constraints, which were defined based on the requirements gathered during the requirement-gathering sessions.

Architecture diagram

This section is the most important section of an SDD. An architecture diagram can be designed using any available designer tool. The key to designing a good architecture diagram is in the details. Enough detail should be provided in the architecture diagram so that it is readable and can be easily understood by a non-technical person. An architecture diagram can be designed as a workflow or using infographics. It is advisable to have both the existing architecture and future architecture in the same document so that a quick comparison can be made between the diagrams if needed. It also helps to quickly review the solution rather than going through the whole document.

The architecture diagram should clearly show the different steps performed by each type of bot in a multi-bot architecture. It should also include mandatory and non-mandatory steps. This can easily be achieved by color-coding different steps and maintaining a legend for the same. Try to provide as many details as possible in the architecture diagram, as your developers will also rely on this.

The next important section in the SDD is the project details.

Project details

This section gives all the details at a glance about the characteristics of the project. For instance, the section might contain the name and version of the project, the type of bot being developed, whether it's attended versus unattended, whether the project will use any kind of orchestrator, the kind of scalability requirements, and the kind of capacity planning being done.

Within the project details section, there should be a subsection containing a list of all the packages, custom libraries, custom code, and their respective versions. Maintaining this list will always help in troubleshooting and the creation of new bot machines.

The next subsection within the project details section should be related to the bot runtime details. This section contains all the details related to the bot environment, software prerequisites, input data, expected output, how the process will be kicked off, or any schedule for the process. This section also records the steps or procedures to resume in scenarios when a process is stopped abruptly, or the bot machine crashes. It also restores information regarding any external reporting requirements such as queue-based reporting and integration to external systems such as Kibana or other similar platforms.

This section should also document manual error handling and manual overrides in situations when the bot is not able to continue due to some kind of system failure. It should talk about how the process can be rolled back or how it can be continued from where the bot left off. Special consideration should be given to this step when the process involves permanent changes to the application, and a rollback is not possible. The use of the breadcrumb methodology should be implemented in those scenarios. This methodology gives us the exact point where the failure happen and can be traced back to the starting point.

This section also includes policies related to passwords where they will be secured by the security norms. As discussed in the previous chapters in the security section, it is always advisable to store credentials and sensitive information in some kind of credential management system, either provided by the vendor or using third-party software. Detailed information about the bot machine configuration, including operating system, memory size, display size, and any other specific software needed for the bot, including the version of the software, should be recorded in the section.

Assets or variables

As you know, assets or variables are used to restore values used by the bot in different steps of the process. Listing the important variable names and a short description helps provide a list to the end user. This helps new team members or anyone wanting to understand which variable stores what kind of data by referring to this variable list. Variables or assets should be divided into two categories: global variables and local variables. Global variables are variables used to configure data needed by the bot across environments. These can be website URLs, shared folders, and API endpoints. Local variables are variables used internally by the bot and are local to that function or code. Having a separation of these types of variables helps to prevent any kind of ambiguity.

Code structure and modules

In the SDD, how the code is structured and what modules will be developed should be documented in detail. This also helps developers to follow the structured way of writing code and designing their modules. This section should focus on the module name, a brief description of the module, and what kind of input and output arguments will be needed for that module. All this information can be arranged in a tabular format or any other acceptable format per the SDD template.

This section should also include any kind of custom development done using external library packages or modules that are not part of the base RPA product. A data flow diagram showing the internal flow between modules should also be included in the section to help visualize the data flow. The next important section in the SDD is the requirement traceability matrix.

Requirement traceability matrix

In this section, all the requirements gathered during the assessment phase should be listed in a tabular format. Each requirement should be mapped to the steps in the architecture diagram. This matrix will help ensure that all the requirements, whether functional or non-functional, are met within the solution. A sample format of a requirement traceability matrix is as follows:

Requirement ID	Technical Assumption(s)	Functional Requirement	Status	Technical Specification	Module Name	Test Case Number	Tested At	Implemented In	Additional Comments
Req 1	Static web page	Login to the website	Completed	Bot will use the stored credentials to login to the website	web_login	TC1	SIT	Version1	
Req 2									
Req 3									
Req 4									
Req 5									
Req 6									
Req 7									
Req 8									
Req 9									
Req 10									

Figure 6.2 – Requirement traceability matrix

As we review the sections, we need to keep in mind that these sections are basically taken from individual documents as per industry standards. As RPA projects don't have that many details, we tried to convert these individual documents into proper sections and include them in a single document for better handling and easement. In continuation of the SDD, there can be a section called **system integration testing (SIT)** and **user acceptance testing (UAT)** scripts. Let's understand this in detail.

System integration testing (SIT) and user acceptance testing (UAT)

In IT, every development project includes a major step called SIT. This is the same as quality control testing in any other industry. SIT is the most important step to keep the development integrated, find bugs, and ensure that the requirements are met. We saw in *Chapter 2*, while we were reviewing the RPA team structure, how important a tester's role is in automation. A tester's work starts even before the first module is even completed. Based on the module design and the steps, the tester can start building their test scripts. As this is a document-intensive activity, the customer has to invest a lot of time in getting the scripts written, finalized, and approved. As this is the quality check, if anything falls through the cracks or gets missed, it will become a major defect in the UAT phase. While this can be a separate document, the same rule applies to having this embedded in one single document for better maintainability and ease of use. A sample test script template is given here for your ready reference:

Test ID	Test script name	Steps	Status	Executed By	Executed On	Expected Outcome	Result	Defect ID	Additional Comments
TS1	Login to the website	1. Open the web browser and navigate to http://yourwebsite.com 2. Type login id and password 3. Click on login button	<New, Passed, Failed, Retest, Partial tested>	<Tester name>	<date>	1. Bot should be able to navigate to the website and the login page should get displayed. 2. Bot should be able to fetch the credentials from the credential vault. 3. Bot should be able to type the login id and password in the respective fields. 4. Bot should be able to click on the login button. 5. After clicking on the login button the landing page should get displayed.	<Observations>	<Defect id>	
TS2									
TS3									
TS4									

Figure 6.3 – Test script template

There can be situations where you must differ from what has been mentioned here and adhere to the client's processes. It really doesn't matter what process you follow. The main motive here is to have a good SIT cycle to minimize the number of defects in the UAT phase. This is the time to build credibility and show what kind of quality product your team can design and develop. Though this phase is designed to capture all the mistakes and bugs introduced due to incorrect requirements or code that can be rectified, there is always an opportunity to boast about the low number of defects found during SIT and UAT. The question which might come to your mind is why UAT scripts are mentioned in the SDD as, technically, it is a document created and maintained by the business and SME. The main reason UAT is also a part of the SDD is that the same SIT scripts can also be used for UAT with some modifications. This will help the client to save time in building the UAT scripts. As technically, UAT scripts are just for documentation and approval as nobody runs the scripts; it is just that the input and output of the bot execution are recorded. You will see that other than a few extra scripts or nuances to the scenarios, almost all the SIT scripts can be used as UAT scripts. Now let's talk about the planning and execution of these scripts. SIT scripts are executed when a module is ready for testing. As and when new modules get added, the previous scripts also need to be executed. This ensures that proper integration is being done and working. This execution of the previous scripts is known as *regression testing* and this type of testing is very important to ensure that integrating the existing code or module is not broken.

For UAT, the execution should be planned as per the SME or business availability to execute and monitor the outcomes. The UAT team is often not trained to run or execute the bot. For that reason, the tester or a developer has to execute the scripts and scenarios on the business's behalf. During the UAT script execution, the recorded defects should be worked in parallel to UAT so that the fixes can be retested within the defined timeframe.

There can be scenarios where the client may ask to use systems such as Jira, Rally, and Remedy to document the scripts, process, and solution. It does not matter where the documentation is done or how it is maintained. The goal should be to document each and every aspect of the process so that it is available for future reference.

We have seen how each stage of the project has some kind of documentation attached to it. Similarly, in postproduction, another document needs to be created for the support team to follow and maintain the RPA process. This document is called the runbook. Let's now understand what the runbook is and what other sections are included that help the support team efficiently manage the bot.

Runbook

A runbook is a document that contains details about the process and procedure of generic tasks related to the bot. It includes scenarios and steps on how to resolve and fix those scenarios. This document will have scenarios such as what to do in situations that are common in RPA projects.

Some of the common scenarios which can be included in a runbook are as follows:

- Steps to follow if the bot is not running.
- Steps to follow if there is a system error or exception. This should list all of the system exceptions documented earlier in the SDD and the steps to resolve them.
- Steps to follow if a new configuration item needs to be added to the bot.
- Steps to follow if a new enhancement is requested by the business.
- Steps on restarting the bot execution if it stops abruptly.
- A list of contacts to reach out to for specific issues such as the bot machine not responding, not starting, crashing abruptly, and similar scenarios.

Once the document is created, it is very important to walk through it with the support team so that they understand the process, common issues, and challenges and how they can be resolved following this document. This helps in resolving and answering any questions from the support team. The runbook can be in the form of a Word or Excel document. The goal should be to make it detailed and precise and tailored to the current process. The support team might ask you to add a few extra pieces of information regarding the bot and process. This helps in providing complete documentation for any known scenarios and issues.

This brings us to the end of the chapter. Proper documentation is very important for the maintenance and future references. For the document templates, you can refer to any RPA vendor website, as they provide a ton of documents and templates, which are free to use and can be extended as per the project's need.

Summary

In this chapter, we saw what documents are created at each phase and how each of them has an important role in the completion of the project. Documentation is the key to the future maintenance of the bot, and for that reason, it should never be avoided. Documentation can be in any form, such as a Word document, or can be in a documentation system such as JIRA or Rally. Test scripts can also be maintained in testing software such as HP ALM. The goal should be to have a proper mechanism to test and track the defects so that a stable product is delivered.

In the next chapter, we'll see how our solution architect gets involved in the development phase and helps the team with proper guidance and governance.

Questions

1. Which document is created in the analysis phase?
2. What is the difference between AS-IS and TO-BE process maps?
3. What are nonfunctional requirements?
4. What are the different ways to create documentation?
5. Which document is created for the support team to help them manage and maintain the bot?

7

RPA Development Phases

In the previous chapter, we saw how documents play an important role in the life cycle of RPA projects. In this chapter, we will deep-dive into the development phase and build our knowledge of development activities. As we all know, development is the most important phase in any project. This is the phase that brings concepts to reality. This is the phase that allows us to implement all that we have learned up to this chapter and helps us follow our RPA recipe. The first step in the development phase is to review a design with a team and get some feedback and opinions. This not only helps in giving the team the opportunity to ask questions but also helps the SA to understand the gaps that the team might identify in the solution that you have designed. Before we jump into the nitty-gritty of solution discussion with the team, let's review what this chapter will cover. In this chapter, we will review the following topics:

- **Proof of concept** (POC)
- Wireframing
- Guiding the team
- Enforcing best practices
- Governance
- Integration testing
- Managing the development timeline

Continuing with the design review with the team, there may be a lot of confusion and plenty of questions from a team as to why you have designed a solution the way you have, or whether you can do it differently. Being an SA, you are not only a technical person but also a thought leader and should always be open to suggestions. Be ready to explain and answer questions in a simple and calm manner. Keeping your cool will help to ensure a healthy conversation. Sometimes, the questions might seem very novice, and that is OK, as the team is curious and wants to learn from your experience, so there's no need to be frustrated. Base your answers on facts and figures, and don't influence your answers just because you have the authority. This is an opportunity to that help you build your rapport with your team and win their trust.

Let's review this using a scenario.

You are walking the team through your design, and in your design, you have mentioned using an open source library to automate a specific task. One of your senior developers said they were able to do the same thing using an API from a third party, in a fraction of the time and with minimal effort. Now, everyone on the team wants to know and understand what the rationale behind choosing an open source library over a ready, off-shelf API is. Your response should be plain and simple – you did consider the API option, and while evaluating the solution, you found that though using the API is easy and involves less effort, it will be costly in the long run. The API is not economical for scaling and also restricts future expansion, as you have to be dependent on the third party. You continue to explain that once you develop the solution using the open source library, it becomes a reusable component and can be used for future projects. The team agrees on that and moves on.

Let's review the answer given by the SA. First of all, the SA did consider the other solutions as well and did not conclude the discussion without exhaustive research. This is one of the key responsibilities of an SA, which they demonstrated very clearly. Secondly, the solution was not targeted at the current project or solution but was more of a strategic approach, including scalability and reusability. This shows the holistic view an SA has, which is the second most important trait for them. Lastly, the SA also kept in mind the cost and economic aspect of the project so that the maximum ROI can be realized and explained the rationale behind their decision, meticulously. This shows the good traits required of an SA.

The next step in the development phase is performing a POC. Let's see how it goes!

POC

You may wonder why we are covering a POC at this stage and whether this should be covered by the SA during the solution stage. Well, you are right – this POC is not for the components, new technology, or any open source library but more for the application and other components that are involved in the process. Doing a quick POC will give you the confidence that there will be no roadblocks or impediments as the development advances. This needs to be taken care of at this stage to avoid any issues later, as then you will have neither the liberty to change your course of action nor the time to go back to the whiteboard to redesign the process.

Let's understand this using a scenario.

You are working on an RPA project that involves three applications – one is a home-grown application developed on dotnet, the second application is a third-party application that is accessible only through a VPN, and the third application is based on a desktop thick client.

You have started your development without a quick POC, based on your gut feeling and past experience. Your developer reports to you that this application can't be automated with the automation strategy you have selected, as part of the application is developed using Adobe Flash. You call for a team meeting, where it is discovered that this functionality was embedded into one of the screens that was developed by a different team. You gather more information and get to the bottom of this. You talk to your analyst who wrote the PDD, and they say it looked similar to other pages, "*so we assumed that it was the same technology.*" This assumption will cost you your project timeline and a ton of embarrassment. It's good to have a gut feeling and good confidence in the project you're working on, but to avoid situations such as these, avoid relying just on them. When it comes to a homegrown application, always double-check the technologies used for every component that will be automated.

Let's assume you worked your magic and were able to pass that hurdle. The next obstacle is with the third-party application. Your automation was full-swing when you were called for a meeting by the RPA program sponsor. You might remember what an RPA sponsor is from the previous chapters. In this meeting, the sponsor informs everyone that the project has to be put on hold for an indefinite amount of time. He continues that he was contacted by the third-party vendor, and they explained that their major concern was that the vendor's website was being accessed by bots. It is strictly written in their contract that no bot or spider is allowed to access the website without written permission. They say that the bots make the website slow and degrade performance. As this is a common website used by multiple clients, this leads to major issues for other clients. The vendor suggested that if they wanted to use the bot, then they would have to sign another contract and use their APIs to get the job done rather than the portal. This added another layer of complexity in terms of cost and signing the contract.

This could have been avoided or tackled had the team done a quick POC at the beginning. When you don't do a POC, you tend to miss these aspects, and they are very likely to fall through the cracks. These types of issues can lead to the cancelation of a whole project. *Also, when dealing with third-party applications, always read their licensing agreement and legal clauses to be sure there are no such restrictions to using automation.*

There can be another scenario where you are dealing with a **Completely Automated Public Turing test to tell Computers and Humans Apart (CAPTCHA)**, a security mechanism and challenge-response system that prohibits an automation to run without performing some human intelligence-based steps. For example, it can ask you to type some letters, numbers, or symbols. These letters, numbers, and symbols will be shown as an image so that automated bots can't read it easily. They will add some impurities as well to the image so that OCR can't be used, such as adding a colored background or extra graphics. This is an anti-bot security mechanism. When an application involves the use of a CAPTCHA, then the SA needs to discuss the options with the vendor or the application team to see whether the CAPTCHA can be bypassed or handled using an API call, where the bot can satisfy the CAPTCHA request behind the scenes by providing a security token of some kind. It is a complicated design, model design, and form of development, and security considerations should be in place.

Let's now see some of the ways you can build a successful POC in record time. I've summarized it in the following steps:

- **Study the user manual and other documents**: Let's assume that you are trying to do a quick POC on functionality that involves an open source library. The first thing you should do is read the documentation and study it for any clause that might become a roadblock for future use of code. This involves reading the feature list, installation instructions, any hardware and software needs, future enhancements, open issues and bugs, the community size, the support available, the response time from the community, and the license agreement. Finding an open source solution on the internet can be done by a 10-year-old kid, but then vetting it so that it doesn't become a viable lawsuit is where you, as an expert, come into the picture. Focus on the type of license agreement, as there are many license types, and as an SA, you should visit `https://opensource.org/licenses` for more insight into the types of licenses.

- **Initiate a security scan**: Every organization or client you will work for has a team of security experts who can help you achieve this. This is a very important step before you even start your POC. You raise a request or follow whatever process your client has for these types of requests and then scan the piece of open source software you are trying to use for any potential malware, virus, or malicious code. We need to understand that the internet is full of gems and garbage. You might stumble upon a very lucrative piece of software but it ends up having a virus or malicious code, which can not only ruin your and your company's reputation but also cost your client a lot of trouble and money. This can go very wrong very quickly. Remember, *haste makes waste*. So, follow the procedure and get it certified. This should be followed for every piece of software you plan to use in your process. Do not attempt to do this on your own. There is a team of experts dedicated to do this for a reason.

- **Separate environment**: Now that you have the library scanned for vulnerabilities, you can safely use it for your POC. While preparing the POC, keep it separate from the existing code so that it doesn't break anything, and at the same time, if it doesn't work, it can be discarded easily without any harm.

- **Validate your solution**: Once the POC is ready, validate it for not only the current use case but also for any future use cases so that the POC can be converted into a reusable component. This is the added value that clients are looking for, and that is what you have been hired for.

- **Review and socialize**: Once the solution is tested and you are satisfied, share it with your team and get feedback from them. It is very important to keep your team in the loop, as your developers are the ones who will convert your POC into full-blown code. Also, keep your project manager and other concerned parties in the loop so that they also know the value you are adding. Seeing is believing, and that is what you need to do at every step of the process.

- **Minimum Viable Product (MVP)**: Set boundaries for your POC. An open source library or product can be leveraged in many ways, but you need to set the boundaries so that you can add a time limit for your POC and don't run out of time to accommodate each and every functionality there is to utilize. Focus on the current need, but also build the knowledge base so that other functions can be utilized in the future. This is where the concept of an MVP comes into the picture and helps you define the scope of the POC.

Now, as we understand the importance of the POC and the difference between doing a POC at the development stage and during the design stage, let's see how the POC should be performed. This type of POC is very disintegrated, and it is only for the developer to unearth this kind of issue early in the development stage. This is like checking a live wire with a tester to see whether the current is flowing. This doesn't take much time but can save a project; as the saying goes, *a stitch in time saves nine*. This task should also be divided between the developers so that it can be quick.

Now, we performed the POC for all the doubtful components, and we decided that these components should be verified before development starts in a full-fledged form.

The next step now is to work on the wireframe.

Wireframing

Wireframing is a concept and technique used for user interface design or software design where a visual aspect is involved. It doesn't mean that it can only be used in user interfaces. The wireframe concepts can also be used to write code. You can call it templates or code snippets.

This is an important step that ensures that each developer uses the same style of coding. If you remember in the initial chapters, we discussed that design is modular, and each developer ends up developing one or two modules. Now, if you don't set a standard for development, then everyone can come up with their own ideas, which can become a mess when maintaining the code base. It will also become a bottleneck for scaling. To avoid all this, we should build a wireframe. This can be a simple flow of data or a process based on a module the developer is working on, but it should be under the guidance of the SA.

You might have read about the **Robotic Enterprise (RE) framework** in UiPath and got it confused with wireframing. They are two different concepts. Wireframing is more about designing the internal working of a module rather than a workflow. The following figure shows a wire frame for a web application module:

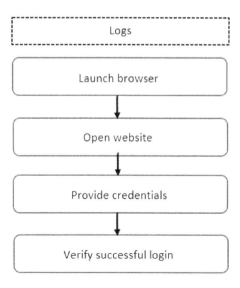

Figure 7.1 – Wireframing

Having a wireframe also helps to streamline the development process by giving the developer the time to focus on implementing the best practices, rather than investing time in structuring the code. It brings consistency and flow to the development process. Sometimes, when there is a roadblock and a solution is not clear, this technique can be used to save time by building the wireframe so that once the solution is clear and tested, the blanks can be filled in rather than just waiting and wasting time.

Let's review an example to understand this scenario.

One of the steps in your process is to download reports from a website and extract data from it for further processing. When your developer started the development, they realized that the report format kept changing. The report is in PDF format, and the format is not standard. The challenge is that the data to be extracted is unstructured and not specific. They bring this to you for a solution and approach. While you are figuring out the best possible solution, you tell the developer to continue with their development. Now, as this is the only module assigned to them and there is a lot of work left in order to continue with the work, the developer has only created a wire frame for this piece of code and will then move on with the rest of the development.

This will help in two ways. Firstly, it will not waste the developer's time due to the clarity of the solution, and secondly, they will be able to continue their development without leaving blanks, which can be confusing when coming back to fill the gap. A wireframe also helps by leaving enough details so that it can be filled in later without losing momentum. The following diagram shows how a wireframe helps in saving time and keeping momentum, helping a project move forward.

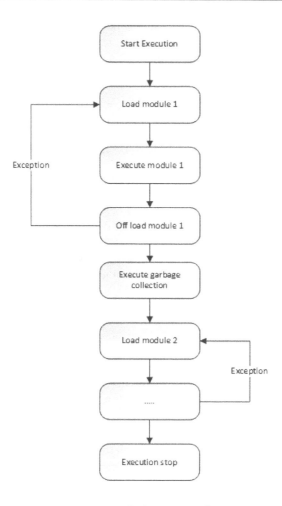

Figure 7.2 – Code execution flow

From the previous diagram, we can clearly see how code is executed and how we can split the different modules to achieve the modularity we always planned in our design. Now, let's see how the preceding workflow came into the picture. It is possible only when we have a wireframe for our design. This helps us to visualize the concept and the control flow of the code. It can clearly show us the failure points so that we can put more emphasis on exception handling and make the code robust. It also helps to find where the code splits so that it can be modularized and later used as reusable components.

Now, you can either do twice the work of creating an execution diagram, such as *Figure 7.2*, or instead, you can use your code as an execution diagram with the use of wireframing. It serves a dual purpose – it gives you the visual structure of your code as well as helping you thinking ahead. It goes without saying that *a picture is worth a thousand words*, and that is what a wireframe diagram will help you achieve and visualize.

Your wireframe becomes your blueprint, which can then be used either as a template or become a part of your coding standard. It can also become an aid for teaching and preaching the best practices to your team. Also, it can be used to explain the approach to your client and project manager. It also helps you to quickly identify the failure points by visually seeing the complete blueprint and then taking measures to be proactive.

Let's now move on to the next activity that the SA has to perform during the development phase – being a *guide* and a *mentor*.

Guiding the team

We read about this function of the SA in previous chapters, but in this chapter, we will do a deeper dive into how an SA can proactively help a team before they even ask for help. This helps in two ways – it eliminates the deliverables being delayed and helps to mitigate the shy nature of developers who will avoid asking for help. The SA's primary job is to make sure that developers get all the help they need. The SA is the caretaker. If developers make mistakes, it comes back to you. Do not, in any situation, think that they are responsible. Think of this as a student-teacher relationship. If a student fails in any subject, it is not entirely the student's fault but also the teacher's.

So, now let's see how an SA can sharpen their instincts to sense and detect that a developer needs help:

- **Experience**: A lot can be learned over time and with experience. SAs use their experience as one of the tools to detect these knowledge gaps. But what if you have just started your career and have not gained enough experience to become a Jedi and play mind tricks? What if you just got promoted from senior developer to SA? Well, the best way to read and understand the situation is to talk to the person or developer. Explain to them that they will not be judged because they asked, say, how to read a specific cell from a data table. Everyone needs a little help. They might have already googled it and not even come to you. But not all questions are answered by Google. For example, fetching data from a data table can be achieved in numerous ways, but there is only a couple of ways to achieve speed and robustness. You, being an SA, might already know that your developer is new or doesn't have enough experience and will tend to opt for an easy solution to get the job done. That immediately opens an opportunity for you to talk to them and ask them to explain to you their approach. Then, after you have listened to their approach, propose your approach with the pros and cons and with due respect. This will not only demonstrate your leadership but also your in-depth knowledge of the subject. Then, next time, a developer will not hesitate to come to you for help or suggestions. This is how a good SA builds rapport and trust within a team.

- **Mentor**: You might recall reading this in the earlier chapters, and at the risk of sounding redundant, I will reiterate – the SA is not only a technical professional but also a leader and a mentor. Their responsibilities also include tending to and guiding a team. Being a mentor and leader, the first responsibility of an SA toward their team is to be transparent. Being transparent means being open and communicative as often as needed so that a developer knows what is going on around them. They shouldn't feel left out. You might wonder how it helps the developer or the team. Well, being transparent gives the sense and feeling of being appreciated and respected. This feeling can't be created instantaneously and comes with the consistent practice of being transparent.

  With good communication, the next best thing that an SA can do is provide constructive feedback. Continuous feedback helps to boost a team's confidence and morale. This helps in better inter-team communication and collaboration. Feedback can't always be positive; sometimes it will be negative, and that gives the SA the opportunity to help developers learn and understand what went wrong so that next time, it can be avoided. This, in return, helps the SA to build a strong team that can deliver results faster, better, and cheaper. Collaboration between teams and team members is very crucial to build a healthy working environment and helps in sharing knowledge. One of the ways to promote collaboration is to schedule bi-weekly or monthly sharing sessions, where the SA can invite team members to present what they are working on and discuss any challenges they might be facing in their work. This promotes knowledge-sharing which is the fuel for growth. It also helps to cross-train developers and makes them aware of what else is going on so that, if needed, they can be deployed as a replacement. No one likes a micro-manager, so an SA should be able to trust the team to do their job and not become too scrutinizing. Having confidence in your team and delegating tasks will help you as an SA to grow with others. Delegation doesn't just mean assigning and forgetting about a task; it means being in the loop and take updates while not becoming a micro-manager.

- **Development best practices**: If you are reading this book, then you have been involved in the RPA field in one way or another. In this field, you might have heard about development best practices. In this section, we will talk about them in detail:

  - **A variable naming convention**: This might seem trivial, but being an SA is always about consistency, reliability, and standards. As I have mentioned multiple times throughout the book, anyone can write code, but there is good code and there is bad code. Both types of code might run and perform as expected, but poorly written code will end up having issues later in maintenance and extension, which leads to more challenges. As these challenges will be faced when the original developer is long gone, the issue arises of no one having a clue what the code is trying to do. Let's understand this with the help of the following diagram:

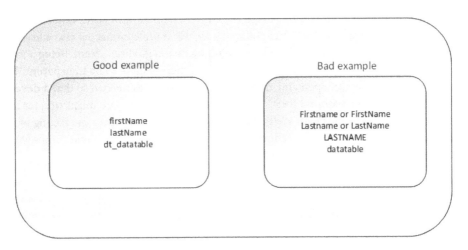

Figure 7.3 – A variable naming convention

In the preceding figure, we can clearly see the differences between the good and bad code examples. The best practice is to use a camel-style naming convention for the variable shown on the left-hand side of the image. The variable should not start with var in front of it, such as var_.

- **Arguments or start and end parameters**: In UiPath, these are called *arguments*, and in Blue Prism, they are referred to as *start and end parameters*. The concept remains the same. Whenever we want to take data from one workflow to another, we use arguments. Similarly, in Blue Prism, when data is needed to start a business object and then the output of the object needs to be collected into a variable, then it is defined in the start and end stages. Let's understand this with the help of the following figure:

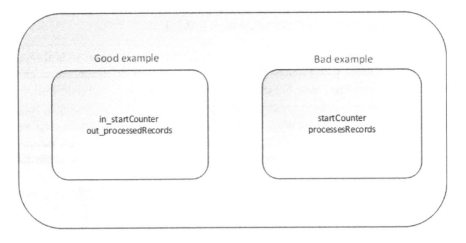

Figure 7.4 – The argument naming convention

- You may wonder why is it not good to follow the same naming convention as that for variables. The reason is to differentiate between variables and arguments or start and end parameters. By doing this, it becomes easier to identify which variables are used for what reason. Technically, all of them are the same. You can follow the same naming convention for variables and your code will still work, but as I said, having clean code that is readable and easier to maintain should follow some best practices. In the preceding example, we added the in and out prefixes to our variable names so that they can be easily identified for their purpose. In UiPath, we have a concept of two-way arguments and that means you can add an io in your variable to denote the same, which stands for input and output.

- **Exception handling (try and catch block)**: Exception handling is the key to writing any robust code. It is language-agnostic. Every programming language has some standard that should be followed to implement exception handling efficiently. As we know, most of the RPA tools are dotnet-based, and in dotnet, we use the `try`, `catch`, `finally`, and `throw` blocks. We will not go into the dotnet way of implementation, but the best practice is not to leave any block empty. Leaving an empty block might work but is not considered a clean and efficient way of developing. To understand this better, see the following diagram:

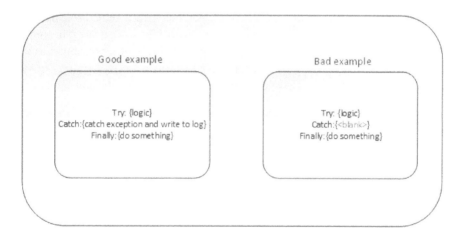

Figure 7.5 – The best practice for writing the try and catch block

- It is very likely that developers will only focus on implementing the exception block and forget to write it out to a log. This can still work and will not throw any errors, but is not considered a best practice. In the long run, it can become a challenge to debug the code. If there is an exception that was captured, it might not be very clear what that exception is all about. Writing it explicitly helps to make the debugging process easier.

- **Empty code blocks**: While writing code, it is very easy to leave blank code blocks, known as sequences in UiPath terminology and pages in Blue Prism terminology. You might think it is not a big deal and doesn't harm the code in any way, but, in reality, it does. If you study the internal architecture of how code is processed and loaded into memory, then you will realize that all RPA software scans the code sequentially and then loads it into memory for execution. This means that all the blank code clocks also get loaded into the memory and end up consuming memory, which is not very efficient. One or two empty blocks might not make a difference, but when best practices are not followed, this can become a problem when you are experimenting and keep leaving the empty or unused code, which can also lead to memory corruption. Keeping clean code and cleaning it after your experiments is the best practice.

- **Strong selectors or elements**: All RPA software works on the basis of selectors or elements. These are unique identifiers within the RPA software that know which field or button to access and act on. Not having a strong selector or element can lead to ambiguity, which leads to bot failure. Now, let's understand what some of the best practices are to make selectors and elements strong. The first thing to keep in mind is to avoid text-only-based selectors and elements. Text is considered a weak method of identification and is also slow. Internally, a code processor has to use many different methods to determine whether the target is the right selector or not. Instead, the use of indexes (idx) is a better way to make the selector strong. One thing to keep in mind while using idx is it should not be greater than 2; otherwise, it loses its effectiveness. If idx is greater than 2, then either avoid using it or use it with a combination of other strong attributes. When $idx <= 2$, using it in combination with the text selector makes the selector stronger. There are other attributes as well that can be used to derive a strong selector, such as `match index`, `ordinal`, `Xpath`, and `match reverse` attributes. Avoid using any attribute that has dynamic or custom data.

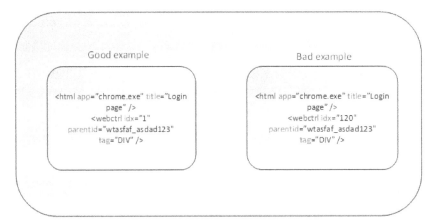

Figure 7.6 – An example of a strong selector

- **Orphan activities**: It is very common while in development to experiment and find the best possible way to implement logic. It can be due to multiple activities available from many different community developers. Sometimes, you might just forget to clean unused activities, which are called orphan activities. They have no link whatsoever to any preceding or succeeding code block. They are just there, eating up code space and becoming garbage. Again, the same rule applies to empty code blocks. They get processed and loaded in memory during execution and might become the root cause of a common error known as memory leaks. They are hard to detect and find when we make the mistake of leaving blank code blocks, empty sequences, and orphan activities. The best practice states that you should always scan your code before the end of each day and remove all this garbage. This makes you a better developer and builds a healthy habit, with good development practices.

- **Nested IF-THEN-ELSE**: Again, this is a very common mistake made by developers when trying to build complex logic. It might feel OK to have nested `IF-THEN-ELSE` blocks, and that is the case if you keep them at the limit of two or three, at a maximum. Having a nested `IF-THEN-ELSE` block with more than three levels will complicate things and is inefficient. If you feel that the logic needs more nested statements, then try to rethink it with other concepts, such as switches or flowcharts. These are some of the alternatives to ensure a better code standard, rather than a complex `IF-THEN-ELSE` loop, which can be a headache to even debug.

- **Unused variables and dependencies**: We all know that every programming language uses variables as a means to store data temporarily or permanently. Variables are extensively used across code to better control the data flow and perform operations on the data. When developing, developers can easily create any number of variables and arguments and forget to use them efficiently. These variables are left unused and become part of garbage collection. Although they will not have much effect on the program execution, they can later make the code tough to maintain and extend. UiPath provides an easy way to get rid of these unwanted variables from the toolbar itself, but knowing that you need to follow the best practices will help you to remember that option. The same goes for the dependency check or package check as well. Make sure that you remove and get rid of any unused packages, activities, and dependencies so that the code base is clean and free from the garbage. It also helps to keep the size of the code to a minimum and, thus, aids faster execution.

- **Use of wait stage**: In RPA, most of the time, we perform actions through a user interface. While humans can time themselves and perform an activity according to the screen displayed, bots on the other hand are more dependent on just executing the step that is next. Bots don't have all the senses humans have, so they can't see what is on the screen. They just click or type based on the selector or element. There are many things that a bot can't handle or control when it launches an application and tries to perform an action on it. What can be done from a development standpoint is to tell the bot to wait for the application or web page to respond. This is not all; we also need to tell the bot that not only does it need to wait for the application but also wait until the specific element is available for it to act, and that is called an *intelligent* or *dynamic wait*.

Intelligent waits are when we tell the bot to wait for the specific element of interest to be fully loaded and ready for it to act. This can be set in the configuration section. This helps to avoid hardcoding the wait time. You can never predict the loading time of an application or page, as it depends on so many factors that are out of our control. The best way is to just let the page wait for the element to appear. So, the best practice is to never use a hard or static wait and always use an intelligent wait. There are many different variations of this, such as *wait to be ready*, *element exists*, and so on. Never rely on your gut feeling when for the past few days, you have been working on the application and it has responded under a certain time frame. That can change anytime when in production, and you will end up having to add these `wait` conditions. So, make it a good practice to add an intelligent or dynamic wait in all the places where you can. There might be some scenarios where you can't and that is OK, but other than that, there should not be any exceptions. Sometimes, your intelligent wait might also fail, and that means that there is an underlining problem with the application, which is worth reporting rather than you trying to fix it in your code.

- **Adding activity names and comments**: Developers are burdened with writing good logic, formatting code, making it readable, following all the best practices in the world, and on top of that, adding extra comments for almost every line of code so that it makes sense to whoever is reading or trying to understand the code. It all seems simple but is easier said than done. In reality, they tend to skip or forget the basic thing, which is adding activity names and comments. It is common for developers to forget or miss this important step, and that is why it is an SA's job to review, comment, and provide timely feedback. The SA should regularly review code and not wait until the end of the development cycle, at which stage it becomes near to impossible to get all the necessary changes done in time. Now, let's see how the activities, sequences, stages, and blocks should be named to make the flow easier to understand. Let's review the following diagram to understand the best practice:

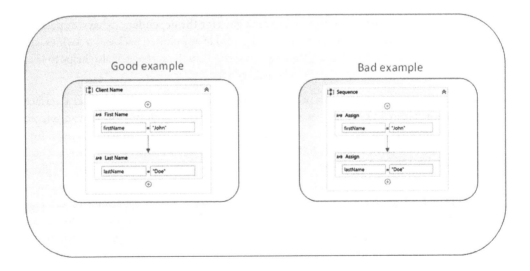

Figure 7.7 – Activity and sequence names

As we can clearly see, without the names of the sequence and the activities, it is not clear what these names are used for. The best practice is to name every sequence and activity appropriately.

- **Use of print or log messages**: Every developer wants to see the output of code in some form so that they know what they coded and what the requirements are. For this, the common approach is to use print or log messages. Sometimes, the same approach is also used to view some sensitive data for troubleshooting or just to make sure that the correct data is being used within the process. During this, there can be numerous scenarios where the developers might forget to remove those debug statements and log messages, which could expose some sensitive data to the common eyes. To avoid this, the focus should be to remove statements immediately after there is no use for that data. This is more about developing good habits rather than a best practice. An SA can enforce these good habits by educating a team about them and providing some kind of quick reference guide, which becomes a way to remind the developer to follow those good development habits.

So, this list of topics provides some of the best practices that an SA has to focus on to deliver robust and stable code. Building rapport with a team helps to achieve these goals, as the team will then not be afraid or shy to discuss the impediments with the SA, and they can guide the team.

Now, let's see how we can build governance around development activities so that there is some kind of tracking for daily progress.

Daily checkpoints

It has been proven that what is out of sight is out of mind. Developers like to work in their silos undisturbed, and that brings out their efficiency and efficacy. But at the same time, an SA needs to be in touch with developers to keep track of progress. The question is, how can we achieve that without disturbing the developers' creative thought process? One way that has been very effective is having daily calls or scrum calls. It doesn't matter which project management methodology is used; daily calls are a must. Now, twice a week or three times daily is the magic number. This works in two ways. First, it helps the SA to understand who is facing challenges without wasting precious development time, as every developer has to join the mandatory call and speak about what they did yesterday and what the plan is for today. This also helps the developer to become more responsible and, at the same time, plan their work better. It also provides the developer a platform to speak openly and discuss any challenges they might be facing, or whether they need any guidance.

Interrupting developers while they are in their deep state of developing code is not a good idea, as they might lose that precious thought process. Rather, have calls at a pre-defined and scheduled time so that everyone knows that by that time, they need to keep themselves free and ready to provide updates. It also keeps developers focused on the work at hand and what is scheduled as per the requirements.

SAs can get help from a project manager or a scrum master to schedule and run these meetings. The best time is to either have them at the start or end of the day so that the rest of the day is free from any distractions.

Now, let's see what key points should be considered and how these daily checkpoint calls should be managed:

- Have the meeting at the same time daily. This makes it easier for the team members to plan ahead of time.

- Have a predefined format for the participant to speak, for example, as follows; start with what you did it yesterday, followed by any challenges, and then what the plan is for today. Every participant, especially the developers, should be given 5–10 minutes to provide their updates. This will limit the time of the call and will not extend it unnecessarily.

- If any participant has any doubts and wants to discuss them further, a separate call should be facilitated between them and SA.

- If there are any new ideas or change of plans, they should be discussed in a separate meeting.

- Encourage the team to come prepared, and make sure the meeting starts and ends on time. This will bring structure to the team and help them value time management.

- Whether face-to-face or video, any format is acceptable. The key to a successful checkpoint call is attendance. If anyone is not able to attend, they can send a note with their updates to the team so that progress can be recorded.

- It is easy to drift away from the topic hand and for a meeting to discuss other things. SAs should keep this in mind and take steps to stop this from happening, taking these discussions offline. A PM or scrum master can help keep a team focused on the agenda, but the SA should also make every effort to not extend the discussion.

- A round-robin or alphabetical order can be introduced for participants to speak. This will make sure that participants know when to speak and when to stop. Encourage them to time themselves for better timekeeping.

- The use of tools such as Jira, Rally, or any other similar tool can also be used to run these meetings, with visuals of team members' activities and tasks. Displaying the tasks on a screen for the team member who is speaking helps them to focus and provides a more accurate and structured status.

As we saw, governance is the key to successful delivery on time. It helps to analyze progress and then take action when needed. So, we started with the POC, worked on best practices, and developed the code – what's next? Next is to do integration testing. As we saw earlier, an SA will distribute work among developers. Each developer will work on their own module, and once all these modules are combined, the code is complete for the bot. How we do that is what we will see in the next topic, which is integration testing.

Integration testing

So, we are ready to test, and this will be our first integration test to find out how our team and SA did in their commitment to a better, faster, and cheaper bot. Let's find out by arranging a series of steps that will help to perform this very important test and streamline it. As the name suggests, *integration testing* involves connecting all the modules and code snippets to make them work in tandem and get the desired outcome. It is very important to perform this type of testing from time to time so that we don't leave any loose threads. The best practices to perform integration testing are as follows:

- **Test data**: Data is the most important factor in testing, and good-quality data is what we need to perform these tests. When we talk about good quality data, we mean production-grade data and nothing that is cooked or man-made. This data should be of sufficient size so that you can perform a few iterations of this test. It is always advisable to prepare at least three times the amount of data for your testing, based on the initially estimated data needs. There are different ways of gathering and preparing the data, and an SA can work with the PM and application teams to figure out what would be the best way to get the data for testing.

  Data can be very sensitive, and its sensitivity arises from the standards under which it falls. For example, **Protected Health Information** (**PHI**) is a standard of data that is governed under the **Health Insurance Portability and Accountability Act** (**HIPPA**) of 1996, a federal law that states that PHI data can't be openly used for any purpose without the consent of the owner of the data, which will be the individual themselves. Unless you have the approval to use data in an open form, every corporation has the mandate to safeguard the data, and no unauthorized personnel can see that data. Similarly, **Personal Identifiable Information** (**PII**) is also protected and should not be publicly used or available. Some examples of this include credit card numbers, addresses, phone numbers, and social security numbers.

- **Test scenarios**: You may wonder why scenarios are needed now. Isn't it for **System Integration Testing** (**SIT**) and **User Acceptance Testing** (**UAT**)? The short answer is *no*. Having scenarios will help you test your integrations based on the requirements and what is expected. For example, let's say you are testing that the bot should be able to read email and load its contents in the queue. You run the bot with a few emails and it does load the data, but it tries to load it from the unwanted emails as well.

  Well, what do unwanted emails mean? This is where your scenarios come into the picture. Using the same example, let's assume that you have to read specific emails from a recipient from a shared mailbox that receives thousands of emails, which are important for other teams and processes. If you start reading and processing all of them, then the purpose of the intelligent bot will be defunct. It can also result in affecting other teams, as all their emails are now marked as read, which is not what we wanted. So, if you have thought about creating scenarios, you will realize that testing only with the emails that you want to read is not the right approach, so you should also add some unwanted emails to mimic a real-life scenario. This is the level of thought leadership an SA has to bring to a team. So, build your test scenarios and think about what you are testing. This will also help you to minimize the bug list. You might think that this is what the SIT team and tester are for, and the answer is *yes*. However, the scenarios you are creating are only the basic ones, just to prove that requirements are met. There are many more things that can go wrong, and that is where testing experts will help you find those undercover bugs.

- **Don't wait until the end**: This might sound surprising, but in RPA, we don't wait for the development to completely finish, as we don't have the time and freedom to do so. Remember the faster and cheaper aspects that we discussed earlier? We suggested trying to run as many activities in parallel as you can, and testing is one of them. Test as you build, and that is where collaboration comes into the picture. Multiple developers working on different modules need to talk to each other and find a time and way to test their modules, as and when functionally and technically feasible. One module can perform multiple functions, but we need not wait for all of them to be completed. For example, in a multi-bot architecture, if developer A is working on reading and loading the data from an email to the queue and developer B is working on reading the queue and processing, then as soon as developer A creates and prepares the queue, a quick test should be done by developer B to make sure that their code is able to access and read the queue. If there are challenges, then resolve them right away, rather than waiting until the end when there are other things to take care of and you will be out of time. It goes without saying that "a stitch in time saves nine." Follow the cycle of develop > test > fix. Also, you don't have to test all the scenarios, as the SIT phase is there for a reason. Focus on the core functionality and the rest will be taken care of by the SIT. It is like **continuous integration/continuous development (CI/CD)** where you keep testing and developing. Build a testing harness so that you can plug and play with different modules and not run an entire end-to-end test. This saves time and energy.

To conclude, always do a POC even if your gut says that it will work as expected, as that can save a lot of efforts in the long run. Always approach development using wireframing, which is a great practice for development. Having daily checkpoints is a great way to keep track of daily activities that might become a major roadblock if not handled on time. Perform testing as you develop and don't save it until last, as you will never know which integration point may fail and lead to an entire project failure.

Summary

This brings us to the end of this chapter. To recap, we reviewed the POC and its strategy and importance. We saw what wireframing is and how it can help to streamline development. We also discussed the different ways an SA can guide teams and some of the important best practices that the SA can enforce to make developers work efficiently. Having daily checkpoints is a great way to have governance over development activities and help build a collaborative environment for a team. Lastly, we discussed the importance of integration testing and some of the steps and best practices that can be followed to have a smooth development experience.

In the next chapter, we will discuss how an SA can go above and beyond its duties and bring the *wow* factor to deliverables. We'll see what customer obsession means and how the SA should develop their thought leadership to achieve it.

Questions

1. Why should we do a POC and go against our gut feeling?

2. What makes wireframing so important before development starts?

3. How does wireframing help in development?

4. What are the best practices that can be followed while developing?

5. How can an SA introduce a collaborative culture to a team?

6. How do we prepare for integration testing?

7. What are some of the key points to consider before we start integration testing?

8

Customer Obsession in the RPA Journey

Sayings such as *"the customer is king"* and *"the customer is god"* are not uncommon. Even the great Mahatma Gandhi once said, *"A customer is the most important visitor on our premises. They are not dependent on us. We are dependent on them."*

These mantras all come from wisdom that has been shared with us for ages. The importance of the customer is a belief in many cultures around the world, and it has significant importance in the success of a business and people who greatly believing the success of a business.

In the modern world, this is known as *customer obsession*. But what does it mean and how does it help an SA? In every business school, we are taught about customer needs, how to solve complex problems, and how to achieve great success in any business. All this directly or indirectly focuses on helping our customers get what they want. With the rise of industrialization, this relationship between the customer and vendor has been the key to every successful business. Any business vendor can provide services or products. However, unless there is a customer who is willing to buy or purchase the services or products, there is no value. There can be many vendors providing the same service, but customer satisfaction comes when the vendor believes in customer satisfaction and not simply providing the service. This becomes the key differentiator for a customer to choose and stick with a vendor.

In this chapter, we will build on this philosophy and see some of the strategies that an SA can implement to showcase this philosophy to their customers. The topics for this chapter are as follows:

- A demonstration and early feedback
- Keeping them engaged
- Being an influencer
- **User Acceptance Testing (UAT)**
- The wow factor

All these topics will help to develop the leadership of an SA and help build rapport with the customer or client. Think of a situation where you might have something to offer but there is no one to buy it from you. This shows that we, as vendors, are dependent on our customers and clients, and they give us the opportunity to show what we can deliver with consistency and great quality. This should be a principle that every SA follows religiously.

As I said, there may be many vendors ready to serve a customer, but what makes you the best is defined by the level of obsession an SA can demonstrate for their customers. How far an SA is willing to go to give the best of the best service to their customer is defined by this obsession. Customer obsession is an attitude that can only be practiced when you believe in it. If you think that just delivering code is going to bring the same feeling, then you are mistaken. The customer should feel that you are fully committed to their cause, and many opportunities will show up during the entire engagement with a customer to show your commitment. In this chapter, we will focus on some of them, which will help you to identify more opportunities to show customer obsession in your endeavors.

The first step is to show our clients that we care about what their opinions are and that we are always willing to hear from them, which can then be put into practice. So, how do we do this? The best way is to do a show-and-tell session or, as we call it in IT, a demo.

A demonstration and early feedback

With the popularity of the agile methodology of project management, it has become inevitable to show a client what is going on behind the scenes. You may share status reports verbally for a couple of meetings, but at some point, clients may want to see what is being cooked up by your developers. For this very reason, we plan demos.

Demos are a great way to provide a live status and gain insights into how a client feels about how everything is coming along. Demos help to send out the message that **what you see is what you get (WYSIWYG)**. This gives the client an opportunity to think and make any adjustments to the project, even if minor, to suit their needs. It also satisfies the clients that they will not end up with a completely different outcome compared to what was envisioned at the beginning.

Let's understand this using a scenario.

Let's go back to our banking client from *Chapter 2, Case Study of a Bank Client*, the bank of Plutus. Imagine you are working on a new project and have started your development phase. The process involves three different applications – web, desktop, and mainframe. You thought of dividing your sprints based on the applications and modules. Now, the best way to plan for the demo is to make it a milestone for every sprint. After every sprint, plan for a quick 30-minute demo for the client to understand how they feel about it and build confidence.

There may be many questions on your mind, such as, why do we need to do so many demos? Why do we need frequent feedback? The answer to both of these is in the definition of *customer obsession*. If you understand it correctly, then you can answer it on your own. But I will try to help you if you can't.

The first thing that these demos do is to make your client feel that they and their input are very valuable to you. It's not the case that you won the project and now you can do whatever you feel like. It also helps keep the client focused on and attentive to the project. The client might not only be working on this project; they might have multiple other projects to focus on. How can you get their valuable time to focus on your project and showcase your dedication? You can get all you need with just two demos or maybe one at the end, but then you are missing the key aspect of customer obsession, which is gathering timely feedback and incorporating it on a timely basis.

You will receive either timely feedback, based on demos, or at the end of the development phase. If you go with the second option, then you will end up having a list of minor changes and enhancements that you will not have any time to accommodate, and that will not look good to the client. They will feel that they missed the opportunity to have a say before the development commenced. So, make sure you have a good number of demos scheduled for the client to provide their feedback and for you, as an SA, to have the time to accommodate those changes. Having a dedicated time frame for feedback and then incorporating it into the next sprint is a great way to provide automation that is useful to the client from day one, bringing in some good ROI.

You might ask a question about the client's feedback, but this will also open room for some changes that might not be accommodated in the entire development cycle. That is exactly why we limit feedback and changes to a minimum, focusing on minor changes or tweaks. Generally, an SA is good at accessing efforts on the fly, and based on your development capacity, you can propose and set an expectation with your client that any changes requested should fit within a bucket of hours. This bucket of hours is the reserved hours for these kinds of unseen requests and can only accommodate x number of hours for every sprint. This will help achieve two things. First, the client will know they have a say and will get a few minor tweaks and changes incorporated without changing any timelines or extra budget. Secondly, it will limit them to thinking about the "must have" rather than the "good to have changed/nice to have" and prioritize them, ensuring a win-win situation. This is what is expected from an SA concerning customer obsession. You were able to demonstrate your willingness to go the extra mile but, at the same time, within reason. Going back to our scenario, you should plan for three demos at the end of every sprint. A final demo can be planned with a bigger audience, once all the initial requirements and all the minor changes and tweaks are incorporated.

Now that we understand the significance of demos and early feedback, the next step is to prepare for a successful demo. It is very common to get into snags when doing demos or live presentations. Anything can go wrong. Though we can't predict the future, with proper planning, some of those mishaps can be avoided. Benjamin Franklin once said, *"If you fail to plan, you are planning to fail!"* So, let's plan the demo so we can avoid failing.

Planning the demo

The first thing you would want to do is list down the functionalities according to the development plan and review them with the team, ensuring that they have been tested and vetted by the developers and yourself.

This is very important and should be planned way before development starts. Your team should know and understand the concept of these demos and their importance so that they work toward that goal. It is like a milestone in the development phase that the team should focus on in every sprint.

The following are the steps you need to follow to plan the demo:

1. *Review each and every requirement* that you plan to demo to the client and get them tested thoroughly. Try to incorporate some of the negative test results as well so that you cover all the testing scenarios.

2. *Do a dry run*. This is very important. Demos are not only about showing how the bot is running but also about doing a voice-over so that your audience can understand what is happening on the screen. It can be overwhelming for clients and hard to understand the real working of a bot if there is no narration for the steps. The best way to do this is to start with a slide deck to set the narrative and expectations of what the client is going to see in the demo. This will help to keep focus and not get distracted by questions that might relate to future functionalities. This helps to run a smooth demo.

3. Ask the team to *record the demo*. It isn't uncommon that when you are ready to demo, something goes wrong. It can be that your bot is not responding or the bot machine itself crashes. This can be very disappointing and lead to dissatisfaction. When a client comes to a demo, they want to see something in action so that they feel satisfied. It's like going to a movie theater and buying a ticket but then the movie projector breaks, and you end up returning home without watching the movie. So, always have a backup.

4. *Rehearse the demo* a few times so that you can set your narration of the steps and do a smooth voice-over. You might feel confident that you can pull this off and don't need practice, but I have seen too many freezes with live demos. People get nervous and forget what they have to say. So, to avoid these situations, rehearse, and do it with your team members so that they can be your audience.

5. *Record a clean execution of the bot*. In case of an emergency where your live bot is not available for some reason, you will have something to fall back on. Keep the recording handy. I would recommend keeping a copy of the recording in a couple of different places and not only on your laptop or the local machine. What if the laptop itself crashes or gets hung? If you have a copy of the demo saved in other locations, then you can easily overcome this snag by asking one of your team members to run the recording for you so that you can do a voice-over. Also, have a designated person that can take over if you are not able to see your screen due to the laptop or machine that you are logged into not working.

6. Try to *time the demo based on the bot execution time*. Always plan some time for Q&A. It is very important to answer any follow-up questions and gather feedback.

So, the next time you plan a demo, keep the aforementioned steps in mind to plan a successful demo. While I am confident that you, as an SA, will manage to get a client to focus on your demo during that moment, that's not all that is required. You want the client to be engaged more often. How do we keep the client engaged? Let's see how we can keep the client more involved in the business in a few easy steps.

Keeping the client engaged

Before we even try to answer how to keep your client engaged, we should try to answer *why* we should keep them engaged and interested. The main reason for an SA to keep the client engaged is so that they can always get early feedback and try to adhere to the principle of customer obsession. Unless you are working closely with your client and sponsor, you might lose some of those opportunities to network and connect, and even future projects. *Out of sight is out of mind*. Having your clients focused on a project gets you better and faster support from other teams as well. Any escalation or urgent need can be sent to the proper channels in a timely fashion. Now that we have understood the *why* part, let's see *how* we can keep the client engaged:

- **Planned meetings**: These can be facilitated by a project manager or a scrum master. This is a quick meeting between a client, sponsor, and SA to discuss the progress, impediments, and challenges that a team might face. This showcases open communication and collaboration between the client and yourself. It gives you the opportunity to share progress and also ask for any help and guidance for you or your team. At the same time, it gives the client an opportunity to ask questions and provide feedback, if any was missed during the regular demos. As the RPA projects are short-lived, it becomes inevitable that meetings are not frequent, and this meeting helps in achieving a regular cadence. The frequency can be set as per need, but a biweekly meeting is preferred.

- **Communication**: Proactive communication is always appreciated. Though it is not ideal for a client to invest a lot of time and join daily cadence meetings with an SA and the team, it is still very important to include them in all the important communications. Apart from the planned meeting, the SA should request for a distribution list to be created, with one including the clients' email addresses for regular communication. This helps to bring immediate attention to any issues that need client involvement or just use them for FYI purposes. This also establishes open communication. It is always preferable to overcommunicate rather than trying to filter and ending up with missed communications. Communication is the key to the successful delivery of any project. History tells us that more than 90% of projects fail due to poor communication, so make sure you remember these three important points – communicate, communicate, and communicate.

- **Understand before being understood**: Steven Convey offered this principle, and it is very important to build that trust with a client. The principle is very simple and straightforward. By following this principle, SAs can build trust in the client that they are being heard and their perspective is being respected. This leads to some great insights, and an SA can uncover a client's hidden requirements, which you might not be able to extract from them in the initial requirement sessions. This helps them to open up to you and really speak their mind.

- **Explain and educate**: There can be moments when a client is not knowledgeable enough to understand what you are saying or what you mean. This can lead to wrong assumptions. Make sure you take the time to educate the client and explain relevant concepts to them in simple language. Using a lot of technical terms might throw them off, so try to explain using business language wherever you can. Always make sure you were understood correctly by checking with them in between your educational sessions so that you don't lose them.

- **Going above and beyond**: One key trait that an SA needs to possess to be distinct from others is the willingness to go above and beyond. This doesn't mean that you deliver what was not even in the scope and requested; it is more about paying attention to details and providing something extra that shows an attitude of going above and beyond. For this very reason, an SA should be a very good listener. The more you listen, the more you can understand those hidden client needs and pain points. There will be moments when, during the conversation, you will hear a lot of challenges, including those that the client might not even know exist, and by actively listening, you can unearth those hidden gems. For example, let's say you are in a meeting actively listening to some of the pain points and requirements for a project. The client says that the volume of emails they get daily becomes overwhelming for them to manage, and they need automation to take care of all of them in a timely manner. While it is very clear that we need to process all the emails in the inbox daily, there is another hidden requirement that was not expressed explicitly, which is the ability to see and review what was processed during the day at a glance. This is where the SA should propose providing a report at the end of every day so that the client can easily see what was processed and deal with that overwhelming situation. This is what I mean when I talk about *going above and beyond*. This is not a requirement, but giving that report will showcase a willingness to do whatever it takes to help the client. It also shows that you were actively listening to the problem and have ready solutions to cater to it.

These are some of the ways an SA can keep a client engaged and pave their path to being an influencer. Being an influencer gives the SA an opportunity to become a part of the "inner circle" of the client's team. The SA as part of the inner circle can become a trustworthy advisor, and all this brings more work and long sustainable business for the SA's employer. This is why it is always recommended to build your persona not only as a technical guru but also as a techno-functional guru. Let's do a deep-dive and understand how to become an influencer and how that impacts business and personal growth.

An SA as an influencer

What is an influencer? Why would an SA want to be an influencer? An influencer is an individual who can persuade another human being to do something. This can be very powerful. If you possess this kind of power, you can influence decisions, and that too, at your will. Well, you may think that this is too much of a sci-fi, Jedi-type mind trick. But the main focus is to build a rapport with your client so that they let you help them to make decisions. They might even lean toward you for some of those decisions, and this is called the power of influence.

Being an SA, you are still a third-party vendor resource, but as you gain trust, you get to participate in those "special meetings," which leads to you being more valuable. If you are valuable to the client, then you definitely are the apple of your employer's eye. I think you get the idea; now, let's see how an SA can work toward achieving this goal. Let's be clear – this is not a covert operation, nor am I suggesting joining a cult or a secret society. This is a proven technique where an individual takes their place within a client's group and gets recognized, all in the name of more business and future growth. This is perfect for the SA, as they are experts, specialized in their field of knowledge, and have the authority and great insight into their subject. Throughout this chapter so far, you have already started working toward this goal of being an influencer. As it has been said, *Rome was not built in a day*; similarly, this is a journey, and it might take more than a couple of projects before you even get any recognition, and even then, being an influencer is way ahead in the future.

As I said, you have already started working toward the goal of being an influencer by providing the best service, delivering a project on time and within budget, and most importantly, having customer obsession. Let's review some of the proven ways to become an influencer:

- **Have an opinion**: When it comes to automation, an SA will definitely have an option, and that matters, as their opinion is set based on technical and functional facts. Sharing your thoughts on why a specific process should come first for automation or why a client should select a specific vendor gives them the perspective that they are looking for, which is one of the reasons you have been hired for the job.

- **Share your ideas**: Sharing your ideas helps a client the most, as many times they don't even know what to ask. Being a wonderful observer, you can chime in with your ideas, backing them up with some great experience, and that can invoke a thought in the client's mind about the next project idea or how to save more money. So, don't hesitate to speak about the ideas you have and get them validated. Don't be afraid that they might be shot down. It might not be something that the client is looking for at the moment, but that will at least let them know that you have ideas to share, and that is what gets your foot in the door.

- **Become a storyteller**: Influencers always tell stories, either their own or ones they may have read or heard somewhere. The moral is to be able to tell any story that can give meaning and full insight to a client and help them in any way. No one can experience everything in this world on their own, but they can definitely benefit from others' experiences. This is exactly what an SA should do by bringing in the success stories from their experience or others'. Narrating a success story and then deriving a conclusion to give the client the confidence that they are on the right track is the key to being an influencer.

Becoming an influencer is a journey that every SA should pursue, as that becomes the ladder to success. Being an influencer doesn't mean that you get to do whatever you want or get some kind of veto vote. It just means that you get to share your thoughts with the client, which is appreciated and considered in the final decision-making. UAT is also a way to show your customer obsession.

You might be thinking, how come this project phase can help you live your customer obsession dream?

Let's find out in the next topic.

UAT

So, we may be confused about how UAT can be a good phase to showcase our customer obsession. Well, to understand this, we need to review the definition of customer obsession. Customer obsession is to listen to your customer and see things from their perspective and enhance their user experience. Now, as we can see from the definition, it is very clear that customer obsession is also about the customer experience, and that can be greatly enhanced by enhancing the UAT phase, as that is the only phase where the customer will be heavily involved.

In RPA projects, 90% of the work is done by project management and development teams. The business or client gets involved only when there is requirement-gathering, decision-making, and UAT. We already looked at the requirement-gathering and decision-making phases and how to facilitate them in the previous chapters. Now, let's see how we can add value by presenting a customer with a better user experience.

We all know what UAT is and have been through that phase so many times. It is when a client tests functionalities and evaluates whether the product has been developed according to the requirements given by the client. There are many ways of executing a successful UAT, but there is only one way to make it a great user experience for the client. Let's review the steps:

1. The first thing we need to understand is that not all clients are the same and will have their own processes to follow for UAT, but no one will ever refuse a helping hand, and that is what we provide to the customer.

2. As we know, an RPA team is small and has very limited bandwidth to spend on a project. Any help is greatly appreciated. Let the team know that you and your team will help them plan and facilitate the UAT.

3. Start by sharing the templates and data you gathered for your SIT. That will help the team and save a ton of time. It will also give them the ideas to write their test cases, as you have already provided most of them, which were used for the SIT. Do you realize that we have already provided a better customer experience by giving them all they need for the UAT?

4. The test cases or scenarios are pretty much the same for both the SIT and UAT. So, using the same ones with some variations and new data points will help them execute the UAT faster and smoother.

5. RPA testing is a bit different. Not everyone knows how to run a bot and perform testing in the development IDE, or run the bot from the orchestrator or command center. Again, it's another opportunity for you and your team to help the client by running the bot for them and complete the UAT. They see and verify the results on their screen, thus giving a hands-off UAT experience.

6. Acceptance criteria, what to expect, and what the real results are captured in the template you have provided, and that helps to quickly review the results and open any defects.

So, we saw how we can use the UAT phase to our advantage and add it to the continuous journey of our customer obsession principle. The next step in this journey is to surprise the client with something that they always wanted but were never able to technically achieve. There can be many factors that may have been a hindrance, but you, being a true believer in customer obsession, will make that dream come true. This is called the *wow* factor.

The wow factor

Every client has a list of must-have and good-to-have functionalities and features that they want you as an SA to consider. Definitely, the *must-haves* are things that are not negotiable, and without those functionalities and features, automation is not of much use to the client. But there is always a list of *good-to-have* things or a dream list of functionalities that, if added to the must-have list, can make the automation even better and more usable. It will make the client super happy, as they will not have expected this, giving them a surprise, and who doesn't like good surprises? Also, getting extra for the same amount of money before a deadline is always welcome. It shows the willingness to go above and beyond.

I'm sure you get the idea. Now, the question is how to work on the wow factor, and how to identify what it takes to create that wow factor but, at the same time, not break the bank breaker or put too much burden on your team. The following are some of the proven ways by which you can identify and implement the wow factor without much resistance:

- **Active listening**: This is key to finding that specific functionality or feature that has the potential to become the wow factor. A lot of the time, you'll find clients casually speaking their minds, but many times, what they really mean is what they are describing. There might be a scenario where the client is trying to explain the process and then narrates a situation or a short story that has a lot of significance to the process and shows how that affected their work or process.

  Being an SA, one of the key skills is active listening. The more you listen, the better you can understand what a client is saying or wants automation to do. This leads to many hidden requirements, and those are valuable features. Let's understand this using an example. Let's say you are in a session with the client and they are explaining a process to you. While explaining it, they told you that last year there was a shortage of resources, as their key resource decided to leave the company. They were in shock, as the resource played a key role in the consolidation of all the tickets that were processed by all the departments. Now, as the resource left, the client did provide a knowledge transfer, but that was not enough. The one person who took over was not able to fully understand the process, and it took them a while to fully understand how to perform the task. You patiently listened to the story and then asked a few follow-up questions. How many departments are there? Are they all going to use automation? Will there be any exceptions where any of the departments still want to be manual?

  You got all the answers, including that there will be 10 departments and all will be using the automation, and there are no exceptions. You made a note of it, and then that meeting ended. You realized that the situation that was narrated to you can happen again, and this can still be a challenge if automation is in place, as there is no requirement for a consolidated report that can be generated for all the departments.

Your design might already produce a report for each day that tickets are processed. Now, if you just consolidate those reports and provide an overall report, this problem can be solved. It might take some extra steps, but as this solves a problem that the client took time to explain, that will be significant to the client. Since there are emotions attached to that instance, this final consolidated report can be that wow factor. This is how active listening can help you find those wow requirements.

- **Having a business understanding**: It is very important for an SA to have some business understanding if they are not experienced in that domain. You can read about it, talk to some experts and colleagues, and gain some knowledge. The reason why this is important is that the client will use a lot of business language while explaining the process and scenarios. If you are not familiar with that lingo, then it will be tough to understand, and you will end up asking some basic questions, which might not impress the client. So, the best bet is to gain knowledge. Now the question is, how will this help in the wow factor? So, once you have a better understanding of the client's business and you understand some real-life scenarios, you will be able to correlate some of those with your design and bring more value to automation. Let's understand this with an example. The banking client that we established in *Chapter 2* has asked you to work on a new process that is related to the credit card process. When you talked to one of the SMEs, they explained to you that the process they have selected involves a lot of interaction with the bank's credit card customers.

The process is about the credit card getting declined when the customer tries to use it online. Now, if you are not from a banking domain, you might not be able to think deeply about this process. Also, bank processes are different in different countries. You might be familiar with some but not all. If the client says that there may be many reasons why the credit card transaction can be declined and doesn't give you the specifics, then you should be knowledgeable enough to know at least a few basic reasons.

We still do not have the wow factor, but we are at least building our knowledge so we can get closer to it. Now, as you worked toward understanding all the reasons and getting a complete understanding, you realized that whenever the customer calls the bank because their credit card has been declined, the first question they ask is why this happened, and if there is no satisfactory answer, then the customer may get angry and even close their account, which gives the bank a bad reputation. So, to add the wow factor to your automation, whenever the customer calls in and asks for a reason, you can get the automation to present a predefined reason for each scenario of a card being declined, written in plain English. The customer care rep can read that back to the client, which explains the reason and keeps the customer happy. Previously, the customer care rep had to explain it in their own words to the customer, which was misleading and frustrating for both parties.

When you explained and showed this extra addition to the client, they were shocked and super happy, as you were able to not only interpret the real challenge but also went above and beyond to incorporate that without being asked, making the automation more valuable.

- **Always think in the business's interest**: Having a mindset of always thinking about how to benefit a client with the knowledge you possess and the skill set you have will always lead to those moments that can then be translated to a wow factor. As I said, it all starts with the attitude and mindset to help the client and solve their problems. Solve your client's problem and you will be in business. Solve their problems and go above and beyond and you will *always* be in business.

Every business wants bang for its buck, and if you can bring the sense that a client is getting something extra, then their business is yours – not only for that year or season but for years to come. These are some of the byproducts of customer obsession and going that extra mile to create the wow factor.

Summary

To summarize, an SA should follow the principle of customer obsession to always be in business. It is an essential ingredient to deliver the best service to a customer and deliver that wow factor that they were never expecting. Being an influencer gives an SA the opportunity to be a part of the client's inner circle and be more resourceful. Their input is valued and, thus, this helps to build a long-term relationship. Keeping the client/customer as your central focus will automatically lead you to customer-centric leadership, which becomes the base of your success.

We have seen how RPA helps automate mundane and repetitive work, but what about the processes that need human intelligence? What if the process you are trying to automate needs cognitive thinking and is not rule-based? In our next chapter, we will cover some new tools and technologies that are the next generation of process automation.

Questions

1. Why is early feedback important?
2. How do we plan for a successful demo?
3. What are the different ways an SA can keep a client engaged?
4. How does customer obsession help to win more business?
5. How do we identify the features or functionalities that can become the wow factor?

Part 3:
Tool Agnostic Approach

In this part, we will explore the concept of the tool-agnostic approach and its far-reaching benefits for the entire RPA ecosystem. We will uncover the power of a tool-agnostic approach, enabling a seamless migration of architecture between different tools and promoting flexibility throughout the RPA journey.

This part has the following chapters:

- *Chapter 9, What is the Future of RPA?*
- *Chapter 10, How to Make Automation Intelligent?*
- *Chapter 11, Reusable Components*
- *Chapter 12, RPA as a Service (RPAaaS)*
- *Chapter 13, Finding the Best Solution*

9
Intelligent Automation

Since its inception, **robotic process automation** (**RPA**) has come a long way. During this journey, there were early adopters of RPA and followers of early adopters. As with every technology, RPA has also reached a point where the early adopters have exhausted all the processes that can be automated through the "vanilla RPA" or the standard rule-based RPA. The entire industry realized that if they wanted to continue to reap the benefits, then RPA needed an overhaul and a boost.

There was a need to have more than what base RPA can do. By this time, all the early adopters had already invested millions in the technology and wanted to get more out of it before it could be considered dead or obsolete. As we know, "necessity is the mother of invention," and so it is true for RPA, and this gave birth to a new version of RPA called RPA 2.0 or Intelligent Automation. In this chapter, we will focus on what **intelligent automation** (**IA**) is and how it has revolutionized the automation industry. Some of the topics that will be covered in the chapter are as follows:

- What is IA?
- The differences between RPA and IA
- Components of IA
- Design considerations for IA
- Chatbots

By the end of the chapter, we will have learned how RPA has evolved to become more cognitive and use human-like intelligence to solve more complex problems and automation. We will also learn about the different tools and techniques that make the RPA and IA.

What is IA?

The words themselves give the meaning of what IA is. Intelligent automation became the need for the industry as we moved more toward automation. Automation is everywhere, and we have been using automation for the past few decades, but the question is: can we ever bake that human-like intelligence into automation so that we can offload those cognitive tasks and processes of humans to machines? The answer is simple: *yes, we can*, but only to an extent. So, as the industry was trying to figure out what could be done to cater to the plethora of processes that still needed to be automated and how much money could be saved, engineers were trying to figure out whether it was something they could add or strap to RPA so it could become a next-generation automation technology. This produced the idea of amalgamating two technologies into one to achieve this, which is when IA was born.

IA is an amalgamation of RPA, **artificial intelligence (AI)**, and **machine learning (ML)**. It became the next generation of automation tools that can now add human-like intelligence to an extent and expand the automation footprint to more high-stake processes. With the recent pandemic, companies and industries have realized that they need technology that can keep the organization running in case of these types of emergencies. When the human workforce is not capable of working, then machines can take over and do some of that work, keeping the companies alive and floating. This also became one of the influences and fuel to invest more in IA and its technologies so that if we ever face a challenge similar to COVID, then we have a plan B to act on rather than the whole industry becoming paralyzed.

Let's understand IA and its capabilities through an example. We all have been using email systems for decades. Email has become the backbone of the 21st-century digital communication system to the extent that it has surpassed the volume that a human can handle. Assume you are responsible for an appeals and grievance department. The daily volume of emails you receive can be between 1,500 to 2,500. This is a lot of emails to read and reply to from angry and frustrated customers. To get the job done, you have four full-time resources working eight hours a day just to reply to emails. Now, imagine if an automated system could do that job for you and help you use your human resources in a more valuable process or activity.

This is where IA comes to the rescue. With IA, you can build a system that can reply to each email based on the email's intent and in a human-like language. The end user will not even be able to differentiate whether the email is written by IA or a human. This is the power of IA. Now, let's break down this scenario into pieces and see what technologies are involved in creating an IA solution like this:

Figure 9.1 – Process automation using IA

As we can see, the end-to-end solution not only includes RPA but also ML. It is a combination of technologies that gives the capability to mimic human-like behavior. The following diagram shows how IA is an amalgamation of two different technologies:

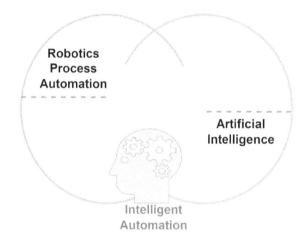

Figure 9.2 – Intelligent automation

Now that you understand what IA is and its significance in taking rule-based automation to the next generation of automation, let's see what the major difference between RPA and IA is. We might want to understand the differences because it can sometimes be confusing and even challenging to classify when you are reviewing the processes as to which bucket it falls into. Knowing the technology needed upfront makes it easier to plan and build the right automation. It also helps identify the low-hanging fruits versus something that will take some time to design and develop.

Understanding the difference between RPA and IA

To understand the fundamental differences between RPA and IA, let's review the following comparison table:

Robotic Process Automation	Intelligent Automation
Technology	**Technology**
Based on scripts (bots) that can mimic human manual steps	A combination of technologies such as intelligent **optical character recognition** (**OCR**), ML, AI, and **natural language processing** (**NLP**) can mimic human intelligence
Strategy	**Strategy**
Helps to automate the manual, repetitive, and rule-based tasks that are mundane and do not require any human intelligence	Takes RPA to the next level by adding the human intelligence-like capability
Development effort	**Development effort**
RPA is considered to be a low-code or even a no-code technology. RPA software gives you the capability to develop without even knowing how to code.	IA is known for its complexity. It is highly complex and needs a lot of coding and development. It takes longer to develop and needs more highly skilled resources. Often, it requires more complex integrations.
Dependency	**Dependency**
RPA is very dependent on the user interface, which is brittle and adds to the maintenance costs	IA, on the other hand, is not dependent on the user interface and works based on technologies such as ML, which is dependent on data
Human dependency	**Human dependency**
RPA is not human-dependent. It doesn't need humans to make decisions on its behalf. It is rule-based. Once the automation is designed, developed, and deployed, it can run forever with timely maintenance.	IA needs human help from time to time. We are still far from achieving AI, which is a replica of human intelligence. We need human intervention to correct the machine, called **Human-in-the-Loop** (**HITL**).

As we have seen the major differences between RPA and IA, let's now review some of the components of IA.

Components of IA

IA is comprised of many technologies used in lifting the capabilities of traditional automation and technology such as RPA. It is an umbrella under which advanced technologies such as AI and ML coexist. IA brings modernization to automation, and each of these technologies complements the other and becomes an ecosystem. IA is also known as **IPA** where "*P*" stands for the process, which makes sense, as RPA was used more for task automation, but IA or IPA is used for end-to-end automation. Let's dive in and review some of these components, which become the core of IA.

AI and ML

When we talk about human-like intelligence, we refer to AI and ML. This concept and technology have been under development for the past few decades, but only in the last few years has it come to a point where we can really understand its use and implement it in automation.

Let's talk about ML, as that is one of the cores of AI. ML, as the name suggests, is the technique where machines are taught to find patterns and make predictions based on historical data. We use this technology in combination with statistical algorithms to build intelligence into automation.

Let's understand this with an example. Assume you are working on a process that involves extracting and collecting data from invoices. Invoice processing is the most common use case for companies that are trying to automate using ML and AI. So, the first step is to download the invoices and categorize them so we know which invoice is related to which type. There can be utility bills, vendor invoices, payments, and so on. Now, downloading and collecting the invoices can be automated by RPA as that is rule-based, but what about categorizing them? For that, you will need something that can mimic the human review step and understand the intent of the invoice. For this step, we use ML. There are many ML models and algorithms that can be used, but for our ease of understanding, we will just call it an *ML model*. A model is based on data; we show the machine where on the invoice the relevant data is located and how to extract it. Then we give the model information about how to categorize it based on the data it has extracted. Let's say the utility bills have a header named ABC Utility Company. Now, the machine knows that when it extracts that specific text from the bill, it can put it in a folder named `Utility`. This is called the classification model. The machine has learned the steps of what humans do. They also open the bill, eyeball it, and try to find the specific information on the bill, which tells them the type of invoice.

Combining this, we get automation that can now download the invoices and then extract and classify them into categories as humans do, and this is what is known as IA. There is a lot to it, but this gives you an idea of how machines work. While reading the preceding example, you might think that this is a simple task, but it is easier said than done there. Training a machine to do what you expect it to do takes a lot of experimentation, trial, and error. A machine is like a kid that needs continuous learning for it to be productive. Teaching it once or twice is not going to help, and that is why experts say *data is the key to any ML algorithm*. The reason is simple: it takes a ton of data, and it requires good data to teach the machine.

Returning to the topic, we saw how ML can add that extra capability and can automate the processes that are heavily dependent on humans; processes that are not rule-based and need cognitive thinking from humans can now be automated to an extent.

OCR and Intelligent OCR

We have used OCR and have also referred to it many times in the previous chapters. To recap, it is a technology that helps extract data from images. Data or text typed or printed and then converted into an image can easily be extracted with great accuracy, but what about handwritten text?

Let's use the same example of invoice processing to understand this technology as well. Let's assume you received an invoice from a vendor that is a small mom-and-pop shop. They are old school and don't have a computerized system to print the invoices. They do handwritten invoices. This is a challenge. There are two ways you can handle it. Either identify the handwritten invoice and send it to a human to work on or implement an intelligent system that can identify the handwritten text and can interpret it correctly. This is one of the most challenging problems for the OCR industry. But, with the advancement of ML and pattern recognition, this is now possible. There are ML models that can, to some extent, extract the handwritten text and understand the intent. There is a lot of complex math involved in making these machines, and understanding that is not our goal, but knowing that there is something that can get the job done is very satisfying. There is still research to enhance the accuracy and efficacy of these ML models but, if needed, it can be implemented to lend a helping hand to your automation. These models and techniques are called Intelligent OCR or **Intelligent Character Recognition (ICR)**.

Computer vision

So, we talked about teaching the machine and how a machine can use OCR and ICR to extract data from different unseen invoices and documents. Now, the next big thing humans use in their daily life that the machine should be able to replicate is the use of vision. If confused, let's understand it using an example.

We humans take most of our actions by senses. We have many different senses, such as sight, hearing, smell, touch, and taste. For getting our work done in the office, we mostly need three of them, which are sight, hearing, and touch, unless you work in the food industry where smell and taste might be the primary senses being used. For the technology we are discussing, we will focus on sight. So, what we see is what we understand, and what we do is based on what we see, and that makes it the most important sense we should have to be able to work on computers. That means 90% of us working on a laptop or PC are using our eyesight to get the work done. So, if we have to automate the steps that need sight, then the technology we have at our disposal is called **Computer Vision (CV)**. You might debate why you need computer vision to click a button or to type your password in the password box, and you are correct. CV is used for very specific tasks, which are not possible by spying on the elements and finding the code behind the user interface. The reason is that there is no code behind the images or screens projected as images.

I know it is confusing, so let's understand this using another example. Assume you are given a task that uses Citrix (virtualization technology), which can virtualize the applications and can publish them as an image to the remote user. The process uses an application deployed on Citrix, and you are asked to automate the functionality. The application needs automation to navigate, click on buttons, type in the textboxes, click on the drop-down menus, and much more. The biggest challenge is that nothing like elements can be exposed to your RPA bot to spy and perform the action. This is where CV is involved.

It uses a fixed screen size (typically, whatever the resolution is set to on the development machine) to determine the coordinates of the desired object. Then, those coordinates are used as the reference to perform the action. Pretty simple? Not exactly; in conjunction with the coordinates, it also uses OCR to extract the text from the desired object and then match it to decide whether the object is what the automation is trying to act on. This makes this an awesome and unique technology and, at the same time, very complex to implement. The next component in line is OCR.

We have discussed the topic many times in the previous chapters, so let's not go into much depth, but just to reiterate, in the automation world, OCR plays a significant role. It becomes the base for data and information extraction steps in any automation when the information is embedded in images or graphics. It becomes evident that you must research and identify the best OCR engine to get the job done when it comes to processes that heavily involve scanned documents, such as invoice processing. Once you have the data or text extracted, then you need some kind of technology so the machine can understand the text and extract meaning from it. Understanding the text, its context, and language is done through a technology called NLP.

NLP

With the advancement of ML, NLP has gained a lot of traction and become one of the most sought-after technologies from the ML stack. It helps in understanding the context, meaning, and language itself. Nowadays, NLP can understand English and other languages such as French, German, Spanish, and Danish. Having this capability at our disposal expands the horizon of IA and the type of processes that can be automated using IA. While NLP can understand and recognize the language, **natural language understanding** (**NLU**) is what helps in understanding the meaning of the sentence or text. This helps the machine to understand the context. Once we teach the machine to understand, we can also teach machines to construct meaningful full replies based on the understanding. This technology is called **natural language generation** (**NLG**). Now, with all these three combined, you can achieve human-like behavior where you can extract the data using OCR, detect the language and understand it using NLP and NLU, and then compile a reply based on NLG. This is how human intelligence is being replicated to an extent in today's words of automation. There is a plethora of use cases in every industry that is benefiting from the use of these technologies. Now, humans don't have to read and go through thousands of written documents to extract the meaning of the document or find errors and mistakes. Machines can do that for humans in a fraction of a second compared to humans doing the same in hours.

This concludes the list of components used in designing an IA solution. Now let's see how these components can be used to design an IA solution and what considerations should be kept in mind while designing such solutions.

Design considerations for IA

Let's first understand one thing: you must draw a line as to how far you want to go in your learning journey. You might be transitioning and want to start with a **solution architect** (**SA**) profile that specializes in only RPA, and that is okay. Rushing through your learning roadmap is not going to help.

So, if you have practiced the RPA solution enough and consider yourself an expert, move on to the next big thing, designing IA solutions. Let's start with understanding the approach of IA design and how an SA can progress their career in designing IA solutions. Think of it this way, you have graduated from college and worked in the industry for some time, and now you want to do your master's degree. There will be a roadmap that is not completely different from what you have learned in your RPA journey, and all your learning will complement your progress. Let's talk about the study topics, as you need to study to understand the technology. There is a lot that needs brushing off from your college days from math to statistics so that you can understand the basics of ML and AI platforms. So, the list goes as follows:

- **Brush up on your understanding of probability, calculus, and statistics**: This is very important so that you can understand the working of the ML models and algorithms. You don't need to master them but you should understand enough so that when you read about the algorithms, they make sense to you. There is a plethora of free resources on the internet and you can look for some YouTube videos to help you to brush up on the topics.

- **Linear programming and linear algebra**: These are the building blocks of ML and AI systems and understanding these topics will help you to select the right solution for the job. There are so many models and algorithms available on a single topic that it will confuse you unless you understand what it is doing under the hood. Again, start with free resources and courses available on the internet, and go for it. There are many good paid-for courses as well. It can sometimes be overwhelming as the math involved is not easy, so have patience and keep going. Consistency is the key to success in this learning path.

- **Learn Python**: Learn Python, which is considered the go-to language for the data science community and ML/AI enthusiasts. As you are already a developer, learning a new language needs practice, and Python is a very forgiving language and easy to learn. All RPA vendors have some kind of mechanism available to integrate the Python code, so this will be very helpful as you will write some code for your IA needs. Some of the important packages that you should focus on are pandas, NumPy, scikit-learn, Flask, matplotlib, SciPy, Beautiful Soup, and any framework such as PyTorch or TensorFlow. This will be continuous learning, so don't stop; keep learning.

- **SQL**: You might already know this from your developer days so you might want to brush up and you should be good to go. This is an added advantage when working with large datasets scattered across different databases or different file formats and storage locations.

- **Data collection and cleanup**: This is the key to any ML model you use. You will need a ton of cleansed data. You will need to understand collecting the data and how it is cleaned and how data is augmented when there is not enough. Additionally, you will need to know how machines can become biased due to having too much or too little data. Read about all these concepts so you can understand and can talk to the data scientist and ML engineers.

- **ML and AI algorithms**: This is when you will have to start working toward gaining knowledge about different algorithms, such as linear regression, **k-nearest neighbors** (**KNN**), K-means, random forest, and naïve Bayes. This will help you understand how these algorithms work and how they are implemented on a large dataset. Also, study some of the NLP models and techniques available, as that will be very handy when it comes to designing NLP-based systems.

Now you are ready to design your IA system. This is all for the sake of understanding the technology and giving requirements to the data scientist and ML engineers so that they can build the service for you. This also helps you identify the right solution from off-the-shelf products on the market. If you don't learn the technology, how will you be able to even think about what fits best for your use case?

Let's understand this using an example. Assume you are given a process that involves a lot of scanned PDFs. The documents are in three different colors, black, blue, and red. Red text is what was added for tracking and special attention. Your automation should be able to detect the red from the black and blue text and then only extract the red and blue text, leaving behind the black text. Take a moment and think about all the technologies we have talked about so far. Which one will fit in this use case? If you thought about OCR and CV, then you are correct. If you have not learned how CV works, how will you be able to identify what should be used for detecting and extracting the red and blue text? This is what is called the application of knowledge.

You will have ML engineers and Python developers to code for you, but to do the design, you need to know the ins and outs of the technology. It will be a continuous learning journey, and the day you stop, your knowledge will become obsolete. With the advancement of technology and new things getting discovered every day, you need to keep up with it. The following diagram shows a representation of the learning journey for someone who wants to move to design IA automation:

Figure 9.3 – The learning path for IA

So, till now, we have seen what IA and IPA are and how an SA can start their journey and add this next-generation technology into their technology arsenal, what components are included in the IA ecosystem, and what the learning road looks like. Once you have completed your learning, you will be ready to design some amazing IA systems. So, is that all that IA can do? Well, technically, there is another type of IA that has become one of the mainstream technology for every company that deals with customers. The technology is called a chatbot. You might have seen chatbots or messengers used by websites and apps to provide you with some answers, and they can be very limited.

In the next topic, we will learn about the advancement of chatbots and how they became an extended part of IA.

Chatbots

With the advancement of the internet and websites and everything being online, customers have started using online platforms more frequently. This resulted in moving the foot traffic from the offices and physical shops to online stores and virtual offices. This industry shift required an agent to be ready to solve queries and talk to online customers.

It started with real humans answering queries and questions, but later, it became less efficient, slow, and very costly. A human takes longer to complete the conversation and sometimes also gets engaged in out-of-topic chats, which can waste time. To avoid this, you need to add more policing to your customer service representatives, which is a costly affair. So, what is the solution? If we analyze the issue, it is mostly human nature that is becoming an issue, and also that human resources are costly, and you need so many as you have a huge customer base. So, if we can have a system that can mimic humans, that should suffice. Well, technically yes, so that led to the rise of chatbots. Chatbots started replacing the initial part of the conversation during inception and even for the next few years. A chatbot will greet, ask a few basic questions, and reply with some standard answers, and when the question is out of their syllabus (recorded questions and answers in the database), they transfer the conversation to a real human. It is rule-based automation. It worked well for the last decade or so, but then with the advancement of IA and all the awesome technologies, it became possible to add human intelligence and experience to the chatbots.

This gave to the rise of intelligent chatbots, also known as conversational AI. As the name suggests, conversational AI can mimic real human conversation with emotions and dialects. This can even decrease the need to transfer the conversation to a real human and can save more time and money. It also provides a smoother customer experience. This is achievable with the advancement of NLP and **text-to-speech** (**TTS**) models. Alexa and Siri are examples of intelligent chatbots that can have a human-like conversation. These intelligent automation or AI chatbots elevate the customer's digital experience. This can be implemented in both **text-to-text** (**TTT**) or TTS and everything in between. Let's understand the basics of AI-based chatbots. The following diagram shows the basic working of the intelligent chatbot and its components:

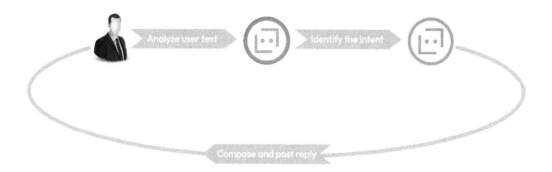

Figure 9.4 – Working of an intelligent chatbot

From the previous diagram, we can see that the intelligent chatbot or agent's first step is to analyze the text, then identify the intent, and then compose a reply based on the chatbot's understanding.

It might seem very straightforward but it isn't. Let's understand it with the help of an example. Using our banking client as an example, let's assume that you have been tasked to design a chatbot for their new web platform. This web platform is an advanced version that should also come with an intelligent agent. The requirements are as follows:

- The agent should first act as a precursor and gather the data, which can then be utilized for customer identification.

- Post identification, the bot should be able to ask basic questions such as, How may I help you? What would you like to do today?

- The agent should also be able to provide a few options on the screen so the customers can simply click on the right option and continue the conversation.

- The agent should not ask for any confidential information and should also not provide any.

- Information such as account balance, next scheduled payment, upcoming payment, and the reason for the recent decline of any transaction are a few services that the chatbot can render.

So, based on these high-level requirements, let's design a chatbot. I am not trying to teach you the complete step-by-step process of designing the intelligent agent, as that is not the intent of this book, but to give you enough so you can understand the complexity of these IA. Let's get started:

1. The first requirement states that the chatbot should be *able to gather and verify some basic info* such as name, address, zip code, email ID, the last four digits of the account number, and so on. We can verify the customer with the combination of these and maybe a few more pieces of info. This is simple; you have some built-in questions and answers, which starts with some greetings. Then it asks these basic questions so the customer can be verified. These questions and their answers can be cross-verified against the bank's backend database and the chatbot can move to the next step.

2. *How may I help you*, or *What is the purpose of your visit today*? Now comes the challenge. Customers can now have a free hand to say whatever. They can say a complete sentence or even choose to reply with one-word answers. Adding to the complexity, the customer can start writing their replies in a different language such as French or Spanish. Well, this is too much for a rule-based chatbot to handle. This all depends on what level of customer experience you want to build. If a different language is detected, the chatbot can simply say *I am not equipped to answer in that language* and can just hand it over to the live agent. But that would defeat the purpose of an intelligent chatbot.

    So, the first thing you might want to do is to take the text from your chatbot and run it through an NLP model that can detect the language. Then, you can reply that the chatbot has detected, let's say, Spanish, and then supply the greeting again in Spanish. Now you can see the beauty of this. As the chatbot has switched language, it has to establish confidence, and greeting the user back in their language of choice immediately builds that. Next, you will need to find the intent of the text. What does the intent mean? It means understanding what the customer wants to do by finding some keywords and phrases. An NLP model trained on a text corpus of a dataset from a banking domain can easily do that. I know I have used some ML lingo but that is to make you familiar with it. Also, I am assuming that you have gone through the learning path and acquired some knowledge about the ML and NLP models. The intent you found is to check the account balance. So, you query the backend database (this is where your knowledge of SQL will come in handy as it's a relational database), and the result is more than one account. Now the chatbot should be intelligent enough to post back the question asking which account, but in the customer's preferred language. You see how this can keep getting complicated. The workflow you have to design can become super complex. So, you post the question, and then the customer replies that they want to know the balance of the checking account. You then take that reply run it through the same workflow of intent | query backend | compose reply | translate to the language, and post it back to the customer.

3. Now that we can solve that query, the chatbot can ask whether the customer needs further help or has any other query. This time, the chatbot can also present some options as the customer might not have known what else can be done through this chatbot. This is where the customer experience comes into the picture. You ensure the customer gets the same feeling as talking to a live agent where the agent asks, What else can I do for you? Or is there anything else I can help you with? Adding an option to talk to the live agent is also recommended, as there can be customers who are not that computer savvy and feel that talking is better than typing their queries. Or there can be other reasons, and they feel talking is better.

    Let's say that at the start of the conversation, the customer types their full account number and details. This is against the chatbot security norms, and the chatbot should be intelligent enough to detect that immediately and redact it. At the same time, it should post back to the customer a warning message that the account number has been deleted for their security, and this information should not be shared without a live agent. This also shows the customer that the proper security is in place and helps build more confidence in automated systems.

4. Let's say that the customer replies that the recent transaction was declined, and the customer wants the reason for that decline. They also add that it was a very embarrassing moment for them, as they didn't have any other means to pay for the transaction. Now, you see there are two intents here: first, to know the reason for the decline, and the other to show sympathy to the customer as any human would do. So, while the text is run through the NLP model, two intents will be detected, and two different replies will be generated. Sympathy statements such as *I am so sorry to hear that, I know how you feel, and it's awful* should be first posted so that the customer feels the human-like behavior, and then the query to the backend made to find the real reason for the transaction decline. Also, there should be guidance on how to avoid these situations in the future so that it completes the intent. These replies, which are composed on the fly based on the intent and entities extracted from the customer message, are what we humans also do. We do the same but don't realize it unless someone points it out. When orchestrated logically, this whole request and response become an AI.

This is just the tip of the iceberg. We saw how chatbots can use NLP and how we can compose the outputs on the fly. We also learned how, with the use of IA, we can enhance the user experience and, at the same time, reduce human involvement in these processes. Nowadays, there are so many off-the-shelf platforms and frameworks that can be used for specific industries and use cases. For example, Rasa, Microsoft Bot Framework, Kore.ai, and many similar platforms can be used to design intelligent chatbots. These platforms are low-code/no-code solutions, so the design and development become easier and less cumbersome.

Summary

To summarize, we discussed the importance of IA and how it can elevate automation to the next level. It helps automate the processes that were not possible earlier due to the involvement of cognitive process steps. We also learned about the differences between RPA and IA and the learning path to progress to an IA SA. Adding this skillset will boost your career.

We discussed the learning curve and the path. We also discussed the next-generation chatbots known as intelligent chatbots or agents. These agents are revolutionizing communication with machines.

In the next chapter, we will study hyperautomation and how it becomes one of the most advanced platforms for automation. We will learn how to design and build solutions using the platform and all the components and technologies used in hyperautomation.

Questions

1. What are the components that make IA intelligent?
2. What are NLP, NLU, and NLG?
3. How do you make a machine understand text?
4. What is Intelligent OCR?
5. What are intent and entity in chatbot design?

10
Hyperautomation: The Future of RPA

In the previous chapter, we talked about **intelligent automation** (**IA**) and how it is revolutionizing industries. But that is not all when it comes to automation and its benefits; there is more to it, and that is what we are going to cover in this chapter. When the industry was taking advantage of IA, or **intelligent process automation** (**IPA**), some people were working on the next phase and trying to figure out what else can be added to the automation ecosystem so it can add more value. We already talked about machine learning and artificial intelligence and adding them to RPA to achieve next-gen automation capabilities. Now, we will see what hyperautomation is – another concept that talks about adding more capabilities to the existing IA and is capable of automating everything automatable in an organization. What does that mean? It means scaling automation to the level where everything can be automated, including the discovery and identification of new automation opportunities.

In this chapter, we will discuss the following topics:

- What is hyperautomation?
- When to consider hyperautomation
- Is hyper-automation the future of automation?
- How to design a hyper-automation solution

Let's dive deeper into the topics. Before we even try to understand what hyperautomation is, we need to understand its significance, why it is needed, and what drives businesses to even think of something beyond IA or IPA.

So, the question is: why do we need hyperautomation? The term hyperautomation was coined by industry gurus who realized that, though we have IA and IPA, there is still a lack of glue to bind them and improve productivity. This concept of improving productivity and increasing the pace of automating more processes compared to previously is what hyperautomation is all about. It helps to build on and expand the same ecosystem that we discussed in the previous chapter, simultaneously improving the productivity and speed of automation. That's enough introduction; let's get right into what hyperautomation is.

What is hyperautomation?

Hyperautomation is like a booster to the existing IA or IPA. It helps in boosting productivity by speeding up automation. It is needed for many reasons. Some of them are as follows:

- Companies that are just starting on their automation journey and have already matured in automation realize that they are not able to keep up with the demand and pace.

- Processes using outdated technology result in an inability to compete with the advanced processes that competitors are utilizing.

- Corporate IT is still working to capacity and can't cater to increasing demands due to a lack of resources, infrastructure, knowledge, and traditional time-consuming deployment techniques.

- A new regulation or compliance is released regularly for industries, and keeping tabs on them and modifying the current system at the same pace is nearly impossible. Hyperautomation provides the capability to produce high-quality products and services with minimal or no human intervention and great productivity and accuracy.

These factors gave birth to a more robust and integrated ecosystem of tools and technologies that can be implemented and used across the board. This ecosystem can now be used to automate any probable process.

For example, let's assume that you have exhausted all the processes based on the curated list of processes. Now, what next? This is where hyperautomation comes into the picture, as now you can even automate the identification of processes that are good candidates to be automated.

Now, think of a scenario. Your organization is starting on its automation journey and doesn't quite know which processes to automate. Having a *process mining* or *process discovery* tool can give you insights into the process, as well as giving you a high ROI and recommendations of whether the process is a good fit. Having this set of tools now automates those very steps that, in earlier automation strategies, were done by humans, if you remember from our second and third chapters. There is a team who reviews the processes and then, based on the preferred method of prioritization, lists the best candidates for automation. It is a human-intensive task. You need to create the process as-is and to-be maps, calculate the ROI, and carry out **cost-benefit analysis** (**CBA**). Now, with the help of hyperautomation, this can all be automated using tools that not only can build all this for you but also will capture the nitty-gritty details of the process, including things that you might have never noticed, having used the same process for years.

Having a tool for the process of discovery and mining can now speed up the process by up to 10x, compared to the traditional way of discovery and mining, where a team had to work for weeks if not months to get a curated list. To add to that, this step needs to be repeated from time to time to maintain a healthy pipeline of processes. If you are a small organization and only have a few processes to automate, then it makes more sense to hire a professional services firm to identify the processes. But if you are a global organization with a plethora of processes and subprocesses, then it definitely makes sense to invest in a good process discovery or mining tool. Some of the famous tools and software available are from RPA vendors themselves, such as UiPath and Blue Prism. Also, other companies have developed tools, such as IBM, Appian, and AntWorks.

So, we talked about adding automated discovery and mining to processes, as well as what else can be done with hyperautomation. Hyperautomation can also be used as a single platform for all your automation needs. That is called **integration platform as a service (iPaaS)**. It can be developed internally or used by a third party, such as Microsoft, Workato, Oracle, SAP, and Boomi. iPaaS is cloud native and can be deployed, leveraged, and managed globally. This brings automation to the next level as now it has no geographical boundaries. This is why hyperautomation is getting a lot of traction among the big players. The following figure shows how all the tools and technologies combined make up the ecosystem that we know as hyperautomation.

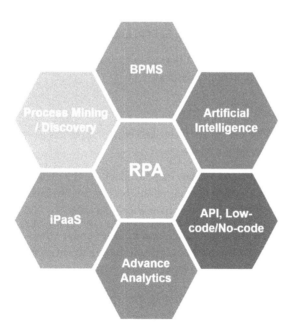

Figure 10.1 – Hyperautomation

In the preceding figure, we can see some new additions, such as iPaaS and advanced analytics. Let's discuss how they contribute to hyperautomation.

Integration platform as a service (iPaaS)

When it comes to automation, integration becomes the glue that keeps everything connected. Integration comes in many different forms, and having so many moving parts working in silos can sometimes lead to a bottleneck for the entire project. How about bringing all these integration services to a common platform and then letting them be available as a service? It becomes a common hub for all types of integration needs, and that becomes an integration platform. Putting this all on cloud-based infrastructure makes it more accessible and easier to integrate with. All this combined and served on a cloud platform is known as iPaaS. This platform can cater to the needs of not just one organization but multiple organizations, thus making it more robust and, at the same time, seamless. Let's now discuss some of the benefits and challenges of iPaaS.

Let's first see some benefits:

- iPaaS is a set of cloud-based tools that can help integrate all kinds of platforms, such as mobile, cloud, and **business to business** (**B2B**), with almost real-time transactions and processing involving huge datasets and many different formats of data.

- Every tool on the platform is highly secure and monitored with a centralized command center by the vendor itself. So, you get security built in and need not worry about the specifics.

- With iPaaS, developers get access to iPaaS platforms and an ecosystem that helps them to integrate and develop applications seamlessly.

Here are some challenges:

- There are so many diverse vendors available and each of them has its strengths and weaknesses. This makes selecting a vendor a challenge.

- There is integrated security and management available on the platform, but still, someone has to manage and monitor it, which can sometimes become overwhelming. Companies also have to adhere to the guidelines and be compliant with state laws.

- Data is always owned by the organization and not the vendor who is providing the platform, security, and monitoring. Organizations have to be cognizant of security breaches and data losses and have to own any such incidents.

Let's now talk about the next topic in hyperautomation, which is advanced analytics.

Advanced analytics

What is advanced analytics? Advanced analytics is the use of next-generation tools and techniques that are way more advanced than traditional **business intelligence** (**BI**) techniques. Advanced analytics helps in gaining deeper insights and finding patterns that can be used in making predictions or generating recommendations. Advanced analytics techniques include data/text mining, ML algorithms, pattern matching, semantic analysis, sentiment analysis, generative networks, cluster analysis, simulation, and neural networks.

As we can see from the preceding definition, advanced analytics is about going above and beyond the traditional ways of doing analytics. It uses ML, data/text mining, pattern matching, and semantic analysis, which all are somehow related to the data science field. Now, you might think that data science and advanced analytics are the same, but they are not. There is quite a difference between the two fields. Although they seem similar and share some tools and techniques, their goals diverge somewhere toward their end.

Advanced analytics is used more for forecasting, such as weather forecasts or hurricane and tornado forecasting, and so on. You get the idea! Data science does a similar type of analysis but goes deeper into the data and tries to find insights that can be helpful for the business to achieve their goals. So, to sum up, data science involves deeper analysis compared to advanced analytics. Data science is also more technical in nature compared to advanced analytics. Let's review a use case for financial institutes that also applies to our own banking clients as well. Every bank or financial institution generates revenue from their customers. Customers using different products, such as credit cards, debit cards, and other financial instruments, build their net worth, and contribute to the financial institution's strengths and growth. So, an all-in-all customer base is the key to success. Banks and financial institutions try to always perform a "what-if" analysis so that they can predict the best and worst situations and be prepared for them. Based on this, let's assume that our banking client came to you and asked for automation that takes in the call data for the past 10 years and then can predict the *customer churn rate*. If you don't know already, the customer churn rate means, in our example, the percentage of customers who are likely to leave the bank and move to a different financial institution.

For this use case, as we already know, *data is key*, and that will help us give all the insights. This data will help us analyze the sentiments of customers who called the bank to make a complaint or for any services. It will give us insight into whether the customer was angry and whether they are likely to leave. Based on this, the bank can take countermeasures, such as providing them with some perks or giving them a special call apologizing for the poor service. This can save a lot of money and keep the bank's reputation intact. So, advanced analytics is used to do a deeper dive into the data and analyze it from every angle to gain insights that can be valuable for the client.

How to design this model will not be covered in depth in this chapter, but we can review the steps.

The following are the steps to solve the previously discussed use case.

1. Gather, collect, and extract lots of data. There is no such thing as enough or too much data. In the ML world, data is the *fuel* and more is always less.

2. Clean the data. Data might be collected from many different sources and there might only be a few attributes that are important. There can be wrong or missing data, and all that has to be fixed before we can even think about analyzing it.

3. Get the data labeled. This includes when a specific customer called, the reason for them leaving, and for how long they were a customer. It's easier said than done and there are many sub-steps involved to achieve this.

4. After the data is cleaned and labeled, we come to the machine learning part. You will need a model that can take in the labeled data and start learning from it so it can find out what types of customers and conversations lead to a churning cycle. You can also learn what kind of proactive measures helped the bank to retain customers.

5. Once that model is able to learn and predict with good accuracy, then you can feed the model prediction to an advanced analytics tool and get some more insights based on the predictions. Based on the machine, the advanced analytics tool can now do some forecasting for you so you should be aware and able to apply some countermeasures.

These were just the steps at a high level and nowhere close to what the real project would look like. The focus of this book is automation and not ML or advanced analytics solutions. So far, we have understood what hyperautomation and its core components are. Now, let's see when we should use hyperautomation. We can't just go and implement hyperautomation whenever we hear about a use case for automation. We need to be sure that it is needed, as implementing it is a costly and time-consuming affair.

When to consider hyper-automation

As we saw, hyper-automation is an amalgamation of technologies. When an organization needs to automate complex processes that involve RPA, ML, advanced analytics, BPMS, and iPaaS, then hyper-automation should be considered. Hyper-automation helps in business process optimization and helps businesses to automate processes that are spread across business units, geo-locations, and continents.

Let's understand this using an example. Assume that your banking client has a central email inbox that receives emails of all types, such as those related to appeals, grievances, complaints, accolades, marketing, requests, and accounts; the list goes on. Now, on average, this main inbox receives anywhere from around 3,000 to 12,000 emails per day. A team of six full-time resources works on reading each of these emails and categorizing or forwarding them to their respective mailboxes for further review based on the intent and sentiments of the email, if applicable. You have been asked to design automation that can automatically read the incoming emails, understand the intent, and then route them to the respective mailbox for further processing. You are also asked to analyze how many types of emails are received every day and month. Also, you will need to find out whether there is a peak time of the year when there are more emails of a specific type. You have to develop this solution for not only the North America geo-location but also Asia and Europe.

If we analyze the use case, it involves all kinds of processes and technologies. Let's review them based on the requirements and see how they can be leveraged for each requirement:

*   **RPA**: The process starts from the email inbox, so we need something to access the email inbox and monitor and read emails, and that is where RPA comes into the picture. This can easily be

achieved using any RPA tool of choice. There is also a requirement of routing the emails based on the intent, and that can also be catered for through RPA.

- **Machine learning**: Next comes understanding the intent of the email. This can be achieved with the help of machine learning. We can train the machine; to be specific, a supervised machine learning algorithm can be used for this use case. For sentiment analysis, there are pre-trained models that can be used as a starting point and then can be trained on specific data to increase their accuracy and efficacy. Once the machine is trained enough to recognize the intent, it can classify the emails and then forward them to the respective departments.

- **Advanced analytics**: This involves finding out how many emails were received every day and month. What are the different intents and sentiments? Find out whether there is a peak time during the year and, if so, find the reason. This analysis can get more complicated when it needs to be split based on geographical locations.

- **iPaaS**: The solution has to be cloud native. The reason is that the solution is not just catering to one geo-location but multiple. Having a cloud-based solution can easily help in scaling the solution vertically or horizontally. It can also help in seamlessly integrating with email systems, machine learning ecosystems, and advanced analytics tools.

So, as we saw in the preceding scenario, integrating different technologies can take simple automation to the next level and not only cater to a local business unit or location but also can be scaled globally.

Let's now look at some of the advantages and disadvantages of hyperautomation.

Here are some advantages:

- When you have to keep up with the technology and human resources aren't available, turn to automation. The challenge of this is that automation involves a high degree of cognitive functions. However, now we have hyperautomation, which can bring the best of all the ecosystems and make this futuristic concept a reality.

- Hyperautomation also helps in achieving more complex automation and adds to the productivity and efficiency of the existing workforce.

- It increases the automation footprint, which otherwise would be next to impossible. As hyperautomation brings all the technologies onto one platform, automation of these complex use cases becomes a reality.

- Hyperautomation can be used to achieve a better customer experience. Using automation helps humans to do the job with more efficiency, reduces the turnaround time, and focuses more on the customer rather than the technology, providing an enhanced customer experience.

- It helps businesses to deep dive into the data, which can give more insights into their business. With advanced analytics, businesses can unlock real insights and find those key points that can boost the business or solve a critical problem.

Now, let's go over some disadvantages:

- The biggest disadvantage of using hyperautomation is the cost. The costs can pile up really quickly. It can be a costly affair when you involve ML and advanced analytics in the mix. It comprises not only the experiments and development cost but also the cost of the infrastructure that you would need to support this type of implementation. Adding to this the other technology needs, such as RPA and iPaaS, can make it really challenging to justify the cost. That is the reason why it is always advisable to spend a good amount of time analyzing the cost and building a CBA, which can then be used to justify the spending and the ROI.

- Another aspect that adds to the disadvantage is the complexity of the process. Using some of the technology from the hyperautomation stack can be challenging, and imagine when the full stack is used for some of the use cases. It can add to the complexity, which leads to challenges of support, among others.

- Hyperautomation not only applies to the software industry but also can be extended to automated machines and medical equipment, such as robotic arms and surgical equipment. Sometimes, the human operating these machines might not be comfortable with using automation, which can lead to a safety concern.

- Having the support of leadership is key to these types of costly automation projects. There can be many situations where the result is not as expected, which can throw off the confidence of the team. Calculating the ROI, and that too from a tangible and intangible form can be challenging.

- Choosing the right solution from off-the-shelf products and services can also be a challenge. Doing exhaustive research and then narrowing down the right product and services can be challenging.

We've discussed the advantages and disadvantages of hyperautomation. There is another challenge, which is that despite all the advancements and technology, machines still can't replace humans in most areas. Machines are not reliable. You can't use data that is only 90% or 95% accurate. You need it to be 100% accurate to be able to call it production-grade data and use it with confidence. For this reason, we ask humans to get involved. But the question is, how do we create an ecosystem where machines and humans can work in tandem? The answer is **human in the loop (HITL)**. As the name suggests, HITL is when machines require the help of humans to review, fix, and validate the data that is extracted or processed by them. This collaboration between the machine and human fills the gap of quality control, bringing the data to 100% accuracy and making it suitable as production-grade data.

Let's understand this concept using an example. Assume that you have been approached by your existing client, the bank, and asked to automate a process that involves data extraction from scanned forms for new account applications. These are forms filled in by people who are not tech savvy. These applications need to go through a process that can extract data with high quality and then be fed to the destination system. After your analysis, this seems to be simple and you start designing the process. It is clear from the process that it will need some type of OCR technology. Now, as you are working with handwritten documents, you will need some type of **handwritten character recognition (HCR)**.

You research and find one of the best in the market and plan to use it for this purpose. Next, you do a quick proof of concept to prove that it is extracting the information with great accuracy. But to your disappointment, it is not consistent. Sometimes it extracts with 100% accuracy, and sometimes 90-95%, which is not good for sending the data to production systems.

So, what can be done? You think of a few things: enhancing the image quality so that the data recognition accuracy is increased, boosting the contrast, and downgrading the color saturation. You do all that can be done to enhance the image to get great results. After these enhancements, you are able to achieve some increase in accuracy, but it is still not up to the mark. Now, it seems the automation will fail due to the data accuracy. So, the next best thing you think of doing is adding another layer of data cleansing using the technique of fuzzy logic.

Fuzzy logic uses algorithms to find the nearest match for a specific word and then gives you a score between 0 and 1. Based on that, a decision can be made and errors can be corrected. So, if the word or words that you are trying to validate are partially extracted, or one of the letters is not correctly extracted, then this technique can help to fix those small errors. For example, if the form had "John Doe" and the OCR extracted "J0hn D0e," getting confused between "o" and "0," then this error can be fixed by fuzzy logic. There are more advanced algorithms that can help with string matching and pattern recognition, which can be useful in this regard. So, you implement all these techniques to the best of your ability. But still, there are a few scenarios where the data can't be extracted because the scanned image quality is very poor or the text is written in bad handwriting. Now what?

You analyze a sample set of 1,000 documents and find that the model is only having a hard time extracting the data from 5-10% of the document. So, the volume of errors is not that huge. Also, the entire document is not a complete waste as there are only a few sections that need a second set of eyes. Well, this is kind of good news as, based on your analysis, any human can review 5-10% of each document in one hour. So, you do that exercise and the automation is able to extract the data with 100% accuracy.

Now, let's visualize this whole process with a diagram.

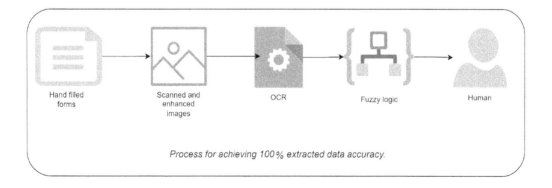

Hand filled forms → Scanned and enhanced images → OCR → Fuzzy logic → Human

Process for achieving 100% extracted data accuracy.

Figure 10.2 – Process for extracting data with a high level of accuracy

Now, when the requirement is to involve the human aspect from time to time as this scenario can repeat itself, then you implement a more permanent solution, which is involving humans on a regular basis based on a platform that can serve the document to the humans and get their feedback and comments. This complete cycle is called HITL.

So, we have proved that machines are not capable of replacing humans but are just there to help and take over mundane and boring jobs. Now, after reading all this and learning about the capabilities of hyperautomation and how the industry is using it for improved productivity and increased efficiency, a question might come to your mind: is hyperautomation the future of automation? Let's discuss it!

Is hyperautomation the future of automation?

With the rise in demand for skills and cheap labor, multi-skilled laborers are like a dream. But with hyperautomation, you can bring all those skills on the same platform, to some extent, leaving the human resources to work on niche skills. When the world was hit by the COVID-19 pandemic in 2020, it posed a threat to industrialization. There was no one available to run machines, factories, plants, and software. This fueled the advancement of automation to eliminate the human factor from the mix.

With the global pandemic, its ever-lasting effect on humanity, and the threat that we could get hit even worse, a human-less system has to be in place to keep the ball rolling. Hyperautomation can provide real-time, in-depth analysis to support business functions that were not possible earlier. It can stop criminal activities in real time and take cybersecurity to the next level. With hyperautomation, it doesn't mean that, in the near future, the work of humans will be done by physical bots, but rather imagining information technology supported by both humans and machines working in tandem. With machines working 24x7, increasing efficiency by 3x, humans can leave time-consuming and tedious tasks to machines. This is why hyperautomation is definitely the future of automation.

That being said, let's now talk about how you should design a hyperautomation process. As stated earlier, hyperautomation is an amalgamation of technologies, and the first thing you need to do is study and try to understand those technologies. You might not be an expert in advanced analytics and can definitely ask for an expert, such as an SME, or for an ML engineer, but you should understand the technology well enough to connect those pieces to build the automation. Let's see how hyperautomation can be designed using an example.

Assume that your client, the bank, asks you to automate a process from the mortgage department. The process involves the underwriter reviewing the mortgage documents and summarizing them to make a quick decision on whether to approve a loan or not. Now, this is a very cumbersome process. The underwriter has to go through and read and review all the documents. As they are the person whose signature will be on the loan approval, they have to review the docs themself. It's complex and time-consuming to review these documents, adding a delay to the process. Typically, it takes anywhere from one to three weeks for an underwriter to review and make a decision on an application. This is a lot of time. Automation can drastically help reduce the time and make the process easy. Let's design the process.

Here are the steps to consider while designing a hyperautomation process:

- Always do a detailed review of the process. If it is not documented, then interview the SMEs, and in this case, the underwriters themselves. By doing this, you can find a lot of pain points that later can serve to indicate your knowledge of the customer.

- Post-review, put the design on paper. Identify the sections and technologies that you would like to propose for each of the steps of the process. This gives you a clear picture and a roadmap for what needs to be worked on next or in parallel.

- Do your research and understand the in-house capabilities. Like I said in earlier chapters, make sure that you look around and try to utilize what is available. Asking for a technology that is not in the current technology stack might not be feasible. Discuss the needs of the process with the stakeholders and get their buy-in. This will make sure that there will be support from them if you need to go looking for resources or technology externally.

In our use case, the first thing you would do is review the documents and try to review as many samples as you can. These should be real documents and not any mockups to give you the real picture of what you are dealing with.

We have discussed, multiple times in previous chapters, that for text extraction from documents, you should use OCR. There can be various document formats, such as loan applications, tax papers, W-2s, payslips, any other proofs of income, and bank statements. Having so many types of documents, you will need some kind of document classification model that can identify the type and then extract the right sections for the relevant data.

To summarize the documents, there are a couple of techniques, **extraction** and **abstraction**. Extraction is the process of finding the relevant sentences and putting them in a proper sequence. Which sentences should be added to the summary can be identified by many different algorithms, one of them being **term frequency-inverse document frequency** (**TF-IDF**). This is the most common algorithm in which the most repeated word is identified and then given a weightage based on how many times it was repeated in the document. Based on that, the sentence is identified in which that word occurred added to the summary considering that sentence to have more importance. Though it is a common algorithm, it has its drawbacks. Abstraction, on the other hand, is a more complex process that uses more advanced algorithms and uses neural networks that are far more accurate but tough to implement. In this technique, the sentences are extracted and then rewritten by the machine without losing its main intent. This makes the summary more human-readable. It also retains the chain of events from the original document, thus making it a real summary.

Then comes the step to handle multiple formats and types of documents. This is a common industry problem and has been solved by many RPA-focused offerings, such as UiPath, Blue Prism, and Automation Anywhere. It is called **intelligent document processing** (**IDP**). This is a pipeline of interconnected functions that starts with training an ML model to identify and classify the documents into categories and types. Based on that, another model will extract the specific sections for pieces of information. Now, when the documents are submitted for automation, they will first get categorized, and then the text extraction process starts.

Once you stitch all these together with other vanilla RPA steps, you will get your initial process. It will take a few iterations to get right, but this is at least your first hyperautomation process designed from scratch. This brings us to the end of this chapter.

Summary

So, to recap, in this chapter, we saw what hyperautomation is and how it is different from simple RPA. What are the other technologies that, combined, help businesses harness the power of hyperautomation for their decision-making and advanced automation needs? Hyperautomation does not have any boundaries and the challenges aren't such that they can't be overcome. Challenges such as cost and skilled labor are always present for any niche solution. But the benefits that the industry can reap from this technology are tremendous.

In the next chapter, we will be discussing a very common but famous concept of development in RPA/IA/hyperautomation, which is reusable components.

Questions

1. What is iPaaS? How is it helpful for hyper-automation?
2. List some of the disadvantages of hyper-automation.
3. What is IDP?
4. When should you consider hyper-automation?

11
Reusable Components

Since the beginning of this book, we have been talking about **robotics process automation** (**RPA**) projects and their short duration. While we already know that RPA projects are short-lived, what's important is that this short duration helps businesses reap the benefits sooner rather than later. But how we make it even faster, better, and cheaper is something to mull over. If a project is scheduled for 8 or 10 weeks as per the project timeline, the code still has to be written and tested, and a complete **software development life cycle** (**SDLC**) has to be followed, but then what can be done to make it even shorter? Is there a way or technique that can be used, implemented, or brought into practice to help? The answer is yes, and in IT, we call this solution reusable components or reusable code snippets.

In this chapter, we will talk about reusable components and how they help in making the development cycle shorter and more robust. We will also talk about some of the use cases and how to design and develop them. The topics that will be covered in this chapter are as follows:

- What are reusable components?
- Faster, better, and cheaper development
- Reusable component use cases
- Building a library

So, let's get into it.

What are reusable components?

The meaning of the words reusable components is self-explanatory. Reusable means it can be used many times, either as is or with minimal modification to get the job done. Components means a piece of code or snippet that covers a single or multiple functionalities that can be used repeatedly in multiple projects. As these code snippets store a distinctive functionality, they are called components. Adding multiple components together, either in series or in parallel, can build a functionality or a set of functionalities. A set of functionalities can then be called an application or a program that covers the end-to-end requirements related to that application or program.

In RPA, a reusable component is a piece of code or a program that can be used multiple times in different automation projects. These components can help to streamline the automation process by allowing developers to reuse and modify existing code rather than starting from scratch each time. For example, if you use an application that stores your credentials for safekeeping, and you need to use that application for every RPA project, then having that code converted into a reusable component makes more sense. This will help you to speed up your development and you will have one less component to worry about as it is already developed, tested, and verified. It also brings consistency and structure to your code base, as well as bringing ease of maintenance, which can become a challenge when you have multiple RPA projects.

The reusability of components is important to the efficiency of **information technology** (**IT**) and the productivity of RPA. You should keep reusable components in mind throughout your design and development process. Reusable components can be used to store configuration information, track information about a step performed in the process, and delegate work between a web browser (user interface) and another web service for more complex tasks that might need a longer time – such as username or state machine validation.

Reusable components aren't just limited to software programming. When people use these template-like building blocks, they spend less time trying to come up with new patterns and shapes to solve problems. This saves both developers' and consumers' cognitive resources. Individuals no longer require the mental space associated with the design or creation of the component because someone else has already done it for them. So, one developer can create a reusable component and then other team members can use it and reap the benefits. That's the whole concept behind reusable components. Now, let's talk a bit about the benefits of reusable components.

Several types of reusable components can be used in RPA, including the following:

- **Functions**: Functions are small blocks of code that perform a specific task and can be called multiple times from different parts of the program. Functions can take input arguments and return output values, which makes them very flexible and easy to reuse.

- **Modules**: Modules are collections of functions and other code that can be imported and used in multiple programs. Modules can help to organize large amounts of code and make it easier to reuse and maintain.

- **Objects**: In **object-oriented programming** (**OOP**), objects are self-contained units of code that contain both data and the functions that operate on that data. Objects can be created and used multiple times, which makes them very useful for building reusable components in RPA.

- **Libraries**: Libraries are collections of reusable code that can be imported and used in different programs. Many programming languages come with a set of built-in libraries, and there are also many third-party libraries available for use in RPA projects.

Using reusable components can greatly improve the efficiency and maintainability of RPA projects. By breaking large tasks down into smaller, reusable components, developers can more easily modify and update the automation process as needed. Using reusable components can help improve the efficiency and maintainability of RPA projects, as well as reducing the risk of errors and bugs. It is generally a good practice to create reusable components whenever possible in RPA development.

Benefits of reusable components

An IT service organization can reduce the risk of problems and save time and money by managing process templates and investing in reusable components. Whether we code or not, reusing information, templates, and components effectively can save costs and reduce the chance of making mistakes due to errors in the code. It also follows the principle of not reinventing the wheel. A perfect example of this is RPA. A system can't be blamed for making a mistake or giving out misinformation when it is following an already-set-out prewritten plan. If a procedure being followed doesn't have to be designed specifically for one company, organization, department, or LOB, then it's worth implementing reusable components or templates rather than having IT do it again and again for the same reasons.

Suppose you have a few RPA projects that you know will have similar data extraction requirements from **Portable Document Format** (**PDF**) files. One common practice for solving this is to find a component that suits your project and reuse it across multiple projects. The importance of components is only amplified when viewed from the perspective of moving from disconnected apps to decoupled apps, and then up the stack to ML abstractions such as natural language processing, which need input datasets.

In the past, it was common to have one component for each task, with a particular set of responsibilities. The result was that once you changed the code, you would have to change the whole component and all its children. However, reuse allows us to change components in such a way that the changes can be made without affecting other components or their children. This is because if we must change something in a component, we make changes in only one place instead of all places where that component is used. Thus, there are fewer things that need to be changed when changes must be made.

In software development, the reuse of code is highly important and is considered a best practice. Reusable components help in reducing development effort. The developer can easily increase or decrease the number of functions that they need, as per their requirements. Also, for every new feature, it will be easier for them to write new components based on the existing component's API. Let's talk about how reusable components contribute toward achieving faster, better, and cheaper development.

Reusable components are essential in RPA for several reasons:

- **Efficiency**: Reusable components allow you to create and use the same functionality multiple times within your automation process, saving time and effort

- **Consistency**: Reusable components ensure that the same steps are followed consistently across different automation processes, reducing the risk of errors and inconsistencies

- **Maintainability**: Reusable components make it easier to maintain and update automation processes, as changes can be made in one place rather than multiple places

- **Scalability**: Reusable components enable automation processes to be easily scaled up or down, allowing for flexibility and adaptability to changing business needs

- **Cost-effectiveness**: Reusable components reduce the need for manual intervention, saving time and resources and increasing the overall cost-effectiveness of automation processes

Let's now see how reusable components help developers develop faster and better code. As the code can be written faster and the quality is better, the development cycle becomes cheaper.

Faster, better, and cheaper development

RPA development is a fast-paced field. A typical time scope for RPA projects may be between 6 and 12 weeks. However, certain factors, such as new requirements, design flaws, or miscommunication, will keep pushing the deadline. Speed is crucial in this era of innovation because it shapes the cost of implementing the solution as well as reliance on outside resources in its deployment process.

Reusable components are one such major technique for reducing the time taken by RPA projects. Apart from reducing costs and the efforts required in remediation due to revisions, they can additionally allow for faster sign-offs for approval. They help to protect against errors arising from typos by comparing an input list with those already coded within a framework tool. In order to efficiently meet deadlines, most companies opt for RPA bots that allow them to perform tasks at scale rather than manually pecking away at repetitive jobs, such as approvals across systems and servers, with human teams. They play a vital role in modern-day software development by using code templates and reconfigurable software architectures.

Reusable components are an integral element in faster and cheaper development. Their ability to create abstract designs, which is a well-researched way of designing easy-to-reuse and maintainable applications. We use these components to achieve abstractions that are independent of the idiom. Abstraction is key in allowing items to be reused across the board with different implementations.

Reusable components help reduce the cost of the development and implementation of RPA projects in many ways. First, they allow you to build more business value from your initial investment by developing reusable components and employing that architecture throughout the project life cycle, instead of building it recursively and then trying to reuse it for future projects. Second, reusable software components allow you to create more modular and flexible systems that are easier to adapt without redesigning when new requirements arise. Having a modular design makes it easy to replace one component with another and allows you to use smaller components when implementing the application. This approach can significantly reduce the need for rework during the life cycle of the project, especially when small changes are made to the application. If a reusable component is replaced by another one or requirements change, another reusable component can be taken out of development without having to rebuild the entire application from scratch.

For developers to share reusable components, they need standards in place. OOP languages allow reusable components, so the standards come from the language itself, which dictates how the program should function. To make these components accessible to others, they are stored in different online repositories in **Web Services Description Language** (**WSDL**), in an XML file that contains information about web services defining operations and associated data schemas (**XSD**). These are some of the generic ways that have been in practice for decades.

With RPA, the same logic is applied but the components can be available in a more packaged format. For example, in UiPath, we can create custom activity sets that can then be packaged as a NuGet package. We can also create smaller and modular scripts based on dotnet, Java, or Python programming languages to achieve the intent. In the Blue Prism world, these packages can be in the form of business objects, processes, and APIs. Every RPA vendor provides some form of development platform that can be used to develop reusable components and bring more value to the table. Their openness leads more customers and developers to use their platform and provides them with a competitive edge against their competitors globally.

Use cases

Let's now go through some use cases that are well suited for reusable components and some examples to get you started.

Use case 1

A common use case that we see very often in the RPA world is the use of PDF files. PDF is a common format in which data and text are shared across the organization. With the wide use of PDF documents, their association with automation is inevitable. PDFs come in many types. There can be text, pictures, scanned images, forms, and many more. All these different types can be a part of the process that you are trying to automate. If there are many processes using a PDF, it makes sense to have a common package, library, or reusable component that can be developed once and reused as and when necessary. Some common operations that involve PDFs are as follows:

- You might have a process that uses PDF documents as a form from the customer. This type of process is categorized as an intake process. A PDF form is given to the customer, which can be either filled out online or printed out and then filled in by hand. This variation of the same PDF form will need separate handling. Forms that are filled in online can be processed simply by copying the required text, but forms that are filled in by hand will need to first be digitized or scanned and then processed. There can be a reusable component to retrieve PDF files from the application storage. It can be a local filesystem or cloud-based storage such as Amazon's S3 bucket or MS Azure Blob storage.

- You can have a completely scanned document that can have just structured or unstructured data. These documents fall under the category of images, and you would need OCR to extract the text.

- You have the same scanned document but this time, the data is in a tabular format. This type of PDF will need special handling.

- Then there are images in a PDF. It can be a cheque, a form, a book, or a new article. All of these can be in the form of a PDF, which can be a part of the process you need to automate.

Wouldn't it be easy if you had a set of activities or code snippets that could be used to process each of these types of PDFs? This brings us to the conclusion that it is a good idea to invest time and money into building a reusable component. This reusable component can be based on an open source package or library or a paid version. The goal is to have something ready to use and not to invest time in figuring out what to do when a similar type of document is involved in a process.

There is a lot of work that has been done by the open source community in this regard and can be used for this purpose. The goal should be to focus on the rich functionality and build something that is future-proof. Thinking ahead is what makes a reusable component useful.

When we talk about PDF documents, one thing that should be kept in mind is that not all PDFs are of the same quality. Especially, scanned PDFs can be very poor-quality. They can be poorly scanned with the wrong orientation or distorted images. What if we can have a reusable component that can fix these PDFs and make them ready before they are used for data extraction and processing? This reusable component can be used repetitively for this purpose. Almost all RPA vendors provide PDF-related actions or activities that can be used to get started. But they might not be what is needed for your use case. Having a tailored solution always helps with faster and more consistent delivery.

Use case 2

We talked about the use of PDF documents and how they are commonly used across processes, which makes them a good candidate for reusable components. This doesn't mean that the use cases are restricted to only having automation scripts or snippets for a type of document, product, or application. The concept can be applied to anything that has recursive usability in the future and where it makes sense to have a reusable component. Let's take the example of our banking client. Each banking organization has some type of mainframe core platform that powers the entire or most of the banking functionalities.

Mainframe systems are a commonly used solution for banks to store data, ensure security, and provide customers with a range of services. Mainframes have an extensive history as a cornerstone of computing in banking and financial institutions. This chapter will explore the various ways they are used and their importance in today's banking landscape. They are also much more secure and resilient than most other technology, making them ideal for handling large amounts of sensitive data and processing transactions quickly and securely. Additionally, mainframes allow for easy integration with a variety of external financial applications, enabling organizations to maximize their potential.

Now, this is something that you can build for your client as a reusable component and can be used in many processes going forward. This can be the start of a library of reusable components, which we will talk about in the next section, but for now, we can just say that this can be a very valuable addition.

Now, let's analyze what the functionalities are that are commonly used from a mainframe system and are beneficial for automation. Before we even jump into the mainframe system, we need to take care of another piece of the puzzle, which is the mainframe simulator. To connect to the mainframe systems, you interact with or go through another piece of software, which is the gateway for you to connect to the mainframe. You will need IBM AS/400 or HP 3000 Series 957 as an emulator. There are various types of emulators available, such as BlueZone or Hercules. Most of these emulators have embedded scripting language that can be used for automating the actions on the mainframe. But then they are limited and adding another level of automation can reduce the efficacy of the automation.

To avoid this, it is recommended to use your primary RPA tool to automate actions directly on the emulator window. With that, you will build a series of actions that can be used repeatedly every time a mainframe is involved in the process. Let's assume you have that part of automation covered. Now come the actions that are native to the mainframe itself. One of the most common actions is to get the coordinates of the screen from where the data needs to be extracted or typed. This, again, is dependent on the configuration of the mainframe system. Commonly, it is set to either 24 X 80 or 32 X 80. This means that if the screen is converted into a graph paper-like display, then each pixel can be represented by the combination of rows and columns, where 24 X 80 or 32 X 80 represents rows X columns.

This is the crux of navigation and identifying the location of a data element on the mainframe screen. Using this, the automation can be given the coordinates in the form of rows X columns or x and y coordinates (graph coordinates). Almost every RPA tool provides existing integration with the emulators and handles to interact with the mainframe systems. Using what already exists, extending the functionality, and converting it into a reusable component will lead to a faster implementation of the automation with minimal changes.

There are many other use cases, some of which are listed here:

- **Creating a standardized login process for all robots**: Instead of having to create a login process for each individual robot, a reusable component can be created and implemented across all robots to streamline the process.

- **Handling error messages and exceptions**: A reusable component can be created to handle any error messages or exceptions that may occur during the automation process. This can save time and resources by not having to write separate code for each error or exception.

- **Data validation**: A reusable component can be created to validate data input during the automation process to ensure accuracy and prevent errors. This can be particularly useful for processes that require large amounts of data input.

- **Data extraction and manipulation**: A reusable component can be created to extract and manipulate data from various sources, such as databases or APIs, for use in the automation process. This can save time and resources by not having to write separate code for each data source.

- **Creating standardized reports**: A reusable component can be created to generate standardized reports on the automation process, such as performance metrics or error rates. This can save time and resources by not having to create separate reports for each process.

- **Alerts and notifications**: A code snippet can help automate alerts and notifications that are sent to the business or support team when a business or system exception is encountered. Having a reusable component will bring consistency and a standard to coding.

We've talked about reusable components and their use cases. Let's now see how you can build one from scratch using UiPath.

Here is an example of a reusable component in RPA using UiPath:

1. Create a new workflow and add a **Sequence** activity.

2. Within the sequence, add the specific actions that you want to include in your reusable component. For example, you might want to include actions to open a specific application, enter data into a form, and save the form.

3. After you have added all the necessary actions to your sequence, right-click on the sequence and select **Convert to Reusable Sequence**.

4. A pop-up window will appear, asking you to name your reusable sequence. Enter a descriptive name and click **OK**.

5. Your reusable sequence is now available for use in any workflow. Simply drag and drop the sequence into your workflow and configure any necessary input or output arguments.

6. To edit or update your reusable sequence, simply double-click on it in the project explorer and make any necessary changes. All workflows that use the reusable sequence will automatically update with the changes.

Here's another example:

1. Create a new workflow in UiPath Studio and add a sequence.

2. Add an **Input Dialog** activity to the sequence and set the message to Enter your name.

3. Add a **Message Box** activity to the sequence and set the message to Hello, [Name]!.

4. Add a **Write Line** activity to the sequence and set the message to Your name has been saved to the database..

5. Save the workflow as ReusableComponent.

Now, this reusable component can be used in any other workflow by simply adding a **Call Workflow File** activity and selecting the **ReusableComponent** workflow. The input dialog will prompt the user to enter their name, and the **Message Box** and **Write Line** activities will display the appropriate messages. This saves time and effort by not having to recreate these steps in each individual workflow. This might not be the exact reusable component you are looking to build but it gives you an idea of how to build one and use it in your automation using UiPath.

Let's now see how the same can be achieved in the Blue Prism RPA tool. This example of a reusable component in Blue Prism checks whether an email address is valid:

1. Create a new process called Validate Email.

2. Add a new input parameter called Email.

3. Add a new decision object and set the condition to **Email matches regex pattern for email addresses**. The regex pattern you can use will look something like so: `/^[a-zA-Z0-9.!#$%&'*+/=?^_`{|}~-]+@[a-zA-Z0-9-]+(?:\.[a-zA-Z0-9-]+)*$/`.

4. Add a new output parameter called **Is Valid Email** and set its value to **True** if the decision is true, and **False** if the decision is false.

5. Save and publish the process.

To use this reusable component, you can add it as an action in another process and pass in the email address as input. The output of the component will be a Boolean value indicating whether the email is valid or not. This can be used in a variety of processes where email validation is needed.

Building a reusable component library

Here are some steps to follow to build a library of reusable components for RPA:

1. Identify the common tasks or processes that need to be automated in your organization. These tasks can be used as the foundation for your library of reusable components. These could include data entry, data manipulation, web scraping, or email processing.

2. Break down each task into smaller, discrete steps. This will help you create individual components that can be easily reused in different automation processes. Determine the specific actions and steps involved in each of these tasks and processes. For example, if you are building a component for data entry, you might need to identify the input fields, the data sources, and any necessary validation or error-handling steps.

3. Create a blueprint or template for each component, outlining the steps and actions required to complete the task. This should include any necessary input and output variables, as well as any dependencies or integrations with other systems or tools.

4. Create a code repository to store all of your reusable components. This can be a local folder on your computer or a cloud-based solution such as GitHub.

5. For each component, create detailed documentation explaining how it works, what input it requires, and what output it produces. This documentation should be stored alongside the component in the code repository.

6. Test each component thoroughly to ensure it works as expected. This will help you avoid issues when using the component in a live automation process.

7. Use version control to track changes to your components over time. This will allow you to easily roll back to a previous version if needed.

8. Continuously review and update your library of components as new tasks and processes are identified and automated. This will help you keep your library up to date and relevant to your organization's needs.

These are some of the steps that you can follow to build a library that will help in the speedy delivery of your projects.

In conclusion, reusable components are a crucial aspect of RPA as they allow for efficient and effective automation processes. By utilizing reusable components, organizations can save time and resources by not having to recreate the same processes repeatedly. Additionally, reusable components can be easily modified and updated to meet changing business needs, making them flexible and scalable solutions. Overall, the use of reusable components in RPA can greatly improve efficiency and productivity within an organization.

Here are some common mistakes that developers make when building reusable components:

- **Overcomplicating the component**: Developers often try to create a highly versatile component that can be used in a variety of scenarios. However, this can result in an overly complicated component that is difficult to use and maintain. It is important to strike a balance between versatility and simplicity.

- **Not considering the context**: A reusable component may work perfectly in one context but not in another. Developers must consider the context in which the component will be used to ensure it is suitable for that context.

- **Not testing the component thoroughly**: It is important to test the component thoroughly before releasing it for use. This includes testing it in different environments, with different datasets and configurations.

- **Not documenting the component**: Documentation is crucial for reusable components. Developers should document the component's purpose, how to use it, and any important details about its behavior or limitations.

- **Not versioning the component**: As updates are made to the component, it is important to version it so that users can easily identify which version they are using and which changes have been made.

- **Making assumptions about how the component will be used**: Developers should avoid making assumptions about how the component will be used. Instead, they should provide clear instructions and guidance on how to use the component.

- **Not considering backward compatibility**: If changes are made to the component, backward compatibility should be considered to ensure that existing applications that use the component are not broken.

By avoiding these common mistakes, developers can create reusable components that are easy to use, maintain, and update.

Summary

To summarize, reusable components help us achieve consistency and stability and give us the opportunity to deliver faster, better, and cheaper software. In the next chapter, we will learn about **RPA as a service** (**RPAaaS**). Why would RPA be used as a service? Who are the service providers and how does that affect the RPA market? What are the different offerings in this regard and how does each of them differ from each other?

Questions

1. What are some of the benefits and the importance of reusable components?

2. What are some of the common types of reusable components?

3. How can reusable components help with faster, better, and cheaper development?

4. What are some of the use cases that you have learned about in this chapter?

5. How do you build a reusable component library and make it available to others?

12

RPA as a Service (RPAaaS)

In this competitive world, companies are always looking for new ways to run their business. They look for software solutions that are reliable, flexible, and customizable and can be tailored to their business needs to make their operations smoother, faster, and cost-effective.

Software as a service (**SaaS**) is the answer to what these businesses are looking for. You may wonder what SaaS is. SaaS is the delivery of software, typically via the internet, which allows users to access it from remote locations and use it on demand from a web browser or an **application programming interface** (**API**). It is a form of software licensing model in which the user does not need to install or update software locally. SaaS applications can be accessed through a web browser or downloaded to be used with some form of client software and access devices, such as desktop software for Windows and macOS platforms; mobile applications for smartphones and tablets; and laptop/desktop applications for Windows and macOS. SaaS is becoming increasingly popular as an efficient way to offer users a range of features, without having to worry about managing complex software.

In this chapter, we will talk about the SaaS model and how the RPA industry is taking advantage of this model to deliver a seamless experience to customers and businesses without the need to own a costly infrastructure and maintain a huge team of human resources. We will also understand the architecture behind **RPA as a service** (**RPAaaS**) and the difference between different implementation types, such as SaaS versus the cloud versus on-premises. We will also talk about the concept of **bring your own process** (**BYOP**). The topics covered in this chapter are as follows:

- Understanding what RPAaaS is

- RPAaaS architecture

- RPAaaS versus the cloud versus on-premises implementation strategies

- BYOP

RPAaaS – an abstraction of SaaS

SaaS is a software licensing model in which software is provided on demand. This is based on the idea that there should be no need for a user to install software on their computer and an even lesser need to install a service (software) onto their systems. Applications are hosted by an organization that may be dedicated to this task or provide the service in exchange for other services. The service provider interfaces with cloud computing resources, manages and monitors your software, fixes issues as they occur, provides 24/7 technical support, and so on.

One of the primary advantages of SaaS is its cost-effectiveness. By subscribing to a SaaS service, businesses and individuals can avoid the high upfront costs associated with purchasing and installing software on their own computers or servers. This can be particularly beneficial for small businesses and start-ups, which may not have the resources to invest in expensive software solutions. Additionally, SaaS providers often offer various pricing plans, allowing customers to choose the level of service that best fits their budget and needs.

Another key advantage of SaaS is its flexibility. Since the software is accessed over the internet, users can access it from any location and on any device with an internet connection. This allows for greater mobility and collaboration, as team members can work together on projects and access important data and documents from anywhere. Additionally, SaaS providers often offer different levels of access and permissions, allowing businesses to control who can access and use certain software.

SaaS providers also often offer automatic updates and maintenance, taking the burden of keeping software up to date away from the customer. This can save businesses and individuals time and resources, as they do not need to worry about downloading and installing updates or troubleshooting software issues. Additionally, SaaS providers often have a dedicated support team available to assist customers with any questions or issues they may have.

However, there are also some potential downsides to SaaS too. One concern is data security and privacy. Since data is stored and accessed over the internet, there is a risk of it being hacked or stolen. SaaS providers must take measures to ensure the security of customer data, such as using encryption and regularly backing up data. Additionally, businesses and individuals must also be careful to choose a SaaS provider that has a strong reputation for data security and privacy.

Another concern is vendor lock-in. Once a business or individual begins using a SaaS service, they may become dependent on it and find it difficult to switch to a different provider. This can be a disadvantage if the SaaS provider raises their prices, changes their terms of service, or goes out of business. It is important for businesses and individuals to carefully consider their long-term needs and choose a SaaS provider that can meet those needs.

Overall, SaaS is a popular and cost-effective solution for businesses and individuals seeking software solutions. Its flexibility, automatic updates and maintenance, and support team make it easy for customers to use and manage. However, it is important for customers to consider data security and vendor lock-in before choosing a SaaS provider. With careful consideration, SaaS can be a valuable asset for businesses and individuals to streamline their software needs. Let's now discuss how the SaaS model can be tailored to fit RPA and can reap the same benefits as other software and technologies. For that, let's first understand what RPAaaS is.

Understanding what RPAaaS is

RPAaaS is a business model that allows organizations to outsource the deployment and management of RPA software to a third-party provider. RPA software is designed to automate repetitive, manual tasks that are typically performed by humans, such as data entry, document processing, and customer service interactions. By outsourcing RPA to a service provider, organizations can gain access to the latest technology and expertise without having to invest in the development and maintenance of their own RPA infrastructure.

RPAaaS is typically offered as a subscription-based model, where the provider charges a monthly or annual fee for access to the RPA software and support services. The provider is responsible for configuring, deploying, and managing the RPA software, as well as providing training and support for the organization's users. This allows the organization to focus on its core business activities and leave the management of RPA to the experts.

One of the main benefits of RPAaaS is cost savings. By outsourcing RPA to a service provider, organizations can avoid the high costs associated with developing and maintaining their own RPA infrastructure. This includes the cost of software, hardware, and personnel. Additionally, RPAaaS providers typically offer flexible pricing plans, which can be tailored to the organization's specific needs and budget.

Another benefit of RPAaaS is scalability. Service providers typically have a large pool of resources and expertise that can be quickly and easily scaled up or down as needed. This allows organizations to quickly respond to changes in their business environment, such as an increase in demand for a particular service or a new regulatory requirement. Additionally, service providers can also help organizations to identify new automation opportunities, allowing them to expand the scope of their RPA implementation over time.

RPAaaS providers offer a range of services to their clients, including the following:

- RPA software deployment and management
- Training and support for users
- Integration with existing systems and processes
- Monitoring and reporting of RPA performance
- Maintenance and updates of RPA software

RPAaaS providers typically offer a range of RPA software options, including both cloud-based and on-premises solutions. Cloud-based solutions are typically more cost-effective and easier to manage, as they do not require the organization to invest in hardware or software. However, on-premises solutions can provide greater control and security over the RPA implementation.

In conclusion, RPAaaS is a business model based on the SaaS model that allows organizations to outsource the deployment and management of RPA software to a third-party provider. By outsourcing RPA to a service provider, organizations can gain access to the latest technology and expertise without having to invest in the development and maintenance of their own RPA infrastructure. The benefits of RPAaaS include cost savings, scalability, and access to a range of services and RPA software options. We now understand how RPAaaS is helpful for businesses, so let's understand how the architecture works and what the components that are involved in RPAaaS are.

RPAaaS architecture

RPAaaS architecture is a model in which an organization manages the deployment, management, and maintenance of its RPA solutions for its clients. It is also known as a *managed service*. RPA as a managed service refers to the outsourcing of RPA services to a third-party provider. This allows companies to focus on their core business activities while the provider handles the technical aspects of RPA. Managed RPA services typically include monitoring and reporting, as well as ongoing support and maintenance. This model is popular among companies that do not have the resources or expertise to manage RPA internally.

The provider offers RPAaaS to an organization, enabling it to automate repetitive and manual tasks without having to invest in the necessary infrastructure and resources.

The RPAaaS architecture typically includes the following components:

- **RPA platform**: The RPA platform is the software that enables the automation of repetitive tasks. It is provided by the service provider and is hosted in the cloud.

- **Automation bots**: Automation bots are software robots that perform tasks. They are created and configured by the service provider and are deployed to the RPA platform.

- **Management console**: The management console is used to manage and monitor the automation bots. It is provided by the service provider and is accessed through a web interface.

- **Integration API**: The integration API enables integration with other systems and applications. It is provided by the service provider and is used to connect the RPA platform to other systems and applications.

- **Support and maintenance**: The service provider is responsible for providing support and maintenance for the RPA platform and automation bots.

The RPAaaS architecture offers several benefits to organizations, including cost savings, scalability, and flexibility. It also enables organizations to focus on their core business while outsourcing the management and maintenance of their RPA solutions.

Let's take an example of a banking client. Let's assume that our banking client wants to leverage RPAaaS for one of their account opening processes. This could involve using RPA bots to gather and verify customer information, such as ID and proof of address, and then inputting that information into the bank's systems. The bots could also be used to perform background checks, calculate credit scores, and determine appropriate account types for the customer. This automation would allow bank employees to focus on more complex tasks, such as providing personalized advice and support to customers, while also reducing errors and increasing the speed at which accounts can be opened.

You might wonder why a banking client keen on data safety and security would put their process on a cloud-based solution. The answer is simple. First of all, the data is already coming from the customer, so as with any other internet platform, it needs to be secured through a channel such as VPN, SSL, or TLS. As the data is not getting saved and just getting transferred from one end to another, there is no risk of data loss, viruses, or hacker attacks. But keeping these types of processes inside of a SaaS platform helps reduce the cost and overhead of maintaining and supporting the process. The following screenshot shows a high-level architecture of RPAaaS.

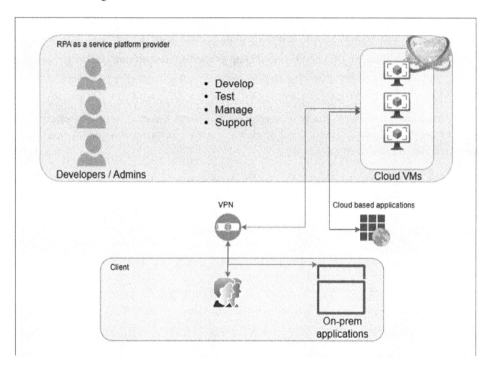

Figure 12.1 – RPAaaS architecture

Let's understand what the preceding architecture comprises:

- **Centralized management system**: A centralized management system is the backbone of the RPAaaS architecture. This system acts as a hub for all RPA-related activities, such as bot deployment, monitoring, and maintenance.

- **Bot factory**: The bot factory is responsible for creating, testing, and deploying RPA bots. This component uses pre-built templates or custom scripts to create bots that can automate various tasks across different systems and applications.

- **Bot orchestration**: Once bots are deployed, they need to be orchestrated to perform specific tasks. The bot orchestration component manages the scheduling and execution of bots, ensuring that they perform their tasks at the right time and in the right order.

- **Bot monitoring and analytics**: To ensure that RPA bots are performing correctly and efficiently, they need to be monitored and analyzed. The bot monitoring and analytics component provide real-time visibility into bot performance, including metrics such as execution time, error rates, and task completion rates.

- **Integration services**: RPA bots need to interact with various systems and applications, such as ERP, CRM, and legacy systems. The integration services component provides the necessary connectors and APIs to enable bots to interact with these systems seamlessly.

- **Security and compliance**: RPA bots handle sensitive data and need to comply with various regulations, such as the HIPAA and **General Data Protection Regulation (GDPR)**. The security and compliance component provides the necessary controls and processes to ensure that bots are secure and compliant.

- **User interface**: To enable users to interact with RPA bots, a user interface is required. This component provides a web-based portal or mobile app that allows users to initiate tasks, monitor progress, and receive notifications.

As we now understand the RPAaaS architecture and its components, you might think about what other options are available for a client. There are three types of implementation that are commonly used in the industry. There is the traditional way of implementing the RPA software, which is the on-premises implementation. Next, we have the public cloud platform, which is offered mostly by the RPA vendors themselves, and lastly comes the option to use the RPA platform as a SaaS implementation. Let's discuss these platforms in detail.

RPAaaS refers to the delivery of RPA software and services through a third-party provider. This means that the provider will handle the installation, maintenance, and updates of the RPA software. This option is ideal for companies that do not have the resources or expertise to manage RPA software on their own.

Cloud RPA refers to the use of RPA software that is hosted on a cloud platform. This means that the software and its data are stored and accessed remotely, rather than on the company's own servers. This option is ideal for companies that want to take advantage of the scalability and flexibility of the cloud, as well as the ability to access the software from anywhere.

On-premises RPA refers to the use of RPA software that is installed and run on the company's own servers. This means that the company is responsible for managing and maintaining the software. This option is ideal for companies that have strict security and compliance requirements, as well as companies that want to have full control over the software.

RPAaaS, cloud, and on-premises are three different deployment models for implementing RPA in an organization. Each of these models has its own set of advantages and disadvantages, and the choice of deployment model depends on the specific needs of the organization. In this chapter, we will explore the differences between RPAaaS, cloud, and on-premises deployment models and the factors that organizations should consider when deciding which model to adopt.

RPAaaS

RPAaaS is a deployment model where organizations outsource the implementation and management of RPA to a third-party service provider. The service provider takes care of the entire RPA implementation process, including the installation, configuration, and maintenance of the RPA software and the development of the automation scripts. This deployment model is suitable for organizations that do not have the resources or expertise to implement RPA on their own.

The following are a few advantages of RPAaaS:

- **No upfront investment**: With RPAaaS, organizations do not need to make any upfront investment in software or hardware. This makes it a cost-effective option for organizations that are just starting with RPA or do not want to invest in a large-scale RPA implementation.

- **Reduced risk**: Outsourcing RPA to a service provider reduces the risk associated with RPA implementation. The service provider is responsible for the successful implementation of RPA and any issues that may arise.

- **Expertise and support**: Service providers have expertise and experience in implementing RPA in different industries and can provide support and guidance throughout the implementation process.

- **Scalability**: RPAaaS is highly scalable, and organizations can easily increase or decrease the number of robots they use as their business needs change.

With pros, there are always a few cons too. They are listed here:

- **Dependency on the service provider**: Organizations that adopt RPAaaS are dependent on the service provider for the successful implementation and management of RPA

- **Limited control**: Organizations have limited control over the RPA implementation and may not be able to customize the automation scripts to their specific needs

- **Higher costs**: RPAaaS can be more expensive than other deployment models in the long run, as organizations have to pay a recurring fee to the service provider

There is another part of RPAaaS that complements the implementation and is called **integration platform as a service (iPaaS)**. iPaaS is a cloud-based platform that enables organizations to integrate their various software applications and systems, both on-premises and in the cloud. The integration platform eliminates the need for custom coding and enables businesses to connect their applications in a secure, scalable, and efficient manner.

In recent years, RPA has emerged as a popular tool for automating manual, repetitive tasks, freeing up employees to focus on more strategic initiatives. RPAaaS is a cloud-based delivery model that enables organizations to implement RPA without the need for significant upfront investment or in-house expertise.

The combination of iPaaS and RPAaaS provides a powerful solution for organizations looking to streamline their operations and improve their overall efficiency. The integration platform enables businesses to connect their RPA bots to their various applications and systems, facilitating the automation of end-to-end processes.

In conclusion, iPaaS plays a critical role in RPAaaS by providing a secure, scalable, and efficient solution for connecting RPA bots to various applications and systems. The combination of iPaaS and RPAaaS offers organizations a powerful tool for streamlining their operations, improving efficiency, and freeing up employees to focus on more strategic initiatives.

Cloud deployment

Cloud deployment is a deployment model where RPA software is hosted on a cloud-based platform. Organizations can access the RPA software and automation scripts through a web browser and users do not need to install any software on their own servers. This deployment model is suitable for organizations that want to implement RPA quickly and easily and do not want to invest in expensive hardware.

The following are the advantages of cloud deployment:

- **No upfront investment**: With cloud deployment, organizations do not need to make any upfront investment in software or hardware. This makes it a cost-effective option for organizations that are just starting with RPA or do not want to invest in a large-scale RPA implementation.

- **Scalability**: Cloud deployment is highly scalable, and organizations can easily increase or decrease the number of robots they use as their business needs change.

- **Accessibility**: With cloud deployment, organizations can access RPA software and automation scripts from anywhere with an internet connection, making it easy for remote teams to collaborate on RPA projects.

- **Automatic updates**: Cloud-based RPA software is updated automatically, ensuring that organizations are always using the latest version of the software.

The following is a disadvantage of cloud deployment:

- **Dependence on internet connectivity**: Organizations that adopt cloud deployment are heavily dependent on internet stability, security, reliability, and sometimes even speed

On-premises implementation

Let's understand the on-premises implementation architecture part by part:

- A central server that acts as the backbone of the RPA system is responsible for managing and coordinating the various RPA components.

- A database stores information such as process definitions, bot configurations, and historical data.

- A set of RPA bots is deployed on individual workstations or servers. These bots are responsible for executing the automation tasks and interacting with the target systems.

- An RPA management console allows administrators to manage the RPA system, including monitoring the status of bots, scheduling tasks, and creating new process definitions.

- A set of connectors allows the RPA system to interact with various target systems, such as enterprise applications, databases, and web services.

- A set of security measures, such as firewalls, encryption, and access controls, ensure the integrity and confidentiality of the RPA system.

- A disaster recovery plan ensures that the RPA system can be quickly restored in case of any unexpected failures or disruptions.

In RPAaaS, there can be a lot of concerns around data security and privacy. How do we make it secure so more and more clients and projects can benefit from this platform? The following are some of the ways an RPAaaS provider needs to make sure that the platform follows the security and privacy best practices:

- **Data encryption**: All data and communication between the RPA service provider and the client should be encrypted to ensure that sensitive information is protected from unauthorized access

- **User authentication**: The RPA service should implement strong user authentication measures to ensure that only authorized users have access to the system

- **Access control**: The service should have robust access control mechanisms in place to prevent unauthorized access to critical data and systems

- **Data backup and recovery**: The service should have a well-established data backup and recovery plan to ensure that important data is not lost in case of system failures or data breaches

- **Compliance with privacy regulations**: The service should be compliant with relevant privacy regulations, such as the **GDPR** and the **California Consumer Privacy Act (CCPA)**

- **Regular security audits**: Regular security audits should be conducted to assess the security of the system and identify potential weaknesses

- **Incident response plan**: The service should have a well-defined incident response plan in place to quickly and effectively respond to any security incidents

- **Role-based access**: Access to the system should be restricted based on the user's role and responsibilities

- **Regular software updates**: The RPA software should be regularly updated to fix any known vulnerabilities and ensure that the system remains secure

- **Education and training**: The service provider should provide regular education and training to their clients on the best practices for maintaining the security and privacy of their RPA systems

The architecture of RPA on-premises should be designed to ensure high availability, scalability, and security while providing a robust and flexible framework for automating business processes.

Overall, the choice between RPAaaS, cloud RPA, and on-premises RPA will depend on the specific needs and requirements of the company. Factors such as budget, resources, and security will all play a role in determining the best option for the company. We talked about all the different styles of implementation, their pros and cons, and their support model. Now, let's talk about what it is that a client needs to do and what their responsibility is. That is where the concept of BYOP comes into the picture.

BYOP

Before we understand what BYOP is, we need to understand the basis on which BYOP is developed. BYOP is developed on the concept of **bring your own device (BYOD)**, which refers to a trend in the modern workplace where employees are allowed to use their personal smartphones, tablets, and laptops for work purposes. This policy has gained popularity in recent years as more and more employees use their personal devices for work tasks. In this section, we will explore the advantages and disadvantages of BYOD and provide some guidelines for implementing a successful BYOD policy.

Here, I've listed the advantages of BYOD:

- **Cost savings**: One of the biggest advantages of BYOD is that it saves companies a lot of money. Instead of having to purchase and maintain separate devices for employees, companies can save money by allowing employees to use their own devices. This reduces the costs associated with device procurement, maintenance, and replacement.

- **Increased productivity**: BYOD has been shown to increase productivity. This is because employees are more likely to be productive when they use a device that they are familiar with and comfortable using. In addition, employees are able to work from anywhere and at any time, which can lead to increased flexibility and greater efficiency.

- **Improved employee satisfaction**: BYOD can also improve employee satisfaction. By allowing employees to use their own devices, companies provide a level of flexibility and control that employees may not have experienced before. This can lead to increased engagement, morale, and job satisfaction.

Here are the disadvantages of BYOD:

- **Security concerns**: One of the biggest disadvantages of BYOD is that it can pose a security risk to a company's confidential information. Personal devices are not always as secure as company-owned devices and can be more vulnerable to hacking and other types of cyber-attacks.

- **Data management issues**: Another disadvantage of BYOD is that it can create data management issues. Employees may use multiple devices, which can make it difficult to keep track of important data and ensure that it is stored securely.

- **Compatibility issues**: BYOD can also create compatibility issues between personal devices and company systems and applications. This can result in increased technical support requirements and decreased efficiency.

Implementing BYOD can be challenging. Formalizing a strategy and following a defined guideline can always help with smooth deployment.

The following are some guidelines for implementing a successful BYOD policy:

- **Develop a clear policy**: It is important to have a clear and concise BYOD policy in place that outlines the guidelines and rules for using personal devices for work purposes. This policy should address issues such as data security, device compatibility, and the proper use of company data.

- **Ensure security**: To mitigate security risks, it is important to implement strong security measures, such as encryption and **mobile device management** (MDM) software, to protect company data.

- **Provide support**: To ensure a successful BYOD program, it is important to provide employees with the support they need to effectively use their personal devices for work. This may include providing training and technical support, as well as access to company systems and applications.

- **Monitor usage**: Finally, it is important to monitor BYOD usage to ensure that employees are using their personal devices in accordance with the company's policies and guidelines.

BYOP follows the same footprints as BYOD and brings the same benefits to the industry. BYOP helps RPAaaS by allowing organizations to utilize their existing processes and workflow within the RPA platform. This means that they can leverage the automation capabilities of RPA without having to completely redesign their processes or spend additional time and resources on process mapping and development. Additionally, BYOP allows organizations to easily integrate RPA into their existing systems and technologies, resulting in a smoother and more seamless implementation. Overall, BYOP helps organizations to more efficiently and effectively implement RPAaaS, resulting in increased productivity and cost savings.

Summary

In conclusion, RPAaaS has revolutionized the way businesses operate and has become a critical aspect of digital transformation. It has proven to be an efficient and cost-effective solution that can help organizations automate routine tasks, reduce errors, and increase productivity. The increasing popularity of RPA services reflects the changing landscape of the business world, where technology plays a significant role in shaping the future of work. Companies that invest in RPA services will be well positioned to capitalize on the many benefits that come with digital transformation and stay ahead of the competition in the ever-evolving business landscape.

In the next chapter, we will see the approach an SA takes to find the best solution. We will see the different types of approaches that can be taken to find the best solution, how this research is done, and how a solution is tested before it can be considered for the final implementation.

Questions

1. What are the advantages of RPA as a service?

2. On what concept is BYOP based?

3. What does BYOP mean and how does it complement RPAaaS?

4. What are the different ways to implement RPA as a service?

5. What are the key components of RPA as a service?

13
Finding the Best Solution

Seeking solutions and finding answers can be a daunting task. But we humans have the power to make it much easier. Are you looking for the best solution to a problem but can't seem to find it? Explore our wide range of resources and get in touch with experts to discover how the ideal solution is found in a process. We understand that you want answers and there are plenty of places to look, but who can you really trust? Who understands your needs and offers viable solutions in a timely manner? How do you find the best solution for your business's needs?

You start by gathering valuable insights from your client and business **subject-matter expert** (**SME**) and examine things from all angles. All of this and more will be discussed in this chapter. As we have seen in the starting chapters of the book, the major role of an SA is to find the best solution, but it is not straightforward. If it were so easy, anyone could do so by just looking on the internet.

As you may have guessed by now, there is a lot that goes into finding the best solution. The journey of finding solutions for a topic, and determining the best solution based on your business needs, is what we are going to learn about in this chapter. We will examine the following topics in this chapter:

- Research – how do we do research? What are the options?
- Known issues and challenges
- Putting your findings to the test
- Socializing the solution and getting early feedback
- Securing approvals for the solution

When faced with a problem, it's easy to feel overwhelmed by the number of possible solutions, along with uncertainty about which one to choose. However, a careful and systematic approach to problem-solving can help you identify the best solution that meets your needs and goals. By considering the available information, evaluating the pros and cons of each option, and weighing the potential risks and benefits, you can make an informed decision that maximizes the likelihood of success. In this process, creativity, flexibility, and open-mindedness are crucial, as they can help you explore new and unconventional solutions that may be more effective than traditional ones. Ultimately, the key to finding the best solution is to stay focused on the problem at hand and remain committed to finding a resolution that works for you.

Research

The word *research* means systematically collecting and analyzing information on a particular topic or problem in order to discover new knowledge or insights. Research can take many forms, including scientific studies, surveys, experiments, case studies, and literature reviews. The purpose of research is to deepen our understanding of a particular topic, test hypotheses, and generate new ideas and knowledge.

The research process typically involves identifying a problem or research question, collecting data or information through various methods, analyzing and interpreting the data, and drawing conclusions based on the findings. It may also involve formulating hypotheses and testing them through experiments or other methods. Research can be conducted by individuals or teams, such as academics, researchers, or practitioners. The results of the research can be used to inform policy decisions, develop new products and technologies, improve social programs, and advance knowledge in a particular field. Doing research is an important way to advance knowledge and understanding in a particular field or area, and to address the problems and challenges facing society. Now let's see what steps an SA can take to progress their research.

Here are some steps an SA can follow when researching a topic:

1. **Identify the research question or topic**: Clearly define what you want to research. Determine the purpose of your research and the specific research questions that you want to answer.

2. **Develop a research plan**: Plan out your approach to the research. Determine what type of research you will conduct, such as primary or secondary research, and the methods you will use, such as surveys, interviews, or focus groups.

3. **Gather information**: Use a variety of sources to gather information on your topic. These sources can include academic journals, books, articles, online databases, and other relevant publications. Be sure to use reputable sources and evaluate the credibility of the information you find, as we'll see next.

4. **Evaluate the information**: Analyze the information you have collected and evaluate its quality and relevance. Consider the source of the information, the author's credibility, and whether the information is current and accurate.

5. **Organize the information**: Organize the information you have collected and create an outline or summary of the key points. This helps to understand the main themes and arguments of the research.

6. **Synthesize the information**: Synthesize the information you have collected and use it to answer your research questions. Identify patterns and connections between the data and draw conclusions based on your analysis.

7. **Write your findings**: Write a report that presents your findings. Use clear and concise language and include all relevant information, including the research question, methodology, data analysis, and conclusions.

8. **Cite your sources**: Cite all of the sources you used in your research. This gives credit to the authors and allows others to locate the same sources and verify your findings.

The steps mentioned earlier give us a generic view of doing research. But, what if we can come up with a framework that can then be applied to any problem you might try to find a solution for? Let's build a framework that SAs can use every time they need to do systematic research on a topic or problem.

Here is a framework for conducting research on any problem:

1. **Define the problem**: Clearly articulate the problem you are trying to solve. This involves specifying the symptoms, causes, and effects of the problem. Be specific about what you are trying to achieve and what success would look like.

2. **Identify the stakeholders**: Determine who is affected by the problem and who might have an interest in the solution. This includes internal and external stakeholders, such as employees, customers, partners, regulators, and investors.

3. **Gather information**: Collect data and information relevant to the problem. This can include existing research, reports, statistics, industry trends, and case studies. Be sure to use credible sources and gather a broad range of information to get a comprehensive view of the problem.

4. **Analyze the information**: Evaluate the information you have gathered and identify patterns, trends, and insights. This may involve using statistical analysis, qualitative research, or other analytical methods to make sense of the data.

5. **Generate solutions**: Brainstorm and develop potential solutions to the problem. Consider multiple options and weigh the pros and cons of each. Be creative and explore new and unconventional solutions, which may be more effective than traditional ones.

6. **Evaluate solutions**: Assess each potential solution and determine its feasibility, impact, and potential risks and benefits. Use criteria such as cost, time, and effectiveness to compare and evaluate the options.

7. **Implement the solution**: Choose the best solution and develop an action plan for implementing it. This may involve developing a project plan, setting goals and milestones, and assigning responsibilities.

8. **Monitor and evaluate**: Continuously monitor the solution and evaluate its effectiveness. This may involve collecting feedback from stakeholders, analyzing metrics, and making adjustments as needed.

The following funnel diagram represents this framework:

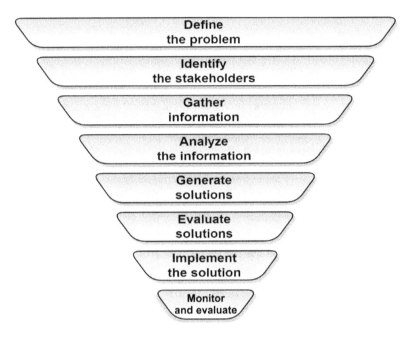

Figure 13.1 – Research framework

By following this framework, you can conduct research on a problem in a structured and systematic way and increase the likelihood of finding an effective solution.

To develop a good, accurate research plan, it is important to understand the challenges, of which there are often many, involved in researching a topic. These might include finding impartial sources of information and conducting effective searches that allow you to find material on the topics of interest. The challenges of research can also vary from person to person. To start with, you will usually find yourself exploring a topic that is unfamiliar but important. Once you have identified the need for information on this topic, you will need to determine where you would like to go with your research. We'll look at this in more detail in the next section.

Issues and challenges while doing research

Researching a topic can be a daunting and intimidating task. You'll find many online resources and books that may help you learn more about the topic, even if you don't read them all from cover to cover. But one of the biggest challenges is finding time to read more than one book, research article, blog, research paper, or even watch YouTube videos fully during your research. There are so many possible avenues for each subject; it's difficult to select the ones that are important to your project. Also, information on some topics can be fragmented, making it difficult or impossible to use only one book as a source and nothing else in your research. Let's discuss in detail the issues and challenges an SA can face while doing their research.

Some of the common issues and challenges you may face when researching a topic are as follows:

- **Narrow or limited information**: There may be limited information available on your topic, which can make it difficult to collect a sufficient amount of data to draw meaningful conclusions.

- **Data reliability and validity**: The data you collect may not be reliable or valid, which can impact the accuracy of your findings. It's important to ensure that the data you use is from credible and trustworthy sources.

- **Bias**: Bias can occur in research when researchers have preconceived notions or opinions that influence their findings. It's important to be aware of potential biases and take steps to minimize their impact on the research.

- **Time constraints**: Conducting thorough research can be time-consuming, and may not be feasible if there are time constraints or deadlines that need to be met.

- **Ethical concerns**: Research involving human subjects or sensitive topics may raise ethical concerns, such as ensuring that participants are fully informed about the research and their rights, and that their privacy and confidentiality are protected.

- **Research methods**: Choosing the right research methods and techniques can be challenging, as some methods may be more suitable for certain research questions or topics.

- **Analysis and interpretation**: Analyzing and interpreting data can also be challenging, as it requires expertise in statistical analysis and data interpretation.

- **Funding**: Research can be expensive, and securing funding can be a challenge, particularly for independent researchers and small research teams.

It's important to be aware of these issues and challenges when doing research and take steps to address them as they arise. This can include carefully designing research methods, ensuring data reliability and validity, being aware of potential biases, and seeking appropriate funding and resources. Let's now examine in more detail the steps an SA can take to avoid these issues and challenges.

To research a topic and be confident when talking about it, you must learn to overcome challenges. There are so many challenges that SAs encounter throughout the research process, including identifying potential sources for your topic, finding relevant information, and evaluating the quality of that information.

The answer to this is very simple: get yourself ready to investigate! The terrain of the modern world seems to get ever more complex, yet our appetite for knowledge has never been greater – how can we possibly make headway in this information-packed landscape? We need to learn how to research and what the best places for doing research are. All of this comes under the topic of critical thinking. SAs should be masters of critical thinking. But what is critical thinking?

Critical thinking is the process of analyzing, evaluating, and synthesizing information and arguments in a systematic and objective manner to make informed decisions and judgments. It involves questioning assumptions, challenging biases, and considering multiple perspectives to arrive at a well-reasoned and evidence-based conclusion.

Critical thinking typically involves several key skills, including the following:

- **Analysis**: Breaking down complex information into its component parts and examining the relationships between them

- **Evaluation**: Assessing the strengths and weaknesses of arguments and information and determining their credibility and relevance

- **Inference**: Drawing logical and well-supported conclusions based on the available evidence

- **Interpretation**: Considering different ways of understanding and explaining information, and identifying underlying assumptions and values

- **Explanation**: Presenting arguments and information clearly and logically, and providing evidence and reasons to support any claims made

- **Self-regulation**: Being aware of our own biases and assumptions, and actively seeking out and considering alternative viewpoints

Here's a diagrammatic representation to help you remember these skills involved in critical thinking:

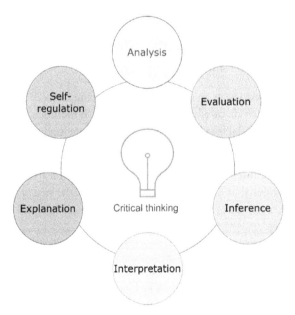

Figure 13.2 – Critical thinking skills

Critical thinking is essential in many fields, including science, business, law, education, and healthcare. It is also important in everyday life, as it helps people to make better decisions and navigate complex situations. By practicing critical thinking, individuals can develop the ability to analyze and evaluate information more effectively, make well-reasoned decisions, and communicate their ideas clearly and persuasively.

Putting your findings to the test

In life, we constantly seek new knowledge and information. Whether it's trying to understand a complex concept, researching a potential purchase, or learning about a new hobby, the process of gathering information can be both exciting and overwhelming. However, one critical step that many people overlook is to put their findings to the test.

Putting your findings to the test means taking what you've learned and verifying its accuracy through experimentation or real-world application. This step is essential because it helps you move from simply having the required knowledge to understanding how that knowledge is applied in practice. Here are a few reasons why putting your findings to the test is so important:

- It helps you gain a deeper understanding of the topic. Reading about a topic or hearing someone talk about it can give you a surface-level understanding, but putting that knowledge into practice can help you gain a much deeper understanding. By testing your findings, you can see how they work in real-life scenarios, identify any gaps in your understanding, and refine your knowledge over time.

- It helps you identify any flaws or errors in your research. No matter how thorough your research may be, there is always the potential for errors or flawed assumptions. By putting your findings to the test, you can identify any flaws or errors in your research and correct them before they become bigger issues. This can save you time, money, and frustration further down the road.

- It helps you build confidence in your knowledge. Putting your findings to the test can be a bit intimidating, but it can also be incredibly empowering. When you see your knowledge working in practice, it helps build your confidence in your understanding of the topic. This can be particularly helpful if you're trying to apply that knowledge in a professional setting or teach it to others.

So, how can you put your findings to the test? The answer will depend on the specific topic and the type of information you're working with. For some topics, you may be able to conduct experiments or simulations to test your findings. For others, you may need to apply your knowledge in a real-life setting and observe the results.

One important thing to keep in mind when putting your findings to the test is to remain open to new information and be willing to adjust your understanding as needed. Testing your findings can be a humbling experience, but it can also be incredibly rewarding as you gain a deeper understanding of the topic and build confidence in your knowledge.

In conclusion, putting your findings to the test is a critical step in the process of gaining knowledge and understanding. By testing your findings, you can gain a deeper understanding of the topic, identify any flaws or errors in your research, and build confidence in your knowledge. So the next time you find yourself with a new piece of information, take the time to put it to the test and see how it works in practice. Now, let's explore techniques to put your research findings to the test with some context.

Let's take an example of researching handwritten-text recognition. We have studied computer text recognition and extraction. But, handwritten text usually takes the form of a scanned image of human handwriting. Let's say your client receives a lot of handwritten appeals and complaints from its customers. Reading all those letters and replying to each of them in a timely manner is very cumbersome and laborious work. What if there was a way to apply technology and make this tedious work feel like a breeze?

To do this, we first need to make the text available digitally to the computers. The first step is to convert physical paper into a scanned copy of the letter. This is very straightforward and there are now many advanced high-speed scanners, which can scan at a speed of ~500 pages per minute. We now have digital versions of complaint letters.

The next step is to read it. The technology for this is called **Optical Character Recognition** (**OCR**), which we studied in previous chapters. But this was for the text generated by a computer, not handwritten by a human. This could be challenging as the handwriting of two people will be at least slightly different. So, we have a candidate for research in order to come up with a solution.

Handwriting recognition is a rapidly growing field that has seen tremendous advancements in recent years. With the increasing popularity of digital note-taking and the need for efficient data entry, handwriting recognition has become an essential tool in many industries. To help you research handwriting recognition and find the best solution for your needs, here are some tips:

- **Determine your specific needs and requirements.** Before you begin your research, it's essential to determine what exactly you need from a handwriting recognition solution. Are you looking for a tool that can recognize handwriting in real time? Do you need a tool that can convert handwritten notes into digital text? Knowing your specific requirements will help you narrow down your search and find the best solution for your needs.

- **Research the different handwriting recognition technologies on offer**. There are several handwriting recognition technologies available, each with its own strengths and weaknesses. Some of the most common technologies include **OCR**, **Intelligent Character Recognition** (**ICR**), and **Natural Language Processing** (**NLP**). Researching the different technologies available and their capabilities can help you better understand which solution is likely to be the best fit for your needs.

- **Read reviews and customer testimonials**. Reading reviews and customer testimonials can be an excellent way to learn about the real-world experiences of others who have used a particular handwriting recognition solution. Look for reviews on trusted websites and forums, and pay attention to both positive and negative feedback. This can help you identify any potential drawbacks or issues with a particular solution before investing in it.

- **Consider the possibilities of integration with other tools and platforms**. If you plan to use your handwriting recognition solution in conjunction with other tools and platforms, such as note-taking apps or productivity software, it's essential to consider how well they integrate with each other. Look for solutions that offer seamless integration with the tools you use regularly to ensure a smooth workflow.

- **Evaluate the accuracy and speed of the solution**. Ultimately, the most important factor in choosing a handwriting recognition solution is its accuracy and speed. Look for solutions that have a high accuracy rate and can recognize handwriting quickly and efficiently. Some solutions may offer a trial period, which can be an excellent way to test the accuracy and speed of the technology before investing in it.

Researching handwriting recognition and finding the best solution for your needs can be a daunting task. However, by following these tips and taking the time to evaluate your requirements and research different technologies, you will be able to find a solution that meets your needs and improves your productivity. Remember to read reviews, consider integration with other tools, and evaluate accuracy and speed to find the best handwriting recognition solution for your needs.

So we found our solution after days of hard work. What's next? We need to get blessings from our stakeholders, and this process is what we call *socializing your solution*. Basically, the concept is simple. The more detail on your solution you provide to stakeholders, the better feedback you will get, as well as getting more endorsements. The more endorsements you get, the better it is.

Socializing your solution

Socializing your solution means sharing and promoting a proposed solution to stakeholders and other interested parties. It involves presenting the solution in a clear and compelling way, explaining its benefits, and addressing any concerns or objections that stakeholders may have.

Socializing a solution is an important step in the problem-solving process, as it helps to gain buy-in and support from key stakeholders, such as executives, team members, and customers. By socializing the solution, you can ensure that all parties understand the problem, are aligned on the proposed solution, and are committed to taking the necessary steps to implement it successfully.

To socialize a solution effectively, it's important to tailor your approach to your audience. This may involve creating different presentations or materials for different groups of stakeholders, focusing on the specific benefits and concerns that are most relevant to each group. For example, executives may be more interested in the financial benefits of the solution, while team members may be more concerned with how the solution will impact their daily work.

Here are some key steps to socializing a solution effectively:

- **Define the problem:** Before you can socialize a solution, you need to ensure that all stakeholders understand the problem you are trying to solve. Clearly define the problem and its impact on the organization.

- **Develop a clear and compelling solution**: Develop a solution that addresses the problem and has clear benefits. Be prepared to explain how the solution will work and the benefits it will provide.

- **Identify stakeholders**: Identify all stakeholders who may be impacted by the solution, including executives, team members, and customers. Determine their concerns and objectives.

- **Tailor your approach**: Tailor your approach to each stakeholder group. Develop different presentations and other materials that address the specific concerns and objectives of each group.

- **Present the solution**: Present the solution to all stakeholders, focusing on its benefits and addressing any concerns or objections that arise.

- **Solicit feedback**: Solicit feedback from stakeholders and be open to making adjustments to the solution based on their feedback.

- **Gain buy-in and support**: Work to gain buy-in and support from stakeholders, addressing any remaining concerns or objections. Develop a plan to implement the solution successfully.

To conclude, socializing a solution involves sharing and promoting the proposed solution to stakeholders and interested parties. By tailoring your approach to your audience, presenting the solution clearly and in a compelling manner, and addressing any concerns and objections, you can gain buy-in and support for the solution, ensuring its successful implementation. So, we socialized our solution and everyone including the stakeholders were happy with it. The solution has a lot of potential not only to cater to the current problem but also to likely future problems.

Does this mean we are all set for implementing the solution? Not yet. There is one last piece of the puzzle still left – to secure the approvals in writing. This is as important as documenting and socializing your solution. Let's see how can we secure approvals and why is it so important as the last step in our research journey.

Securing approvals

Securing approvals from stakeholders means obtaining formal agreement or permission from individuals and groups who have a vested interest in or influence on a project, proposal, or decision. In most cases, stakeholders are those individuals and groups who will be affected by the outcome of the project or decision, such as customers, employees, shareholders, partners, and regulatory bodies.

Securing approvals from stakeholders is a critical step in ensuring the success of a project or decision. By obtaining formal agreement from stakeholders, you can ensure that they understand the proposed solution, its benefits, and its potential impact on them. This can help to build trust and support for the project, reducing the risk of resistance and opposition.

Here are some key steps for securing approvals from stakeholders effectively:

- **Identify stakeholders**: Identify all stakeholders who may be affected by the project or decision. This can include internal stakeholders, such as employees and managers, and external stakeholders, such as customers, suppliers, and regulatory bodies.

- **Determine their interests**: Determine the interests, objectives, and concerns of each stakeholder group. This allows you to tailor your approach to each group and address their specific concerns.

- **Develop a communication plan**: Develop a communication plan that outlines the key messages and channels for reaching each stakeholder group. Be sure to use clear and concise language, and address any potential objections or concerns.

- **Present the proposal**: Present the proposal to stakeholders, focusing on its benefits and addressing any concerns or objections that arise. Be sure to provide relevant information, such as data, research, and examples, to support the proposal.

- **Obtain formal agreement**: Obtain formal agreement or permission from stakeholders, using methods such as signing contracts, voting, or other formal agreements. Be sure to document the agreements in writing and keep copies for future reference.

- **Follow up**: Follow up with stakeholders after the proposal has been implemented to ensure that their objectives have been met and that any issues or concerns have been addressed.

Securing approvals from stakeholders means obtaining formal agreement or permission from individuals or groups who have a vested interest in or influence on a project or decision. By identifying stakeholders, determining their interests, developing a communication plan, presenting the proposal, obtaining formal agreement, and following up, you can ensure that stakeholders are engaged and supportive of the project or decision, ensuring its success.

Summary

Researching a solution and testing it to find the best options involves the process of gathering information and evaluating different alternatives to determine the most effective course of action. Throughout the research and testing process, it is important to remain open-minded and flexible, be willing to adapt to new information, and use data and evidence to guide decision-making.

By following the steps presented in this chapter, you can effectively research a solution and test it to find the best option for your needs. In the next chapter, we will study the best practices for designing solutions and, the different approaches to solution design, and focus on a modular approach.

In the next chapter, we will review some best practices for designing a robust solution. We will do a deep-dive into the concept of modular design and see how it adds robustness and resilience to the design and code.

Questions

1. What are some of the steps you can take to conduct successful research on a topic or subject?

2. What are the challenges you might face while doing research?

3. What are the benefits of socializing your solution?

4. Is it necessary to secure approval? If yes, list some of the steps involved.

Part 4:
Best Practices

In this part, we will delve into industry-proven best practices for defining, designing, developing, implementing, and maintaining RPA solutions. Prepare to gain invaluable insights into each crucial phase of the RPA lifecycle and get ready for the following enlightening chapters that await you:

14
Design Best Practices

A good design is critical for the success of software development projects. It helps to ensure that the software meets users' needs, is reliable, maintainable, and scalable, and enables developers to work more effectively as a team. Good design ensures that the software meets its intended purpose and works as expected. It considers all aspects of the software, from user experience to performance, security, and scalability.

A well-designed software system is more likely to meet user needs and requirements, as well as reduce the risk of errors and bugs. Good design provides a common language for developers, stakeholders, and users. It helps developers to communicate more effectively with each other and with stakeholders by providing a shared understanding of the software system. This makes it easier to identify and resolve issues early on, saving time and resources in the long run.

Software systems are often complex and can be difficult to manage. A good design breaks down the system into manageable components, making it easier to develop, test, and maintain. It also helps to identify potential issues and dependencies between components, reducing the risk of errors and improving overall system performance. It promotes modularity and reuse, allowing developers to build upon existing code and functionality. This saves time and resources, as developers can focus on developing new features and functionality, rather than re-implementing existing code.

We will look at the importance of design, some different design patterns, and the best practices to implement the module design pattern. The following topics will be covered in this chapter:

- Modular design
- Breadcrumbs
- Decoupling the obvious
- Garbage collection
- Exception handling

To achieve a good design, a well-structured format and concept needs to be in place and this is where design patterns come into the picture. Design patterns are general solutions to common software design problems that have been identified and documented by software developers over time. They provide reusable templates that can be applied in various software development contexts and help to ensure that code is well organized, efficient, and easy to maintain.

Design patterns are not complete solutions that can be copied and pasted into code, but rather they are high-level descriptions of the structure and interactions of code that can be used as guidelines for implementation. They are not tied to any specific programming language or platform, but rather describe common solutions to problems that are relevant across a variety of different contexts.

Some examples of well-known design patterns include the **Model-View-Controller** (**MVC**) pattern, the Singleton pattern, the Factory pattern, the module pattern, and the Observer pattern. By using these patterns, developers can save time and effort in creating high-quality software, and ensure that their code is both maintainable and reusable.

Design patterns are a powerful and widely adopted concept in software development. They are reusable solutions to common problems that software developers encounter during the design and implementation of software systems. In essence, they are proven and effective ways of solving recurring problems in software development, based on the collective experience of the software development community.

Design patterns provide a way of creating a common language and shared understanding among developers, enabling them to communicate and collaborate more effectively. By following design patterns, developers can ensure that their code is robust, reliable, and maintainable, as patterns are tried-and-tested solutions to problems that have been proven to work in a variety of different contexts.

There are many different design patterns, each with its own strengths and weaknesses, and each can be used in a variety of different contexts, from object-oriented programming to web development and beyond. By mastering the use of design patterns, developers can improve their coding skills, create more efficient and effective code, and become more valuable members of their development teams. Let's now understand modular design and how it can be achieved in RPA.

Modular design

Modular design is an essential aspect of software development that involves breaking down a software system into smaller, more manageable pieces or modules. These modules can then be developed and tested independently, making the overall software development process more efficient and effective. In this section, we will explore the importance of modular design in software development and how it can be used to build better software.

Why is modular design important?

- **Reusability and scalability**: By breaking down a software system into smaller modules, each module can be reused in different parts of the system or even in other software projects. This makes it easier to scale up the software system or make modifications and improvements over time.

- **Easy maintenance**: When a software system is built with a modular design, it becomes much easier to maintain and update. Since each module is developed independently, making changes to one module does not affect the rest of the system, making it easier to identify and fix bugs or errors.

- **Better collaboration**: Modular design encourages teamwork and collaboration among developers. Different developers can work on different modules simultaneously, making the development process faster and more efficient.

- **Reduced complexity**: Developing a large software system without modular design can be overwhelming and complex. Breaking down the system into smaller modules makes it easier to manage and understand, reducing the complexity of the development process.

How do we use modular design in software development?

- **Identify the modules**: The first step in using modular design in software development is to identify the different modules that make up the software system. This requires a thorough understanding of the requirements and functionality of the software system.

- **Develop the modules independently**: Once the modules have been identified, each module can be developed independently, with its own set of requirements and specifications. This allows developers to focus on developing a specific module without worrying about the rest of the system.

- **Integrate the modules**: After each module has been developed, they can be integrated into the overall software system. Integration testing is crucial at this stage to ensure that the modules work together seamlessly.

- **Maintain the modules**: Once the software system is up and running, it is important to maintain the modules individually to ensure that they continue to function as intended. This includes updating, debugging, and testing each module regularly.

In conclusion, modular design is an important aspect of software development that can help developers build better software systems. By breaking down a software system into smaller modules, developers can make the development process more efficient, scalable, and maintainable.

To implement modular design successfully, developers must identify the different modules, develop them independently, integrate them into the overall system, and maintain them regularly. You might ask whether there is any such design pattern for use in RPA, and the short answer is *yes*. Let's do a deep dive into this design pattern and understand how we can bring its structured approach to RPA.

Module pattern

Module patterns are a way of organizing code in software development that involves breaking up a program into smaller, independent parts or modules. These modules can then be used in different parts of the program, making it easier to manage and update the code. In this section, we will discuss module patterns, their use in the software industry, some examples of module patterns, and how they can be used in RPA.

Module patterns in the software industry

Module patterns are widely used in the software industry as a best practice for developing large, complex software systems. By breaking down a program into smaller modules, developers can make it easier to understand and maintain, as well as allow for greater reusability and flexibility. Some common examples of module patterns include the Singleton pattern, the Factory pattern, and the Observer pattern:

- **Singleton pattern**: This pattern ensures that there is only one instance of a particular class in a program, making it easier to manage and access the class. This is useful for situations where there should only be one instance of a certain resource, such as a database connection.

- **Factory pattern**: This pattern is used to create objects without exposing the creation logic to the client. This allows developers to create objects without knowing the exact class of the object being created.

- **Observer pattern**: This pattern defines a one-to-many relationship between objects, where a change in one object triggers a notification to all the other objects. This is useful for situations where multiple objects need to be notified of a change in another object, such as in a messaging system.

Module patterns in RPA

Module patterns can also be applied to **robotic process automation** (**RPA**), which involves automating repetitive tasks using software robots. In RPA, modules can be used to break down a process into smaller, independent steps, making it easier to manage and maintain. For example, the Factory pattern could be used to create robot objects without exposing the creation logic to the client, while the Observer pattern could be used to trigger notifications to other robots when a task is completed.

The pros of the module pattern are as follows:

- **Reusability**: Modules can be reused in different parts of a program or even in other programs, reducing development time and effort.

- **Maintainability**: Modules are easier to maintain than large monolithic code bases. This makes it easier to identify and fix bugs or add new features.

- **Flexibility**: Modules can be easily swapped in and out of a program, making it easier to modify or improve the program.

- **Encapsulation**: Modules allow for the encapsulation of data and functionality, making it easier to manage and control access to sensitive data.

The following are the cons of the module pattern:

- **Complexity**: As the number of modules in a program increases, so does the complexity of the program. This can make it more difficult to understand and maintain.

- **Overhead**: Creating modules adds some overhead to the development process, as developers must design and implement each module.

- **Interoperability**: Modules may not always be compatible with each other, which can lead to compatibility issues that are difficult to resolve.

- **Performance**: Using modules can sometimes lead to a decrease in performance due to the additional overhead required to manage them.

Let's understand the modular concept using a diagram. The following diagram depicts a typical modular design for the login and logout functionality of a website, along with other steps:

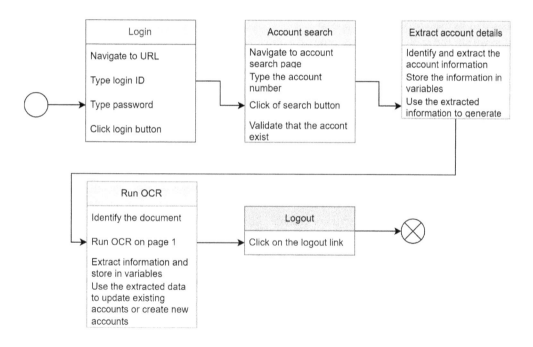

Figure 14.1 – Modular design

It is clear from the preceding diagram that the components are designed and developed so they are self-contained and perform a single action. This helps to decouple the functionality and creates a modular structure. If there is any change in a respective module, then this can be edited without touching the other modules, thus giving better control over the development and testing of the module. For example, a change in the login page does not necessarily affect or trigger testing for the account search functionality or run the OCR modules as the code itself is modularized and is not interdependent.

In conclusion, module patterns are an important aspect of software development that involves breaking down a program into smaller, independent parts, or modules. These patterns are widely used in the software industry and can be applied to RPA to improve automation processes. Examples of module patterns include the Singleton pattern, the Factory pattern, and the Observer pattern, each of which can be used to improve code reusability, flexibility, and maintainability.

When it comes to RPA or automation, one of the key concepts and considerations of design is to save time. Time can be wasted if the bot or automation has to be restarted. There are many potential reasons for restarting an automation, such as catastrophic errors, system freeze, OS crashes, or memory leaks. All these force us to start again from scratch, reducing the efficiency of the automation. How can we solve this problem? This is where the concept of breadcrumbs comes to the rescue.

Breadcrumbs

Breadcrumbs are a common navigation feature found in most software applications. These are small text-based links that are typically displayed at the top of a page or screen, indicating the user's current location within the application. They provide a quick and easy way for users to understand where they are in the application hierarchy and offer a way of navigating back to previous pages or screens.

What are breadcrumbs in software development?

In software development, breadcrumbs refer to a navigational aid that displays a user's location within the application hierarchy. The term "breadcrumb" is derived from the classic fairy tale, *Hansel and Gretel*, in which the siblings leave a trail of breadcrumbs in the forest to find their way back home.

Similarly, in software development, breadcrumbs help users to understand their location within the application and provide a quick and easy way to navigate back to previous pages or screens. Breadcrumbs typically consist of a series of clickable links, starting with the home page and leading to the current page or screen.

Breadcrumbs are especially useful in large and complex applications with multiple levels of navigation. They allow users to quickly understand where they are in the application hierarchy and how to navigate back to previously viewed pages or screens. This feature helps to improve the user experience by making it easier for users to find the information they are looking for and reducing the amount of time they spend searching for it.

Why are breadcrumbs important in modern-day development standards?

Breadcrumbs have become an essential component of modern-day development standards for several reasons. The following are some of the key benefits of using breadcrumbs in software development:

- **Improved navigation**: Breadcrumbs provide a simple and effective way for users to navigate through an application. They help users to understand their location within the application hierarchy and provide a clear path back to previous pages or screens. This feature improves the user experience by making it easier for users to find the information they are looking for and reducing the amount of time they spend searching for it.

- **Increased usability**: Breadcrumbs improve the overall usability of an application by providing users with a clear understanding of how to navigate through the application. They are particularly useful in complex applications with multiple levels of navigation, where users may become disoriented or lost. Breadcrumbs provide a visual cue that helps users to maintain their bearings and navigate through the application with ease.

- **Better user engagement**: Breadcrumbs help to increase user engagement by improving the overall user experience. When users can easily navigate through an application and find the information they are looking for, they are more likely to spend more time using the application. This increased engagement can lead to higher user satisfaction, improved retention rates, and ultimately, increased revenue for the business.

- **Improved SEO**: Breadcrumbs can also improve the **search engine optimization** (SEO) of an application. When implemented correctly, breadcrumbs can provide search engines with additional information about the structure and content of an application, making it easier for search engines to understand and index the application's content. This can lead to improved search rankings and increased organic traffic to the application.

Types of breadcrumbs

There are three main types of breadcrumbs commonly used in software development. These include location-based breadcrumbs, attribute-based breadcrumbs, and path-based breadcrumbs. Let's take a closer look at each of these types:

- **Location-based breadcrumbs**: Location-based breadcrumbs are the most common type of breadcrumb and are based on the user's location within the application hierarchy. These breadcrumbs display the user's current location and provide links to the parent pages or screens. For example, if a user is viewing a product page, the location-based breadcrumb might display **Home** > **Products** > **Product Name**.

- **Attribute-based breadcrumbs**: Attribute-based breadcrumbs are based on specific attributes of the content the user is viewing. For example, if the user is viewing a list of products, the attribute-based breadcrumb might display **Home** > **Products** > **Category** > **Subcategory**. This type of breadcrumb is particularly useful for applications with a large amount of content that is organized based on specific attributes.

- **Path-based breadcrumbs**: Path-based breadcrumbs are based on the user's path through the application and provide links to the pages or screens the user has visited. This type of breadcrumb is particularly useful for applications with complex navigation structures or for users who frequently jump between different sections of the application. For example, if a user visits a product page from the home page, and then navigates to a related product page, the path-based breadcrumb might display **Home > Product 1 > Related Products > Product 2**.

Best practices for implementing breadcrumbs

When implementing breadcrumbs in software development, the following best practices should be followed to ensure maximum effectiveness:

- **Keep it simple**: Breadcrumbs should be simple and easy to use. They should not overwhelm the user with too much information or be difficult to understand. Stick to the standard format of displaying the user's current location and links to parent pages or screens.

- **Make it easy to navigate**: Breadcrumbs should be designed in a way that makes it easy for users to navigate through the application. They should be located in a consistent location on every page or screen and be easy to click on. It's also important to ensure that the breadcrumb links are accurate and up to date.

- **Use appropriate breadcrumb types**: When choosing a breadcrumb type, it's important to consider the type of content the user is viewing and the navigation structure of the application. Location-based breadcrumbs are generally the most appropriate for most applications, but attribute-based or path-based breadcrumbs can be more appropriate for certain types of content or navigation structures.

- **Use consistent terminology**: Breadcrumbs should use consistent terminology throughout the application. This means using the same words and phrases to describe similar content or navigation paths. This consistency helps users to understand the structure of the application and navigate through it more easily.

- **Test and iterate**: As with any user interface element, it's important to test and iterate on breadcrumbs to ensure they are effective. This may involve conducting user testing or analyzing usage metrics to identify areas for improvement. Regularly testing and iterating on breadcrumbs can help to ensure they are always optimized for maximum effectiveness.

Use of breadcrumbs in RPA

Breadcrumbs can also be used in RPA and automation tools to help users navigate through complex workflows and processes. In RPA and automation, breadcrumbs are often referred to as process maps or process flows.

As solution architects for RPA projects, we need to understand the importance of ensuring efficient and error-free automation processes. Breadcrumbs, a term borrowed from web development, can be effectively employed in RPA projects to enhance the visibility, troubleshooting, and error-handling capabilities of automated workflows. In this use case, we explore how breadcrumbs can be utilized within an RPA project to improve process monitoring and facilitate issue resolution.

The main objective of using breadcrumbs in RPA projects is to provide detailed process tracking and auditing, allowing developers and stakeholders to monitor the progress of automated workflows, identify potential bottlenecks or errors, and trace the steps leading to specific issues or exceptions.

Use case scenario: Let's consider a use case where an organization wants to automate its invoice processing system using RPA technology. The process involves extracting invoice data from email attachments, validating the information, updating the company's financial system, and archiving the documents for future reference.

Implementation: To implement breadcrumbs within the RPA project, the following steps can be followed:

1. **Integration with workflow management systems**: Integrate the RPA solution with a workflow management system that supports breadcrumb tracking. This system will capture and store the breadcrumb information generated during the automation process.

2. **Breadcrumb generation**: Within the RPA workflow, incorporate breadcrumb generation at key milestones or significant steps. Breadcrumbs can be created by appending relevant contextual information such as timestamps, activity names, input parameters, or system states. For example, breadcrumbs can be generated after extracting invoice data, validating fields, updating the financial system, and archiving documents.

3. **Breadcrumb storage**: Store the generated breadcrumbs in a centralized repository or database associated with the specific instance of the automated process. Each breadcrumb should include essential details such as the timestamp, activity name, input parameters, and any relevant error or exception messages encountered during the step.

4. **Breadcrumb visualization**: Develop a user-friendly interface or dashboard that enables stakeholders to visualize the generated breadcrumbs. The dashboard should provide a comprehensive overview of the automated workflow, displaying the sequence of activities, timestamps, and any errors or exceptions encountered. This visualization will assist developers and business users in monitoring the progress and health of the automated process.

5. **Troubleshooting and issue resolution:** In case of errors or exceptions during the automation process, the breadcrumbs will serve as a valuable resource for troubleshooting and issue resolution. By analyzing the breadcrumbs leading up to the error, developers can quickly identify the specific step or activity that caused the problem. This facilitates targeted debugging and accelerates the resolution process.

Process maps or flows are visual representations of the steps and actions involved in a workflow or process. They typically include the input and output data, the decision points, and the steps or actions required to complete the process. Process maps or flows are particularly useful in RPA and automation because they help users understand the logic behind the process and identify any bottlenecks or inefficiencies. By following the process map or flow, users can quickly and easily navigate through the process and identify any areas that require attention or optimization.

In RPA and automation, process maps or flows can also be used to automate certain tasks or processes. For example, a process map or flow could be used to automate the process of generating a report by automating the steps involved in pulling the data, formatting the report, and distributing it to stakeholders.

Breadcrumbs, in the form of process maps or flows, are an essential part of RPA and automation because they help users understand and navigate through complex workflows and processes. By providing a clear and concise visual representation of the process, users can quickly identify any areas that require attention or optimization and make the necessary changes to improve efficiency and productivity.

In conclusion, breadcrumbs are a simple and effective way to help users navigate through software applications. They provide a quick and easy way for users to understand their location within the application hierarchy and navigate back. Another concept that plays an important role in designing a robust solution, whether it be software or an RPA bot, is decoupling. Let's now understand what decoupling is and how it helps in achieving a modular design.

Decoupling

In recent years, decoupling has become an important concept in software development, particularly in the context of RPA. Decoupling refers to the practice of separating software components or modules from each other so that they can operate independently. Decoupled software architecture is a design approach that promotes flexibility, modularity, and scalability, which are essential for creating software systems that can adapt to changing business needs.

In this topic, we will explore decoupling in software development, including its principles, benefits, and best practices. We will also discuss how decoupling plays an important role in RPA, a rapidly growing field that involves automating repetitive and manual tasks using software robots.

Decoupling in software development

Software decoupling is the process of separating the software components that interact with each other so that each component can operate independently without any dependencies on other components. Decoupling helps to eliminate tight coupling between components, which can create a brittle system that is difficult to maintain and scale. In a decoupled system, each component can be updated or replaced without affecting the other components, making it easier to maintain and scale.

The decoupling principle is based on the idea of modularity, which is a fundamental principle of software engineering. Modular design involves breaking down a software system into smaller, more manageable components or modules. These modules can then be developed, tested, and deployed independently, making the overall system more flexible and adaptable.

Benefits of decoupling

Decoupling offers several benefits to software development:

- **Scalability:** Decoupled systems are easier to scale because each component can be scaled independently without affecting the other components. This makes it easier to add more capacity to the system as demand grows.

- **Flexibility:** Decoupled systems are more flexible because each component can be updated or replaced without affecting the other components. This makes it easier to adapt the system to changing business needs.

- **Modularity:** Decoupled systems are more modular because each component is self-contained and can be developed, tested, and deployed independently. This makes it easier to maintain the system and add new features.

- **Resilience:** Decoupled systems are more resilient because they can continue to function even if one or more components fail. This is because each component operates independently and can be designed to handle failures gracefully.

- **Reusability:** Decoupled systems are more reusable because each component can be reused in other systems or applications. This makes it easier to develop new systems or applications using existing components.

Best practices for decoupling

Decoupling requires careful planning and design to ensure that the software system is modular, scalable, and flexible. Here are some best practices for decoupling:

- **Use interfaces:** Use interfaces to define the interactions between components. This allows each component to operate independently, without having to know the internal details of the other components.

- **Minimize dependencies:** Minimize the dependencies between components to reduce the risk of tight coupling. This makes it easier to update or replace individual components without affecting the rest of the system.

- **Use messaging:** Use messaging to communicate between components. This allows each component to operate independently, without having to wait for the other component to respond.

- **Use asynchronous communication:** Use asynchronous communication to avoid blocking the system. This allows each component to operate independently, without having to wait for the other component to complete its task.

- **Use microservices:** Use microservices to break down the system into smaller, more manageable components. This makes it easier to develop, test, and deploy individual components.

Decoupling in RPA

RPA is a rapidly growing field that involves automating repetitive and manual tasks using software robots. RPA tools can perform tasks such as data entry, data extraction, and report generation, among others. These tasks are typically performed by humans, and they are often time-consuming, error-prone, and require a high degree of manual effort.

Decoupling plays an important role in RPA because it helps to create software robots that are modular, scalable, and flexible. RPA systems typically consist of several components, including the RPA engine, the RPA bot, and the RPA interface. Decoupling these components helps to create a flexible and scalable system that can adapt to changing business needs.

RPA engine

The RPA engine is the core component of an RPA system. It is responsible for managing the RPA bots, executing workflows, and managing the interactions between the bots and the applications they interact with. The RPA engine is typically decoupled from the RPA bots and the RPA interface to ensure that it can operate independently.

Decoupling the RPA engine from the bots and the interface allows the system to scale more easily. The RPA engine can be scaled horizontally by adding more instances, and it can also be scaled vertically by adding more resources to each instance. This makes it easier to handle large volumes of work and to ensure that the system remains responsive even under heavy load.

RPA bots

The RPA bots are software robots that perform automated tasks in an RPA system. The bots interact with the applications they are automating through the user interface, either by emulating user interactions or by using APIs. Decoupling the RPA bots from the RPA engine and the RPA interface ensures that they can operate independently.

Decoupling the RPA bots from the RPA engine and the interface also makes it easier to manage the bots. Each bot can be developed, tested, and deployed independently, making it easier to update or replace individual bots as needed. This makes it easier to maintain the system and to ensure that it remains up-to-date with the latest software and hardware.

RPA interface

The RPA interface is the user-facing component of an RPA system. It allows users to create, configure, and manage the RPA bots and workflows. Decoupling the RPA interface from the RPA engine and the RPA bots ensures that it can operate independently.

Decoupling the RPA interface from the RPA engine and the bots also makes it easier to update or replace the interface without affecting the rest of the system. This makes it easier to provide a better user experience and to ensure that the interface remains up to date with the latest software and hardware.

Best practices for decoupling in RPA

Decoupling in RPA requires careful planning and design to ensure that the system is modular, scalable, and flexible. Here are some best practices for decoupling in RPA:

- **Use microservices architecture:** Use microservices architecture to break down the RPA system into smaller, more manageable components. This makes it easier to develop, test, and deploy individual components.

- **Use message queues:** Use message queues to manage the interactions between the RPA engine and the RPA bots. This allows the bots to operate independently, without having to wait for the engine to respond.

- **Use APIs:** Use APIs to interact with the applications that the bots are automating. This allows the bots to interact with the applications in a more controlled and reliable way.

- **Use containers:** Use containers to package the RPA bots and the RPA engine. This makes it easier to deploy the bots and the engine to different environments and to manage the dependencies between the components.

- **Use version control:** Use version control to manage the source code for the RPA bots and the RPA engine. This makes it easier to track changes, collaborate with other developers, and roll back changes if needed.

- **Use testing frameworks:** Use testing frameworks to test the RPA bots and the RPA engine. This helps to ensure that the system is reliable and free from errors.

- **Use monitoring tools:** Use monitoring tools to monitor the performance of the RPA system. This helps to ensure that the system is running smoothly and that any issues can be quickly identified and resolved.

Decoupling in RPA can help to create a more flexible and scalable system that can adapt to changing business needs. However, decoupling requires careful planning and design to ensure that the system is modular and easy to manage. Developers must also use best practices such as microservices architecture, message queues, APIs, containers, version control, testing frameworks, and monitoring tools to create a robust and reliable system.

To summarize, decoupling in software development is an important concept that involves breaking down a system into smaller, more manageable components. Decoupling can help to create a system that is flexible, scalable, and easier to maintain. In RPA, decoupling plays an important role in creating software robots that are modular, scalable, and flexible. Developers can use best practices such as microservices architecture, message queues, APIs, containers, version control, testing frameworks, and monitoring tools to create a robust and reliable RPA system. By decoupling their systems, developers can create software that is easier to manage, more reliable, and better suited to the needs of its users.

Not all concepts in software development are the primary concepts. Sometimes we have to deal with a by-product, which can become a major obstacle to maintaining the efficiency of the system or automation. Garbage collection is one of them. It is not produced as a piece of software by developers, but has to be managed instead as a by-product of using volatile memory or **random-access memory** (**RAM**) when running our software.

Garbage collection

Garbage collection is an essential process in software development that helps manage memory allocation and deallocation. It automates the process of freeing up memory that is no longer being used by the program, which reduces the likelihood of memory leaks, performance issues, and other related problems. However, the mishandling of garbage collection can lead to a range of challenges, including application crashes, memory leaks, and reduced system performance. In this section, we will explore the challenges that arise from mishandling garbage collection and discuss how it is used in RPA and automation. We will also provide some best practices for handling garbage collection in RPA and automation.

What is garbage collection?

Garbage collection is an automated process that manages memory allocation and deallocation in software development. The process involves identifying and freeing up memory that is no longer being used by the program, which helps prevent memory leaks and other related issues. In programming languages such as Java, garbage collection is handled by the runtime environment, which automatically identifies and frees up memory that is no longer being used.

In addition to reducing the likelihood of memory leaks, garbage collection also helps improve system performance by freeing up memory that can be used for other processes. It also helps simplify programming by automating the process of memory management, which reduces the likelihood of errors and simplifies the debugging process.

Challenges due to mishandling garbage collection

The mishandling of garbage collection can lead to a range of challenges in software development. These challenges include application crashes, memory leaks, and reduced system performance. The following are some of the most common challenges associated with the mishandling of garbage collection:

- **Memory leaks:** Memory leaks occur when the memory that is no longer being used is not freed up by the program. This can lead to a gradual reduction in available memory, which can eventually result in an application crash. Memory leaks can occur due to a variety of factors, including a lack of understanding of the garbage collection process or poor programming practices.

- **Performance issues:** Poor garbage collection practices can also lead to reduced system performance. If garbage collection is not managed properly, it can consume too many system resources, which can cause the system to slow down or even crash.

- **Application crashes:** Garbage collection issues can also cause application crashes. If memory is not freed up properly, it can eventually result in a system crash, which can cause data loss and other related problems.

- **Garbage collection in RPA and automation:** In RPA and automation, garbage collection is used to manage memory allocation and deallocation. RPA and automation tools rely heavily on memory management, as they often involve the use of large amounts of data and complex algorithms. The garbage collection process in RPA and automation is similar to that used in traditional software development.

In RPA and automation, garbage collection is essential for ensuring that memory is properly managed and that system performance remains consistent. The use of garbage collection in RPA and automation helps prevent memory leaks and other related issues, which can cause application crashes among other problems.

Best practices for handling garbage collection in RPA and automation

To ensure that garbage collection is properly managed in RPA and automation, the following best practices should be followed:

- **Understand the garbage collection process:** The first step in managing garbage collection in RPA and automation is to understand the process itself. This includes understanding how memory is allocated and deallocated, as well as how garbage collection is handled by the runtime environment.

- **Use appropriate data structures:** The use of appropriate data structures can help simplify the garbage collection process and reduce the likelihood of memory leaks. When designing RPA and automation solutions, it is important to choose data structures that are efficient and easy to manage.

- **Minimize memory usage:** Minimizing memory usage can help reduce the workload on the garbage collector and improve system performance. This can be achieved by using efficient algorithms and optimizing code to reduce the amount of memory required.

- **Monitor system performance:** Monitoring system performance is essential for identifying issues with garbage collection and other related processes. This includes tracking memory usage, CPU utilization, and other key performance indicators to ensure that the system is running smoothly and that garbage collection is being managed effectively.

- **Test and debug:** Testing and debugging are essential for identifying and resolving issues with garbage collection. This includes testing the system under different loads and conditions to identify potential issues, and debugging code to identify and fix memory leaks and other related issues.

- **Implement proper memory management:** Proper memory management is essential for managing garbage collection effectively. This includes implementing appropriate memory allocation and deallocation processes, as well as employing strategies to manage large amounts of data. One way is to have sub-processes and make sure the unnecessary modules, business objects, and sequences are offloaded from the memory and a garbage collector function is called to free up the previously used memory. This is needed from time to time during the process flow so the memory is maintained healthily.

To conclude, garbage collection is an essential process in software development that helps manage memory allocation and deallocation. Mishandling garbage collection can lead to a range of challenges, including memory leaks, performance issues, and application crashes. In RPA and automation, garbage collection is used to manage memory allocation and deallocation and ensure that system performance remains consistent.

To handle garbage collection effectively in RPA and automation, it is important to understand the process, use appropriate data structures, minimize memory usage, monitor system performance, test and debug, and implement proper memory management strategies. By following these best practices, developers can effectively manage garbage collection and ensure that their RPA and automation solutions are reliable, efficient, and scalable.

We saw how modular design can help with the process of development and simplify integration and use. Breadcrumbs can help in maintaining the status of the process state and allow us to review from the point of failure. Decoupling helps to maintain the modular design, while the resilience of this design and the use of garbage collection both make the code stable and immune to memory leaks and crashes. But there is still an important aspect of development that we have not discussed yet: that of exception handling.

Exception handling

Exception handling is a crucial aspect of software development that ensures the uninterrupted execution of software programs. Exception handling is the process of identifying, managing, and responding to exceptions, errors, and other unexpected events that may occur during the execution of a software program.

When an exception is raised, it interrupts the normal flow of the program and must be handled properly to prevent the program from crashing or producing incorrect results. In this article, we will discuss the importance of exception handling in software development, the challenges faced due to not handling exceptions, how exception handling is used in RPA and automation, and the best practices for doing so.

Importance of exception handling

Exception handling is critical in software development because it allows programs to continue executing even when unexpected events occur. Without exception handling, programs would crash and produce incorrect results whenever an exception occurs. By handling exceptions, software developers can identify and resolve errors, ensuring that the software performs as expected. Exception handling is particularly important in large-scale software development projects, where errors and exceptions can be difficult to identify and resolve.

Challenges faced due to not handling exceptions

When exceptions are not handled correctly, software programs can produce incorrect results, crash, or become unresponsive. These issues can result in lost productivity, revenue, and damage to a company's reputation. Some common challenges that arise due to not handling exceptions are the following:

- **Unreliable software:** When exceptions are not handled correctly, software programs can become unreliable and produce unpredictable results. This can result in lost productivity and revenue for the organization.

- **Inefficient problem-solving:** When exceptions are not handled correctly, it can be difficult for software developers to identify the root cause of the problem. This can result in inefficiencies and delays in resolving the issue.

- **Security vulnerabilities:** When exceptions are not handled correctly, it can create security vulnerabilities that can be exploited by attackers. This can result in data breaches, system compromises, and other security incidents.

Exception handling in RPA and automation

RPA and automation are two areas where exception handling is particularly important. RPA is the process of automating repetitive tasks using software robots or bots. Automation, on the other hand, is the process of using software to automate tasks that are typically performed by humans. In both cases, exception handling is critical to ensuring that the automation process is uninterrupted and that the software performs as expected.

In RPA, exceptions can occur when the bot encounters unexpected data, errors in the input or output, or problems with the system or network. To handle exceptions in RPA, developers must design bots that can identify and respond to exceptions. For example, if a bot encounters unexpected data, it can re-try the task, alert a human operator, or skip the task and move on to the next one as appropriate.

Best practices for exception handling in RPA and automation

To ensure effective exception handling in RPA and automation, developers should follow best practices. Some best practices for exception handling in RPA and automation are as follows:

- **Identify potential exceptions:** The first step in effective exception handling is to identify potential exceptions. Developers should review the system requirements, use cases, and input data to identify potential exceptions.

- **Handle exceptions gracefully:** When exceptions occur, software should handle them gracefully. This means that the software should respond in a way that minimizes disruption to the overall automation process. For example, if the software encounters an unexpected error, it should log the error, notify a human operator, and continue executing the automation process.

*   **Implement exception-handling logic:** Once potential exceptions are identified, developers should implement exception-handling logic. This involves writing code that can identify exceptions, respond to them, and handle them appropriately. Exception-handling logic should be designed to handle both known and unknown exceptions.

*   **Test exception handling:** Once exception-handling logic is implemented, developers should thoroughly test it to ensure that it works as expected. This involves testing the software with a variety of inputs, edge cases, and error conditions to ensure that it can handle exceptions gracefully.

*   **Monitor and review exception logs:** After the software is deployed, developers should monitor and review exception logs to identify and resolve issues. Exception logs can provide valuable information about the frequency and nature of exceptions, which can be used to improve exception-handling logic and prevent future exceptions.

*   **Provide clear error messages:** When exceptions occur, software should provide clear error messages that explain the nature of the problem along with guidance on how to resolve it. Clear error messages can help human operators quickly identify and resolve issues, minimizing disruptions to the overall automation process.

Summary

To summarize, exception handling is a critical aspect of software development, particularly in the areas of RPA and automation. Effective exception handling can help prevent software crashes, improve reliability, and minimize disruptions to the overall automation process. Developers should follow best practices for exception handling, including identifying potential exceptions, handling exceptions gracefully, implementing exception handling logic, testing exception handling, monitoring and reviewing exception logs, and providing clear error messages. By following these best practices, developers can ensure that their software performs as expected and delivers value to their organizations.

In the next chapter, we will talk about the data needed to test automation, the different ways we can get data for testing, how security is handled within an automation, the importance of logging, and how maintaining logs can help with troubleshooting and debugging.

Questions

1. What are the benefits of a modular design?
2. What are breadcrumbs, and how do they help in boosting the efficiency of automation?
3. What is decoupling, and why should it be a focal point in your design?
4. How can you prevent memory leaks and memory crashes in automation?
5. List five best practices to employ when implementing exception handling.

15
Data, Security, and Logs

In the digital era, data, security, and logs are crucial components of an organization's IT infrastructure. Organizations heavily rely on data to make informed decisions and gain a competitive edge. Therefore, possessing high-quality data is crucial for an organization's success. Data quality refers to the accuracy, completeness, consistency, and timeliness of data. Good data quality ensures that organizations make informed decisions based on accurate and reliable data. On the other hand, poor data quality can lead to incorrect decisions, financial losses, and reputational damage. Security is an equally critical aspect of managing data. Organizations gather and maintain sensitive data such as customer information, financial records, and intellectual property. Incidents of data breaches can cause significant financial losses and damage an organization's reputation. Thus, it's essential for organizations to put in place robust security measures to safeguard their data against unauthorized access, theft, and misuse. Logs are records of events or transactions that occur within an organization's IT infrastructure. These records provide valuable information for auditing, troubleshooting, and analyzing system performance. Logs also help organizations identify security breaches, track user activity, and ensure compliance with regulatory requirements.

In this chapter, we will cover the importance of data, and look at how we can collect good data. We will also talk about security: how we can implement security in a **robotic process automation** (**RPA**) project, why security is so important and a different way to implement it, and how logs play an important role help to manage the RPA bots and provide a great insight into the workings and performance of the automation. The following topics will be covered in this chapter:

- Cooking the data versus synthetic data
- Application logs versus custom logs
- Credentials
- RBAC
- Governance and auditing

As RPA becomes increasingly prevalent in modern organizations, it is critical to consider data privacy, data security, and environmental security in RPA projects. These aspects of RPA implementation are crucial in ensuring the successful adoption and implementation of RPA technologies.

Data privacy is a fundamental aspect of RPA projects that involves protecting sensitive data from unauthorized access, use, disclosure, or modification. Organizations need to implement data privacy controls to ensure that sensitive information is handled in a way that is compliant with relevant laws and regulations and that individuals' rights are respected.

Ensuring data security is a crucial aspect of RPA projects because RPA robots frequently access and manage sensitive data. RPA projects need to implement robust security measures to protect data from unauthorized access, theft, or misuse. These security measures may include access controls, encryption, and regular security audits.

Environmental security in RPA projects is another key consideration. RPA robots interact with various applications and systems, and any environmental issues in these systems can significantly impact RPA operations. Organizations need to ensure that their RPA projects are resilient to environmental changes and can handle system failures or disruptions.

To summarize, data privacy, data security, and environmental security are critical aspects of RPA projects. Organizations must implement robust controls and measures to protect sensitive data, ensure compliance with relevant laws and regulations, and mitigate risks associated with system failures or disruptions. By addressing these issues, organizations can successfully adopt and implement RPA technologies while ensuring the safety and privacy of their data. Keeping this in mind, let's explore methods for data collection and what to do when there isn't enough data available. In situations where there is insufficient data, the options are to either cook the data by manipulating it or generate synthetic data artificially.

Cooked and synthetic data

Data is a critical component of an RPA project, as it provides the necessary input for the RPA robot to perform its tasks. The RPA robot uses data to process information, make decisions, and automate tasks. Without data, an RPA robot cannot perform its intended functions.

Cooking the data is a term used to describe the practice of manipulating data in order to produce a desired outcome or result. It typically involves altering the data in some way to make it appear more favorable or to hide unfavorable information.

In the context of RPA and automation projects, cooking the data can be a serious issue because it can lead to inaccurate results and decisions made based on faulty information. This can have serious consequences, particularly in industries such as finance or healthcare where decisions based on data are critical. To avoid cooking the data in RPA and automation projects, it is important to establish clear guidelines for data collection, processing, and analysis. This includes defining data sources, ensuring data quality and accuracy, and documenting any data transformations or manipulations that are performed.

Additionally, RPA and automation projects should incorporate quality control measures such as validation checks and audits to ensure that the data being used is accurate and reliable. This can help prevent errors and inconsistencies that can arise from cooking the data, and ensure that decisions are based on the best possible information.

Collecting data for RPA projects can be done in several ways. One way is to extract data from existing systems, such as **enterprise resource planning (ERP)** systems, **customer relationship management (CRM)** systems, or other databases. Data can also be collected through manual data entry, which involves human operators entering data into the RPA system. However, in some cases, data may not be readily available or may not exist in the required format. In such cases, synthetic data can be created for use in RPA projects. Synthetic data refers to artificially generated data that resembles real data in terms of format and content. This type of data can be created using machine learning algorithms, simulation models, or other techniques.

Creating synthetic data requires careful consideration to ensure that the data is representative of the real-world data that the RPA robot will encounter. The synthetic data must also be generated in sufficient quantities to support the RPA robot's processing requirements. One approach to creating synthetic data is to use data augmentation techniques. Data augmentation involves generating new data by applying various transformations to the existing data. For example, image data can be augmented by flipping or rotating the image, changing the brightness or contrast, or adding noise.

Another approach to creating synthetic data is to use generative models. Generative models are machine learning algorithms that can learn the underlying distribution of real-world data and generate new samples that resemble the real data. These models can be trained on existing data and used to generate new synthetic data that can be used in RPA projects.

However, organizations must be cautious when using synthetic data in RPA projects. Synthetic data may not accurately reflect the real-world data that the RPA robot will encounter, and the performance of the RPA robot may be affected if the synthetic data is not representative of the real data. Therefore, organizations must carefully validate the synthetic data before using it in RPA projects.

In conclusion, collecting data is crucial for RPA projects, and organizations must use various techniques to collect data from multiple sources. Synthetic data can be used if real data is not available, but organizations must be careful to ensure that the synthetic data is representative of the real data and does not affect the performance of the RPA robot. Let's see what steps we can take to collect good-quality data for RPA projects.

Let's assume that you are asked to design a solution for a process that uses ServiceNow as one of the core applications. As this is the first time your client is working on a data-intensive process, they are seeking your guidance as an SA to lay down the steps their team needs to take in order to extract the clean data. The steps to extract and clean or transform the data are outlined here:

1. **Identify the data requirements**: The first step in preparing data for RPA projects is to identify the data requirements for the project. This includes understanding the data fields and formats needed to perform the tasks that the RPA robot will automate. For ServiceNow as a source

application, this includes identifying the ServiceNow tables, fields, and their relationships that need to be accessed by the RPA robot.

2. **Extract data from ServiceNow**: Once the data requirements have been identified, the next step is to extract data from ServiceNow. This can be done using ServiceNow's web services API or through ODBC/JDBC drivers. Organizations must ensure that they have the necessary permissions and credentials to access the data from ServiceNow.

3. **Clean and transform data**: After extracting the data from ServiceNow, it may be necessary to clean and transform the data to prepare it for use in the RPA project. This includes removing duplicates, filling in missing values, and converting data types to match the RPA system's requirements. Organizations may also need to merge data from multiple sources or split data into multiple tables to meet the RPA system's requirements.

4. **Validate the data**: Once the data has been cleaned and transformed, it must be validated to ensure its accuracy and completeness. This includes checking for any inconsistencies, errors, or missing data that may affect the performance of the RPA robot.

5. **Store the data**: After validating the data, it must be stored in a format that is accessible by the RPA system. This includes saving the data in a file format that can be read by the RPA robot, such as CSV, Excel, or JSON.

6. **Update the data**: In some cases, the RPA robot may need to update the data in ServiceNow. Organizations must ensure that they have the necessary permissions and credentials to access the data and update it through ServiceNow's web services API.

We saw how simple steps can be taken to extract good-quality data from a complex system like ServiceNow. These same steps can be followed and applied to most of the applications and systems that use some kind of database to store the data. Now, let's see how data can be sensitive and how we can handle it in RPA projects.

Sensitive data, such as **protected health information (PHI)** and **personally identifiable information (PII)**, require special handling to ensure their confidentiality, integrity, and availability. PHI refers to any health information that can be used to identify an individual, while PII includes any information that can be used to identify an individual, such as their name, address, social security number, or driver's license number.

Organizations that handle sensitive data must adhere to strict regulations, such as the **Health Insurance Portability and Accountability Act (HIPAA)** for PHI or the **General Data Protection Regulation (GDPR)** for PII. These regulations require organizations to implement strict security controls to protect sensitive data from unauthorized access, use, or disclosure.

Sensitive data should only be collected and processed when it is necessary for business purposes, and it should be stored securely using appropriate encryption methods. Access to sensitive data should be restricted only to authorized personnel with a need to know, and it should be audited regularly to detect any unauthorized access or use. Organizations must also consider the use of synthetic data in place of real data for RPA projects involving sensitive data. Synthetic data generation involves creating artificial data that mimics the characteristics of real data. Synthetic data can be used to train machine learning models or to test and validate systems without exposing sensitive data.

Synthetic data generation can be done using various techniques such as data augmentation, **generative adversarial networks** (**GANs**), or differential privacy. However, organizations must ensure that the synthetic data accurately reflects the real data characteristics to ensure the effectiveness of the RPA system. PHI and PII require special handling to ensure their confidentiality, integrity, and availability. Organizations must adhere to strict regulations and implement appropriate security controls to protect sensitive data. Synthetic data generation can be used to replace real data for RPA projects involving sensitive data, but organizations must ensure that the synthetic data accurately reflects the real data characteristics.

We discussed the significance of data and how it's vital for the success of any RPA project. Now, let's delve into the role of logs in the world of RPA and how they can be useful and essential.

Understanding the differences between application and custom logs

Application logs are logs that are generated by RPA applications to record information about their behavior and performance. These logs typically contain information about application events, such as user actions, system events, and errors. They can be used to monitor and troubleshoot applications, as well as to identify areas for optimization and improvement.

The following is a sample application log:

```
2023-04-05 14:33:21,303 - INFO - Application starting up...
2023-04-05 14:33:21,361 - INFO - Connected to database server at
address 192.168.1.100
2023-04-05 14:33:23,112 - ERROR - An error occurred while processing
user request: "Invalid password"
Traceback (most recent call last):
  File "app.py", line 126, in process_request
    raise ValueError("Invalid password")
ValueError: Invalid password
2023-04-05 14:33:23,250 - INFO - User "jdoe" logged in successfully
2023-04-05 14:33:25,017 - WARNING - Request from user "jdoe" took
longer than expected (3.5 seconds)
2023-04-05 14:34:12,512 - ERROR - An error occurred while processing
user request: "File not found"
Traceback (most recent call last):
  File "app.py", line 158, in process_request
    raise FileNotFoundError("File not found")
FileNotFoundError: File not found
2023-04-05 14:34:12,612 - INFO - Application shutting down...
```

This log shows several different types of events that might be recorded in an application log, including information messages (`INFO`), error messages (`ERROR`), and warning messages (`WARNING`). The log also includes timestamps for each event, as well as additional information about the event, such as the user who made the request or the error message that was encountered.

This is just a simple example of what an application log might look like. Depending on the complexity of the application and the needs of the organization, application logs can contain much more detailed information, including performance metrics, system events, and user activity. By analyzing these logs, organizations can gain valuable insights into their application's behavior and performance and take steps to optimize and improve it over time.

Custom logs, on the other hand, are logs that are specifically tailored to the needs of a particular application or organization. These logs may contain additional or different information than standard application logs and may be used to track specific events or performance metrics that are important to the organization. For example, a custom log may be used to track customer interactions with a particular application or to monitor the performance of a specific function or process within an application. The following is a sample custom log that can be added to the RPA process or workflow to have better control over and insight into the process:

```
2023-04-05 14:33:21,303 - INFO - RPA process starting up...
2023-04-05 14:33:22,112 - INFO - Task "Extract Data" started
2023-04-05 14:33:24,508 - INFO - Completed data extraction from source
system: "SAP"
2023-04-05 14:33:25,912 - INFO - Task "Transform Data" started
2023-04-05 14:33:27,817 - INFO - Completed data transformation using
tool: "Python Pandas"
2023-04-05 14:33:29,205 - INFO - Task "Load Data" started
2023-04-05 14:33:30,719 - INFO - Data loaded into target system:
"Oracle Database"
2023-04-05 14:33:31,521 - INFO - RPA process completed successfully
```

In this example, the custom log is used to track the progress of an RPA process that is responsible for extracting, transforming, and loading data between different systems. Each log entry includes a timestamp, as well as information about the specific task that is being executed and the system or tool being used to perform that task.

By analyzing this custom log, RPA developers and operators can gain valuable insights into the behavior and performance of the automation process. For example, they can identify which tools or systems are being used most frequently, or which tasks are taking the longest to complete. This information can then be used to optimize and improve the automation process over time, leading to increased efficiency, accuracy, and productivity.

The main difference between application logs and custom logs is that application logs are generated by the application itself, while custom logs are created by the organization or developer using the application. Application logs are typically standardized and provide a consistent set of information about the application's behavior and performance, while custom logs can vary widely depending on the specific needs and goals of the organization. Both application logs and custom logs are important tools for monitoring and maintaining applications and can be used to identify issues, optimize performance, and improve user experience. When developing an application or implementing an automation project, it is important to carefully consider the types of logs that will be generated and how they will be used to monitor and optimize the application's behavior and performance.

In RPA projects, logs play a crucial role in monitoring and maintaining automation processes. Logs are files that contain information about events, actions, and errors that occur during the execution of an RPA process. They provide a detailed record of what happened during the automation process and can be used to troubleshoot issues and identify areas for optimization.

The importance of logs in RPA projects cannot be overstated. They help RPA developers and operators understand how an automation process is functioning, whether it is meeting its objectives, and whether there are any errors or exceptions that need to be addressed. Logs also provide a means for tracking performance over time and can be used to identify patterns and trends in automation processes.

There are several different types of logs that can be used in RPA applications and automations. Some of the most common types include the following:

- **Audit logs**: These logs record all actions and events that occur during an automation process, including user actions, system events, and errors

- **Debug logs**: These logs contain detailed information about the execution of an automation process, including variable values, function calls, and other debugging information

- **Performance logs**: These logs track the performance of an automation process over time, including metrics such as processing time, memory usage, and CPU utilization

- **Security logs**: These logs record all security-related events that occur during an automation process, including login attempts, access requests, and other security-related events

- **Error logs**: These logs record all errors and exceptions that occur during an automation process, including stack traces and error messages

By leveraging the information contained in these logs, RPA developers and operators can gain valuable insights into the behavior of their automation processes, and take steps to improve performance, optimize workflows, and ensure that their RPA applications are meeting their objectives.

In addition to the types of logs just mentioned, there are other specialized logs that may be used in specific RPA applications or environments. For example, in healthcare settings, there may be specific logs related to patient data privacy and security, while in financial settings, there may be logs related to compliance with regulatory requirements.

Regardless of the type of log used, it is important to ensure that the information contained within it is accurate and reliable. This means establishing clear guidelines for logging, including what information should be logged, when it should be logged, and how it should be stored and analyzed. In addition, logs should be regularly reviewed and analyzed to identify any issues or areas for improvement.

One of the benefits of using logs in RPA projects is that they can be easily integrated with other monitoring and analytics tools. For example, logs can be used to generate real-time alerts when certain events or errors occur or to provide insights into process performance and efficiency. Logs can also be used in conjunction with machine learning algorithms to identify patterns and trends and to develop predictive models that can help optimize automation workflows.

In summary, logs are an essential component of any RPA project, providing valuable insights into the behavior of automation processes and helping developers and operators ensure that their RPA applications are meeting their objectives. By leveraging the information contained in logs, RPA teams can identify and address issues, optimize workflows, and continuously improve the performance and efficiency of their automation processes.

We talked about logs, types of logs, and how to maintain them. Now, let's talk about another very important topic, which is credentials and how to manage them. Before we jump into how to manage them, let's understand what credentials are.

Credentials

Credentials or **login credentials** are nothing but another name for the same old **login** and **password** we have been using for ages. Credentials play a crucial role in RPA projects as they are used to authenticate bots and provide access to systems and applications. However, managing and securing credentials can be a challenging task, and a single mistake can lead to severe security breaches. Therefore, it is essential to follow best practices and use the right tools and technologies to protect sensitive information.

What makes bot login and application credential management so important? Let's look at the reasons:

- **Security**: Bots access sensitive information and systems, so it is essential to ensure that they have the right level of access and that their credentials are secure

- **Compliance**: Many industries have regulatory requirements around access to sensitive data, and bot login and credential management can help organizations comply with these regulations

- **Efficiency**: Proper bot login and credential management can help reduce the time and effort required to manage bot access to applications and systems

Here are some top best practices for bot login and application credential management in RPA and automation projects:

- **Use a centralized credential management system**: Centralizing credential management can help organizations manage bot access to applications and systems more efficiently. This can also help reduce the risk of credential theft or loss.

- **Use strong passwords and multi-factor authentication**: Strong passwords and multi-factor authentication can help ensure that bot credentials are secure and reduce the risk of unauthorized access.

- **Rotate passwords regularly**: Regularly rotating passwords can help reduce the risk of credential theft or misuse. This can also help ensure that only authorized bots have access to systems and applications.

- **Use encrypted communication**: To ensure that bot credentials are secure in transit, it is essential to use encrypted communication channels. This can help protect against credential theft or interception.

- **Use least privilege access**: Least privilege access means giving bots only the minimum level of access required to perform their tasks. This can help reduce the risk of unauthorized access or data breaches.

- **Audit bot access**: Regularly auditing bot access to applications and systems can help organizations identify potential security risks and ensure that only authorized bots have access.

Proper bot login and application credential management are essential components of RPA and automation projects. By following the preceding best practices, organizations can ensure secure and efficient bot authentication. These practices can help reduce the risk of unauthorized access or data breaches and ensure compliance with regulatory requirements.

When it comes to handling credentials in RPA projects, there are some *dos* and *don'ts* that should be followed. Firstly, it is crucial to ensure that all credentials are stored securely and encrypted using industry-standard encryption algorithms. Secondly, credentials should only be given to bots that require them to perform their tasks, and access should be revoked immediately after the task is completed. It is also recommended to use password managers to store and manage passwords and other sensitive information.

There are different ways to secure and store credentials in RPA projects, such as using encrypted files, vaults, or secure databases. The choice of method depends on the organization's security policies and requirements. Some commonly used tools and technologies for securely storing and using login credentials in RPA and automation projects are CyberArk, Microsoft Azure Key Vault, HashiCorp Vault, AWS Secrets Manager, and Google Cloud Secrets Manager.

In conclusion, managing and securing credentials is a critical aspect of RPA projects. Following best practices, such as using password managers, revoking access after tasks are completed, and using secure storage methods, can significantly reduce the risk of security breaches. Moreover, using advanced tools and technologies can enhance the security of credentials and ensure the safe and efficient operation of RPA bots.

We talked about login credentials, and how to save, manage, and maintain them. There is another aspect of security, which is **role-based access control** (**RBAC**). RBAC helps in controlling and maintaining the right access for the bot based on what the humans were doing during the manual process. It helps mimic the same level of access for a seamless transition.

RBAC implementation

As organizations continue to adopt RPA and automation technologies, there is a growing need to implement effective access control measures to protect sensitive data and applications. One such measure is RBAC. In this section, we will explore the basics of RBAC, how it can be applied in RPA and automation, and the benefits of using RBAC for access control.

RBAC is a widely used access control mechanism that restricts access to resources based on the roles of users within an organization. In RBAC, users are assigned roles based on their job responsibilities, and these roles are associated with a set of permissions that allow users to perform specific actions on resources.

How RBAC can be applied in RPA and automation

RBAC can be applied in RPA and automation in several ways, such as the following:

- **User roles and responsibilities**: In RPA and automation, users are assigned roles and responsibilities based on their job functions. For example, a developer may have access to create and modify bots, while a tester may have access to test bots.

- **Resource permissions**: Resources in RPA and automation, such as bots and applications, can be secured using RBAC. Permissions can be granted or revoked based on user roles and responsibilities.

- **Workflow access**: RBAC can also be applied to control access to workflows. For example, only users with specific roles may be able to initiate a workflow or approve a workflow.

- **Audit trails**: RBAC can be used to track user activities and create audit trails. This can help identify any unauthorized access or actions taken by users.

The following are the benefits of using RBAC for access control in RPA and automation:

- **Enhanced security**: RBAC can help enhance security by ensuring that users only have access to resources that are necessary for their job functions. This can help reduce the risk of data breaches and unauthorized access.

- **Compliance**: RBAC can help organizations comply with regulatory requirements by providing a structured approach to access control.

- **Increased efficiency**: RBAC can help increase efficiency by automating access control processes, reducing the time and effort required to manage user access.

- **Improved auditability**: RBAC can help improve auditability by providing an audit trail of user activities, which can be used to identify any security issues or compliance violations.

The following are the challenges in implementing RBAC for access control in RPA and automation:

- **Role definition**: Defining roles and responsibilities for users can be a complex task, as job functions and responsibilities may vary between organizations. It is always advised to use the existing roles from an SME or a user who is using the current process and mimic the same role for the bot or automation.

- **Role management**: Managing roles and permissions can be challenging, particularly in large organizations with a high number of users and resources.

- **Compliance requirements**: Compliance requirements may vary between organizations and industries, and implementing RBAC to meet specific compliance requirements can be challenging.

- **Integration with legacy systems**: Integrating RBAC with legacy systems can be challenging, particularly if these systems are not designed to support RBAC.

Here are a few examples of RBAC implementation in RPA and automation:

- **Bot access control**: RBAC can be implemented to control access to bots in an RPA environment. For instance, developers may have access to create and modify bots, while testers only have permission to test bots. This ensures that each user has access only to the bots required for their job function and reduces the risk of data breaches.

- **Workflow approval**: RBAC can be applied to control access to workflow approval processes in an automation environment. For example, users with specific roles, such as managers or supervisors, may have permission to approve workflows. This ensures that only authorized users can initiate or approve workflows, reducing the risk of unauthorized access.

- **Application access control**: RBAC can be implemented to control access to applications in an automation environment. For instance, users with roles such as administrators may have access to perform administrative functions on an application, while regular users may have access only to the application features required for their job function. This ensures that users only have access to the features and functionalities required for their job function and reduces the risk of data breaches.

To summarize, RBAC is an effective access control mechanism that can be applied in RPA and automation to enhance security, compliance, and efficiency. However, implementing RBAC can be challenging, particularly in large organizations with complex user roles and legacy systems. By understanding the basics of RBAC and its benefits, organizations can develop effective RBAC strategies to secure their RPA and automation environments.

We discussed login credentials, RBAC, and maintaining access for multiple automations in an organization. With potentially hundreds of automations in play, effective governance is crucial to ensure adherence to rules and regulations. Let's now explore the role of governance in RPA and how it's vital to the overall success of the program.

Effective governance

Governance is a crucial aspect of any technology implementation, including RPA and automation. Governance refers to the set of policies, procedures, and controls put in place to ensure that the use of RPA and automation aligns with the organization's goals and objectives. In this article, we will explore the importance of governance in RPA and automation, the key components of an effective governance framework, and examples of how governance can be implemented in RPA and automation.

Why is governance important in RPA and automation?

Governance is essential in RPA and automation for several reasons, such as the following:

- **Ensuring compliance**: RPA and automation often involve the use of sensitive data; therefore, it is crucial to ensure that their use is compliant with the organization's regulatory and legal requirements.

- **Managing risks**: RPA and automation can pose several risks to an organization, such as data breaches and system downtime. Governance can help manage these risks by implementing policies and procedures to mitigate them.

- **Maximizing benefits**: Governance can help maximize the benefits of RPA and automation by ensuring that they align with the organization's goals and objectives.

Here are the key components of an effective governance framework in RPA and automation:

- **Governance structure**: A clear governance structure is essential for effective governance in RPA and automation. This includes defining the roles and responsibilities of the governance team and ensuring that there is clear communication between the governance team and stakeholders.

- **Policy and procedures**: Policies and procedures are necessary to ensure that the use of RPA and automation aligns with the organization's goals and objectives. These should include policies for data privacy, security, and compliance.

- **Risk management**: Risk management is essential for effective governance in RPA and automation. This includes identifying and assessing risks, developing risk mitigation strategies, and monitoring risks on an ongoing basis.

- **Training and awareness**: Training and awareness are necessary to ensure that stakeholders are aware of the policies and procedures governing the use of RPA and automation. This includes training for end users, developers, and governance teams.

The following are some examples of governance in RPA and automation:

- **Access control**: Access control is an essential aspect of governance in RPA and automation. It involves implementing policies and procedures to ensure that only authorized personnel have access to RPA and automation systems. For example, access control policies may require users to authenticate their identity using a two-factor authentication mechanism before accessing the RPA and automation systems.

- **Data privacy**: Data privacy is a critical aspect of governance in RPA and automation. It involves implementing policies and procedures to ensure that sensitive data is protected from unauthorized access or disclosure. For example, data privacy policies may require that all sensitive data is encrypted both at rest and in transit.

- **Change management**: Change management is an essential aspect of governance in RPA and automation. It involves implementing policies and procedures to manage changes to RPA and automation systems. For example, change management policies may require that all changes to RPA and automation systems are documented, approved by the governance team, and tested before implementation.

- **Audit and compliance**: Audit and compliance are critical aspects of governance in RPA and automation. They involve implementing policies and procedures to ensure that the use of RPA and automation systems is compliant with regulatory and legal requirements. For example, audit and compliance policies may require that regular audits of RPA and automation systems are conducted to ensure compliance with regulatory and legal requirements.

- **Vendor management**: Vendor management is an essential aspect of governance in RPA and automation. It involves implementing policies and procedures to manage vendors who provide RPA and automation services. For example, vendor management policies may require that all vendors are thoroughly vetted before engagement and that all vendor contracts include provisions for data privacy and security.

In addition to these examples, it is essential to note that governance is an ongoing process that requires continuous monitoring and improvement. This means that governance policies and procedures should be regularly reviewed and updated to reflect changes in the organization's goals and objectives, regulatory requirements, and technological advancements.

Effective governance is essential for the successful implementation and use of RPA and automation. It ensures that the use of these technologies aligns with the organization's goals and objectives, manages risks, and maximizes benefits. The key components of an effective governance framework include a clear governance structure, policies and procedures, risk management, and training and awareness. These components should be tailored to the organization's specific needs and requirements.

In conclusion, effective governance is essential for the safe and successful implementation and use of RPA and automation. It ensures that these technologies are used in a manner that aligns with the organization's goals and objectives, manages risks, and maximizes benefits. Organizations that implement effective governance frameworks will be better positioned to realize the full potential of RPA and automation while minimizing the associated risks.

Having implemented security measures, RBAC, and governance, we might think that we have everything in place. However, there is another critical aspect of ensuring that these measures are maintained to the highest standards: policing. To achieve this, regular audits must be conducted.

Auditing

Auditing refers to the process of reviewing and verifying the use of RPA and automation to ensure that it aligns with the organization's goals and objectives, complies with regulatory and legal requirements, and manages risks. In this article, we will explore the importance of auditing in RPA and automation, the key components of an effective auditing framework, and examples of how auditing can be implemented in RPA and automation.

Why is auditing important in RPA and automation?

Auditing is important in RPA and automation for several reasons, such as the following:

- **Ensuring compliance**: RPA and automation often involve the use of sensitive data; therefore, it is crucial to ensure that their use is compliant with the organization's regulatory and legal requirements.

- **Managing risks**: RPA and automation can pose several risks to an organization, such as data breaches and system downtime. Auditing can help manage these risks by reviewing the use of RPA and automation systems and identifying any potential vulnerabilities.

- **Maximizing benefits**: Auditing can help maximize the benefits of RPA and automation by identifying areas where RPA and automation systems can be improved or expanded.

The following are the key components of an effective auditing framework in RPA and automation:

- **Governance structure**: A clear governance structure is essential for effective auditing in RPA and automation. This includes defining the roles and responsibilities of the auditing team and ensuring that there is clear communication between the auditing team and stakeholders.

- **Risk assessment**: Risk assessment is necessary to identify and assess the risks associated with the use of RPA and automation systems. This includes identifying the critical business processes that are automated, assessing the potential impact of system failures, and determining the likelihood of specific risks occurring.

- **Compliance review**: Compliance review is essential to ensure that the use of RPA and automation systems is compliant with regulatory and legal requirements. This includes reviewing the policies and procedures governing the use of RPA and automation systems and verifying that they align with regulatory and legal requirements.

- **System review**: System review is necessary to ensure that the RPA and automation systems are operating effectively and efficiently. This includes reviewing the system's design, configuration, and performance, and verifying that it aligns with the organization's goals and objectives.

- **Data review**: Data review is essential to ensure that the use of RPA and automation systems does not result in data breaches or unauthorized disclosure of sensitive information. This includes reviewing data access policies and procedures and verifying that they align with the organization's data privacy and security requirements.

The following are some examples of auditing in RPA and automation:

- **Process audit**: A process audit involves reviewing the automated processes to ensure that they align with the organization's goals and objectives. This includes reviewing the processes' design, configuration, and performance and identifying any areas where they can be improved or expanded.

- **Compliance audit**: A compliance audit involves reviewing the use of RPA and automation systems to ensure that it complies with regulatory and legal requirements. This includes reviewing policies and procedures governing the use of RPA and automation systems, verifying that they align with regulatory and legal requirements, and identifying any areas where they can be improved.

- **Data audit**: A data audit involves reviewing the use of RPA and automation systems to ensure that it does not result in data breaches or unauthorized disclosure of sensitive information. This includes reviewing data access policies and procedures, verifying that they align with the organization's data privacy and security requirements, and identifying any areas where they can be improved.

- **Security audit**: A security audit involves reviewing the RPA and automation systems' security measures to ensure that they protect against unauthorized access or disclosure. This includes reviewing the systems' access controls, authentication mechanisms, and encryption measures, and identifying any potential vulnerabilities that need to be addressed.

- **Vendor audit**: A vendor audit involves reviewing the third-party vendors that supply RPA and automation systems to the organization. This includes reviewing the vendor's security measures and compliance with regulatory and legal requirements, and their overall reputation in the industry. It is important to ensure that the vendor's systems align with the organization's goals and objectives and do not pose any potential risks to the organization.

- **Change management audit**: A change management audit involves reviewing the changes made to the RPA and automation systems to ensure that they are implemented effectively and efficiently. This includes reviewing the change management policies and procedures, verifying that they align with the organization's goals and objectives, and identifying any potential risks associated with the changes.

- **Performance audit**: A performance audit involves reviewing the RPA and automation systems' performance to ensure that they meet the organization's goals and objectives. This includes reviewing the system's efficiency, accuracy, and overall performance, identifying any areas where performance can be improved, and implementing strategies to address these areas.

This brings us to the end of the chapter. As we saw, audits are the key to maintaining the health and integrity of the system. It helps to keep the entire automation on track and avoids introducing any unwanted and unapproved code, data, or process steps.

Summary

Logs, login credentials, governance, and audits are crucial aspects of any technology implementation, including RPA and automation. It ensures that the use of these systems aligns with the organization's goals and objectives, manages risks, and maximizes benefits. An effective auditing framework includes a clear governance structure, risk assessment, compliance review, system review, data review, and performance review. Examples of auditing in RPA and automation include process audits, compliance audits, data audits, security audits, vendor audits, change management audits, and performance audits. By implementing an effective auditing framework, organizations can ensure the safe and effective use of RPA and automation systems while minimizing risks and maximizing benefits.

Logs, login credentials, governance, and auditing are essential components of any technology implementation, including RPA and automation. These measures help ensure that the use of these systems aligns with the organization's goals and objectives, manages risks, and maximizes benefits. An effective auditing framework comprises a clear governance structure, risk assessment, compliance review, system review, data review, and performance review.

In the next chapter, we will talk about the **key performance indicators** (**KPIs**) and how they play a vital role in measuring the effectiveness of automation. We will talk about the different KPIs and how to implement them.

Questions

1. What are the benefits of having logs and what are their types?

2. How do we maintain the highest level of consistency and compliance in RPA projects?

3. What are the challenges of implementing an RBAC solution?

4. What are the different ways to secure credentials?

5. What are the different types of audits?

16

Key Performance Indicators (KPIs)

Key Performance Indicators (**KPIs**) are measurable values that demonstrate how effectively a company is achieving its business objectives. They are quantifiable metrics that are used to evaluate the success of a particular activity or process. KPIs can be applied to any aspect of a business, including finance, marketing, sales, production, and customer service. They allow businesses to monitor their progress and make data-driven decisions that improve overall performance. In this chapter, we will see how KPIs can be applied to RPA and automation.

KPIs are essential for businesses because they provide a framework for measuring progress toward specific goals. Without KPIs, it is challenging to determine whether a business is on track to achieving its objectives. KPIs allow businesses to identify areas of weakness and make strategic changes to improve their overall performance. They also provide a way to measure success objectively, which helps motivate employees and drives continuous improvement. In this chapter, we will talk about the different types of KPIs, how to measure them, and how they are used to measure the ROI and effectiveness of automation. To provide a comprehensive understanding of the subject, the following topics will be discussed in the chapter:

- **Straight-through processing (STP)**
- Using exception metrics in KPIs
- Accuracy
- **Bot handling time (BHT)**
- Utilization
- Reliability (MTTF, MTBF, and MTTR)

Before we jump into the specific list of topics, let's see the different types of KPIs that can be generated to quantify and measure success.

Some of the most common KPIs include the following:

- **Financial KPIs**: These metrics measure a company's financial performance, including revenue, profitability, and *ROI*

- **Marketing KPIs**: These metrics measure the effectiveness of a company's marketing efforts, including website traffic, leads generated, and conversion rates

- **Sales KPIs**: These metrics measure a company's sales performance, including the number of sales made, the value of sales, and the average order value

- **Production KPIs**: These metrics measure a company's production efficiency, including throughput, cycle time, and defect rate

- **Customer Service KPIs**: These metrics measure a company's ability to provide quality customer service, including response time, customer satisfaction, and resolution rate

Choosing the right KPIs for a business can be a challenging task. It is essential to select metrics that align with the company's overall goals and objectives. KPIs should be **specific, measurable, attainable, relevant, and time-bound** (**SMART**). They should also be actionable, meaning they provide information that can be used to improve performance.

In addition to selecting the right KPIs, it is essential to establish benchmarks for each metric. Benchmarks provide a way to compare performance over time and against industry standards. They also provide a way to set targets and measure progress toward specific goals.

In conclusion, KPIs are critical for businesses of all sizes and industries. They provide a way to measure progress toward specific goals, identify areas of weakness, and make data-driven decisions that improve overall performance. Choosing the right KPIs and establishing benchmarks are essential for success. By using KPIs effectively, businesses can drive continuous improvement and achieve long-term success. The first KPI that a solution architect (SA) and the management focus on is how many documents were processed without issues, or how many iterations were run without any human intervention. This metric alone tells a lot about the stability, consistency, and reliability of the automation as a whole. This takes us to the first KPI, known as STP.

STP

STP is an automated process that involves end-to-end processing of a transaction with no manual intervention. The concept of STP has been around for a long time, but it has gained more attention in recent years due to advancements in technology and increasing demand for faster and more efficient processing of transactions. STP is used in various industries, including finance, healthcare, and insurance, to streamline processes and reduce operational costs. In this chapter, we will discuss how STP is used in **RPA**, its pros and cons, and how to set up STP KPIs.

RPA is the use of software robots to automate repetitive tasks and processes. STP is an essential component of RPA and automation because it allows faster and more efficient processing of transactions.

RPA software robots can be programmed to perform a range of tasks, from data entry to customer service, and STP ensures that these tasks are performed accurately and without manual intervention.

STP is used in RPA and automation to reduce the time and cost associated with processing transactions. By automating the process, organizations can eliminate manual errors, reduce the need for manual intervention, and speed up the process. This results in increased efficiency, improved accuracy, and cost savings.

Let's now quickly see the pros and cons of STP.

Here are the pros:

- **Faster processing**: STP allows faster processing of transactions by eliminating manual intervention, which speeds up the process
- **Improved accuracy**: By eliminating manual intervention, STP reduces the risk of errors, resulting in improved accuracy
- **Cost savings**: STP reduces the need for manual labor, resulting in cost savings
- **Improved customer satisfaction**: Faster processing times and improved accuracy result in improved customer satisfaction
- **Scalability**: STP can be easily scaled up or down depending on the volume of transactions

And these are the cons:

- **Complexity**: Implementing STP can be complex and requires significant investment in technology and infrastructure
- **Technical issues**: Technical issues can arise when implementing STP, which can result in downtime and delays
- **Lack of flexibility**: STP is designed to be a rigid process, which can make it difficult to make changes to the process
- **Inability to handle exceptions**: STP is designed to handle standard transactions, and exceptions can be difficult to handle
- **Lack of human oversight**: STP eliminates the need for human intervention, which can result in a lack of human oversight

Setting up STP KPIs

KPIs are essential for measuring the effectiveness of STP. The following are some of the KPIs that can be used to measure the effectiveness of STP:

- **Processing time**: This KPI measures the time it takes to process a transaction from start to finish

- **Error rate**: This KPI measures the number of errors that occur during the processing of transactions

- **Cost savings**: This KPI measures the cost savings that result from the implementation of STP

- **Customer satisfaction**: This KPI measures the level of customer satisfaction with the STP process

- **Scalability**: This KPI measures the ability of the STP process to scale up or down depending on the volume of transactions

To set up STP KPIs, you need to define the metrics that you want to measure and determine how you will measure them. You will also need to establish a baseline for each metric and set targets for improvement. Regular monitoring of the KPIs will help you to identify areas for improvement and take corrective action if necessary.

To summarize, STP is an essential component of RPA and automation that allows faster and more efficient processing of transactions. While there are pros and cons to implementing STP, the benefits outweigh the drawbacks, making it a worthwhile investment for organizations. Setting up STP KPIs is essential for measuring the effectiveness of the process and identifying areas for improvement. By regularly monitoring and analyzing KPIs, organizations can optimize their STP processes to achieve maximum efficiency, accuracy, and cost savings. As technology continues to advance, we can expect to see even more applications of STP in various industries, further streamlining processes and reducing operational costs. Another type of KPI that is used to gauge the stability of the automation and RPA relates to exceptions. There are many types of exceptions, but in RPA we mostly track two types of exceptions, which are business and system exceptions. Let's understand how these exceptions play a vital role in KPIs.

Using exception metrics in KPIs

RPA software robots can automate tasks that are typically performed by humans, such as data entry, invoice processing, and customer service interactions. However, like any other technology, RPA is not foolproof and can experience exceptions that require human intervention.

What are exceptions in RPA?

In RPA, exceptions are unexpected events that occur during the automation process that require human intervention to resolve. These exceptions can arise for various reasons, such as system errors, input data errors, incorrect processing logic, and changes in the application's user interface.

Business exceptions

Business exceptions refer to exceptions that occur due to problems with the business process itself. These can include errors in the data being processed, invalid input values, and missing information. For example, if an RPA robot is processing invoices, a business exception may occur if the invoice data is missing or incorrect, or if the invoice does not match an existing purchase order.

System exceptions

System exceptions refer to exceptions that occur due to issues with the system itself. These can include problems with network connectivity, application crashes, and system timeouts. For example, if an RPA robot is automating a login process and the system experiences a network outage, a system exception would occur, and the automation process would be interrupted.

Impact of exceptions on business processes

Exceptions can have a significant impact on business processes, as they can cause delays in processing, errors in data, and additional costs associated with manual intervention. In some cases, exceptions can even lead to complete automation failures, requiring the process to be restarted from scratch. These delays and errors can negatively impact business performance, leading to decreased productivity, decreased customer satisfaction, and increased costs.

Using exceptions in KPIs

In RPA, exceptions can be used as KPIs to measure the effectiveness of the automation process. By tracking exceptions, organizations can identify areas where the automation process is not working as expected and make improvements to increase efficiency and accuracy.

Building exception metrics in RPA

To build exception metrics in RPA, organizations must first identify the types of exceptions that are relevant to their business processes. These exceptions can be classified as either business or system exceptions and can be further categorized based on the specific types of errors that occur.

Once the exceptions have been identified, organizations can begin tracking them using RPA software. This can be done by logging each exception as it occurs and assigning it a unique identifier. The exceptions can then be aggregated and analyzed to determine the frequency and severity of each exception type.

To use exceptions as a KPI, organizations can set targets for the number of exceptions that are acceptable within a given time period. For example, an organization may set a target of no more than five business exceptions per week. If the number of exceptions exceeds the target, the organization can investigate the root cause of the exceptions and make changes to improve the automation process. Next comes the accuracy of the process. You might ask "isn't that the same as STP?" The short answer is "No." STP is the measurement of completing the process from end to end without human intervention; that does not mean that it is correct or correctly processed. Accuracy is defined as completing the process according to the defined norms. Let's talk about this in detail in the next section.

Accuracy

Accuracy and efficiency are two critical factors in RPA that determine the success of the automation process. In this section, we will discuss why accuracy and efficiency are important for RPA, as well as how they can be measured and used as metrics and KPIs.

Why is accuracy important for RPA?

Accuracy is the ability of the RPA system to perform tasks without making errors. Accuracy is essential because it ensures that the automated process is working correctly and the results are reliable. If the RPA system is not accurate, it can lead to serious consequences for the business, such as incorrect financial reporting, legal compliance issues, or customer dissatisfaction.

Inaccurate RPA systems can also lead to wasted time and resources. If an RPA system is making errors, it can take longer to complete a task, and humans may need to intervene to correct the mistakes. This defeats the purpose of RPA, which is to save time and reduce costs.

How to measure accuracy in RPA

There are several ways to measure accuracy in RPA. The most common method is to compare the results of the RPA system with the results produced by a human performing the same task. This method is called **human validation**.

Another way to measure accuracy is through the use of "process metrics." Process metrics measure the performance of the RPA system as it completes a process. For example, a process metric for an RPA system that performs invoice processing could be the percentage of invoices processed correctly without human intervention.

How to use accuracy as a metric and a KPI

Accuracy can be used as a metric and KPI in RPA to measure the effectiveness of the automation process. The accuracy metric can be used to determine whether the RPA system is performing the task correctly and producing reliable results. The KPI can be used to set a target level of accuracy and track progress toward that target over time.

For example, if an RPA system is processing invoices, the accuracy metric could be the percentage of invoices processed correctly without human intervention. The KPI could be set at 95% accuracy, and the RPA system could be monitored regularly to ensure that it is meeting this target.

Why efficiency is important for RPA

Efficiency is the ability of the RPA system to complete tasks quickly and with minimal resources. Efficiency is important because it allows businesses to save time and reduce costs. If the RPA system is not efficient, it can take longer to complete tasks than it would for a human to perform the same task. This negates the benefits of automation.

Inefficient RPA systems can also lead to wasted resources. If an RPA system is taking longer to complete tasks than necessary, it may be using more resources than it needs. This can lead to increased costs and lower ROI for the business.

How to measure efficiency in RPA

There are several ways to measure efficiency in RPA. The most common method is to measure the time it takes for the RPA system to complete a task. This can be done by setting up a stopwatch or timer and recording the time it takes for the RPA system to complete the task.

Another way to measure efficiency is through the use of **resource metrics**. Resource metrics measure the resources used by the RPA system to complete a task. For example, a resource metric for an RPA system that performs invoice processing could be the amount of CPU and memory resources used during the process.

How to use efficiency as a metric and KPI

Efficiency can be used as a metric and KPI in RPA to measure the effectiveness of the automation process. The efficiency metric can be used to determine whether the RPA system is completing tasks quickly and with minimal resources. The KPI can be used to set a target level of efficiency and track progress toward that target over time.

For example, if an RPA system is processing invoices, the efficiency metric could be the time it takes to process each invoice. The KPI could be set at a certain time limit, and the RPA system could be monitored regularly to ensure that it is meeting this target.

Accuracy and efficiency as complementary metrics

While accuracy and efficiency are both important metrics in RPA, they are also complementary to each other. In other words, an RPA system that is highly accurate may not be efficient, and an RPA system that is highly efficient may not be accurate.

For example, an RPA system that is highly accurate may take longer to complete a task because it is performing additional checks and validations to ensure the accuracy of the output. On the other hand, an RPA system that is highly efficient may sacrifice accuracy by completing tasks quickly without performing thorough checks.

Therefore, it is important to balance accuracy and efficiency in RPA. This can be done by setting targets for both accuracy and efficiency and monitoring the RPA system regularly to ensure that it meets these targets.

Other metrics and KPIs for RPA

In addition to accuracy and efficiency, there are other metrics and KPIs that can be used to measure the effectiveness of RPA:

- **Cost savings**: This metric measures the amount of money saved by using RPA instead of human labor. The KPI could be set at a certain percentage of cost savings, and the RPA system could be monitored regularly to ensure that it is meeting this target.

- **Error rate**: This metric measures the number of errors made by the RPA system during a process. The KPI could be set at a certain error rate, and the RPA system could be monitored regularly to ensure that it is meeting this target.

- **Throughput**: This metric measures the number of tasks that can be completed by the RPA system in a given time period. The KPI could be set at a certain throughput rate, and the RPA system could be monitored regularly to ensure that it is meeting this target.

- **Scalability**: This metric measures the ability of the RPA system to handle an increasing workload. The KPI could be set at a certain level of scalability, and the RPA system could be monitored regularly to ensure that it is meeting this target.

- **Customer satisfaction**: This metric measures the satisfaction of customers with the results produced by the RPA system. The KPI could be set at a certain level of customer satisfaction, and the RPA system could be monitored regularly to ensure that it is meeting this target.

In conclusion, accuracy and efficiency are two critical factors in RPA that determine the success of the automation process. Accuracy ensures that the automated process is working correctly and the results are reliable, while efficiency allows businesses to save time and reduce costs. These two metrics are complementary to each other, and it is important to balance them to achieve the desired results. In addition to accuracy and efficiency, other metrics and KPIs can be used to measure the effectiveness of RPA, such as cost savings, error rate, throughput, scalability, and customer satisfaction. By monitoring these metrics regularly, businesses can ensure that their RPA systems are meeting their targets and delivering the desired results.

BHT

BHT is a metric used in RPA that measures the time it takes for an RPA bot to complete a specific task or process. It is different from **average handling time** (**AHT**), which measures the time it takes for a human agent to handle a process.

BHT is calculated by measuring the time it takes for the bot to complete a specific task from the moment it receives the input data to the moment it produces the output data. This includes the time spent on data processing, data entry, validation, and any other steps involved in the automation process. BHT can also include any wait times, such as time spent waiting for a response from an external system or user input.

BHT is a useful metric for measuring the performance of an RPA system because it provides insight into how quickly and efficiently the bot is completing tasks. By tracking BHT over time, businesses can identify areas for improvement and optimize their automation processes to reduce handling time and increase efficiency.

BHT can be used as a performance metric in several ways:

- **Setting targets**: By setting a target BHT for specific processes, businesses can ensure that their RPA systems meet their performance goals. Targets can be based on historical data, industry benchmarks, or other factors.

- **Comparing bots**: By comparing the BHT of different bots performing the same task, businesses can identify which bot is most efficient and effective. This can help businesses optimize their bot selection and deployment strategies.

- **Monitoring performance**: By monitoring BHT regularly, businesses can identify trends and patterns in their automation processes. This can help businesses identify areas for improvement and optimize their RPA system to reduce handling time and increase efficiency.

- **Identifying bottlenecks**: By analyzing BHT data, businesses can identify bottlenecks in their automation processes that are causing delays or inefficiencies. This can help businesses optimize their processes to improve performance and reduce BHT.

Here are some common examples of BHT:

- **Invoice processing**: Many companies use RPA to automate their invoice processing tasks, such as data entry and validation. BHT can be used to measure the time it takes for the bot to process each invoice, from the moment it receives the data to the moment it produces the validated output. By tracking BHT over time, the company can identify areas where the bot is taking too long and optimize its automation processes to reduce handling time. For example, they might find that the bot is spending too much time on data validation, and they can optimize the validation rules to reduce the processing time.

- **Customer service**: RPA can also be used in customer service to automate tasks such as responding to customer inquiries or updating customer data. BHT can be used to measure the time it takes for the bot to handle each customer interaction, from the moment it receives the inquiry to the moment it produces the response. By tracking BHT, the company can identify areas where the bot is taking too long and optimize its automation processes to reduce handling time. For example, they might find that the bot is spending too much time waiting for user input and can optimize the user interface to reduce wait times.

In both of these examples, BHT is a critical metric for measuring the performance of the RPA system and identifying areas for improvement. By optimizing their automation processes to reduce handling time, companies can increase efficiency and productivity, reduce costs, and improve customer satisfaction.

Overall, BHT is a critical metric in RPA that provides insight into the efficiency and effectiveness of automation processes. By tracking BHT over time and using it as a performance metric, businesses can optimize their RPA system to reduce handling time, increase efficiency, and achieve their automation goals. Next, we'll discuss the utilization of the underlying bot hardware and infrastructure. Having a sense of utilization can give better insights into what kind of ROI can be expected from the overall RPA program. Let's talk about it in the next section.

Measuring utilization of underlining bot hardware

Utilization of bot machines or **Virtual Desktop Infrastructure** (**VDI**) in RPA refers to the percentage of time that an RPA bot is actively working on tasks versus the time it is idle or waiting for tasks. In other words, it measures how effectively the bot infrastructure is being used to automate tasks.

Optimizing the percentage of utilization is important for increasing efficiency in RPA. The higher the utilization percentage, the more tasks the bot infrastructure can handle, leading to increased productivity and cost savings. However, increasing utilization too much can lead to performance issues and decreased efficiency.

There are several ways to optimize the percentage of utilization in RPA:

- **Increasing task volume**: One way to increase utilization is to increase the number of tasks that are automated by the bot infrastructure. This can be achieved by identifying additional processes that can be automated, or by increasing the volume of tasks within existing processes.

- **Improving process efficiency**: Another way to increase utilization is to optimize the efficiency of the processes that the bots are automating. This can be achieved by reducing the number of steps in a process, simplifying the data input requirements, or optimizing the validation rules used by the bot.

- **Load balancing**: Load balancing is a technique that's used to distribute workloads evenly across bot machines or VDIs. By ensuring that each machine is working at optimal capacity, load balancing can increase the overall utilization percentage of the bot infrastructure.

- **Scaling the infrastructure**: Scaling the bot infrastructure involves adding more machines or VDIs to handle increased workloads. By adding more capacity, the overall utilization percentage can be increased, allowing more tasks to be automated.

- **Prioritizing tasks**: Prioritizing tasks based on their importance or complexity can help ensure that the bot infrastructure is being used to its maximum potential. By prioritizing high-value or high-complexity tasks, the utilization percentage can be optimized, leading to increased efficiency and gains.

RPA vendors such as UiPath, Blue Prism, and Automation Anywhere offer various features and tools to increase the utilization of bot infrastructure. These tools can help businesses achieve higher efficiency and cost savings in their RPA implementations. Let's take a look at some of the different ways these vendors help increase bot utilization:

- **Cloud-based infrastructure**: Many RPA vendors offer cloud-based infrastructure, which allows businesses to easily scale their bot infrastructure up or down depending on their workload. This helps ensure that bots are always working at optimal capacity, increasing the overall utilization percentage. Cloud-based infrastructure also helps businesses avoid the cost and complexity of managing their own hardware.

- **Multi-bot orchestration**: Multi-bot orchestration allows businesses to automate complex processes that require multiple bots working together. By coordinating the tasks of multiple bots, businesses can increase the efficiency and utilization percentage of their bot infrastructure.

- **Load balancing**: Many RPA vendors offer load balancing features that automatically distribute workloads evenly across bot machines or VDIs. This helps ensure that each machine is working at optimal capacity, increasing the overall utilization percentage.

- **Bot scheduling**: Bot scheduling features allow businesses to schedule bots to work during peak workload times or when hardware resources are available. By scheduling bots to work when the infrastructure is most available, businesses can increase the utilization percentage of their bot infrastructure.

- **Unattended automation**: Unattended automation allows bots to work without human intervention. This allows businesses to automate processes that occur outside of normal business hours, increasing the overall utilization percentage of the bot infrastructure.

- **License pooling**: License pooling allows businesses to share licenses across multiple bots, increasing the overall utilization percentage of the bot infrastructure. This allows businesses to avoid the cost of purchasing additional licenses for each bot.

The impact of these features on license utilization can vary depending on the vendor and the specific features used. For example, cloud-based infrastructure and license pooling can help reduce license utilization by allowing businesses to share licenses and avoid the cost of managing their own hardware. On the other hand, multi-bot orchestration and load balancing can increase license utilization by allowing businesses to automate more complex processes and distribute workloads across more bots.

In conclusion, RPA vendors provide various tools and features to help businesses increase the utilization of their bot infrastructure. These features can have different impacts on license utilization depending on the vendor and the specific features used. Businesses should carefully consider the impact on license utilization when evaluating different RPA vendors and features. The utilization percentage of bot machines or VDIs is a critical metric for measuring the efficiency and effectiveness of RPA. By optimizing the utilization percentage through techniques such as increasing task volume, improving process efficiency, load balancing, scaling the infrastructure, and prioritizing tasks, businesses can achieve higher efficiency and gains in their RPA implementation.

The last metric that we are going to discuss in this chapter is reliability. The processes an SA is asked to automate are mostly high-value processes that are already running in production. Thousands of people can be affected by this automation, and there is a lot of dependency on the reliability of RPA automation. That is what makes reliability one of the most important metrics to measure and track. It helps build confidence in automation.

Reliability metrics

Reliability metrics are a set of quantitative measures used to evaluate the reliability of a system. Reliability refers to the ability of a system to function without failure over a given period of time. Several reliability metrics are used in the field of engineering, and three of the most commonly used metrics are MTTF, MTBF, and MTTR.

Mean Time to Failure (MTTF)

MTTF is a measure of the average amount of time for which a system or component will operate before it fails. It is calculated by dividing the total operational time of the system or component by the number of failures. For example, if a system has been operating for 10,000 hours and has experienced 5 failures, then the MTTF would be 2,000 hours (10,000/5). This metric is used to assess the reliability of a system and to predict the expected lifespan of a component or system.

Mean Time between Failures (MTBF)

MTBF is a measure of the average amount of time between failures of a system or component. It is calculated by dividing the total operational time of the system or component by the number of failures. For example, if a system has been operating for 10,000 hours and has experienced 5 failures, then the MTBF would be 2,500 hours (10,000/(5-1)). This metric is used to assess the reliability of a system and to predict the expected time between failures.

Mean Time to Repair (MTTR)

MTTR is a measure of the average time it takes to repair a failed system or component. It is calculated by dividing the total downtime of the system or component by the number of failures. For example, if a system has been down for a total of 10 hours due to 5 failures, then the MTTR would be 2 hours (10/5). This metric is used to assess the maintainability of a system and to identify opportunities for improvement in the repair process.

MTTF and MTBF are both measures of system reliability, but they are used to answer different questions. MTTF is used to predict the lifespan of a component or system, while MTBF is used to predict the expected time between failures. MTTR, on the other hand, is used to measure how quickly a failed component or system can be repaired, which is an important factor in maintaining high levels of system availability.

These metrics are used in different industries, including RPA, to measure the reliability of a system or component. By monitoring and analyzing these metrics, RPA developers can identify areas for improvement and optimize system performance. For example, by tracking MTTR, RPA developers can identify bottlenecks in the repair process and make changes to reduce downtime. Similarly, by tracking MTBF, RPA developers can identify components that are more likely to fail and prioritize maintenance efforts to prevent failures from occurring.

To summarize, reliability metrics such as MTTF, MTBF, and MTTR are important tools for measuring the reliability and maintainability of a system or component. These metrics are used to identify areas for improvement and optimize system performance, ultimately leading to increased system availability and reduced downtime.

Summary

KPIs and metrics play a crucial role in measuring the success and efficiency of businesses. STP is a metric that's used to determine the percentage of automated transactions without the need for manual intervention. The higher the STP, the more efficient the process and the lower the operational costs.

Exceptions can be used to determine the number of transactions that require manual intervention or handling. By tracking exceptions, businesses can identify areas that require process improvement and training to reduce errors and improve efficiency.

Accuracy is a metric that's used to measure the level of correctness in data or processes. Accurate data is essential for informed decision-making, and inaccurate data can lead to costly errors and missed opportunities. Ensuring data accuracy requires regular monitoring and validation of data inputs and processes.

Efficacy is a metric that's used to measure the effectiveness of a process or system in achieving its intended goals. It is essential to regularly measure efficacy to identify areas for improvement and ensure that systems are operating as intended.

Utilization is a metric that's used to measure the level of resource utilization in a system or process. By monitoring utilization, businesses can optimize resources to maximize efficiency and reduce costs.

Finally, reliability is a metric used to measure the ability of a system or process to consistently deliver results. Ensuring reliability requires regular monitoring and maintenance to minimize downtime and reduce the risk of errors and disruptions.

Overall, KPIs and metrics are essential tools for businesses to measure performance and identify areas for improvement. By tracking STP, exceptions, accuracy, efficacy, utilization, and reliability, businesses can optimize their processes and resources to achieve their goals and improve their bottom line.

In the next chapter, we will talk about how can we implement reporting and analytics, which can help the end user have a greater utilization of the automation. We will also talk about data retention, alerts, and notification and how to develop a cost-benefit analysis model.

Questions

1. What is the reason for having KPIs?

2. What is STP, and how can you achieve higher STP rates?

3. How is reliability measured, and what metrics are measured for it?

4. Define utilization and describe the different ways to increase bot utilization.

5. What is BHT, and how is it different from AHT?

17

Reporting, Analytics, Efficiency, and Efficacy

RPA has gained significant attention in recent years as a tool to automate routine and repetitive tasks across various industries. RPA technology is designed to mimic human actions and can perform a wide range of activities, including data entry, report generation, and rule-based decision-making. However, like any other technology, implementing RPA projects requires a significant investment, and organizations need to consider the **cost-benefit analysis** (**CBA**) and **return on investment** (**ROI**) before embarking on such initiatives.

CBA is a process used to evaluate the costs and benefits of a particular project or investment. This analysis helps organizations determine whether an investment in RPA technology will generate sufficient benefits to justify the cost. The CBA involves identifying all the costs and benefits associated with an RPA project and comparing them to determine whether the project is financially viable. Costs can include the cost of RPA software and hardware, implementation costs, and ongoing maintenance costs. Conversely, benefits can include improved productivity, increased accuracy, reduced errors, and cost savings.

ROI is another critical factor that organizations should consider when evaluating the viability of RPA projects. ROI measures the financial return an organization can expect from an investment in RPA technology. Calculating ROI involves comparing the expected benefits of the RPA project with the costs of implementing and maintaining the technology over a specific period. The ROI calculation helps organizations determine whether an RPA project is financially feasible and will generate the desired returns.

In this chapter, we will explore the CBA and ROI calculations for RPA projects. We will examine the various costs and benefits associated with RPA implementation and the factors that organizations need to consider when calculating ROI. We will also provide some guidelines to conduct a CBA and ROI calculation for RPA projects. By the end of this chapter, you will have a better understanding of how to evaluate the financial viability of RPA projects and how these processes help a business make informed decisions about whether to invest in this technology. Some of the topics covered in this chapter are as follows:

- CBA and ROI
- Queue reporting
- Keeping the history
- Data retention
- Analytics
- Alerts and notifications
- Resilience
- Discovering the unknowns
- Monitoring the health
- Updates and upgrades
- Change management

Let's dive into the first topic of this chapter, which is CBA and ROI.

CBA and ROI

The purpose of CBA is to determine whether the benefits of a project outweigh its costs and whether it is financially viable. In the context of RPA projects, CBA is crucial to determine the feasibility of implementing RPA technology within an organization.

CBA is important for RPA projects because it helps organizations make informed decisions about whether to invest in RPA technology. Implementing RPA projects can be expensive, and organizations need to ensure that the benefits of the technology outweigh its costs. CBA helps organizations identify all the costs and benefits associated with RPA implementation, providing a framework to compare these costs and benefits to determine the financial viability of the project.

Developing a CBA for RPA projects involves several steps, which include the following:

1. **Define the scope of the RPA project**: The first step in developing a CBA is to define the scope of the RPA project. This involves identifying the processes that will be automated using RPA technology, and the expected benefits of automation.

2. **Identify costs**: The next step is to identify all the costs associated with RPA implementation. This includes the cost of RPA software and hardware, implementation costs, and ongoing maintenance costs.

3. **Identify benefits**: Once the costs have been identified, the next step is to identify the benefits of RPA implementation. This can include improved productivity, increased accuracy, reduced errors, and cost savings.

4. **Assign values to costs and benefits**: After identifying the costs and benefits, the next step is to assign values to each of them. This involves quantifying the costs and benefits in monetary terms.

5. **Calculate the net present value (NPV)**: The final step is to calculate the NPV of the project. NPV is a financial metric that takes into account the time value of money and provides an estimate of the project's profitability.

CBA is a crucial process in determining the financial viability of RPA projects. It helps organizations make informed decisions about whether to invest in RPA technology by identifying all the costs and benefits associated with implementation. Developing CBA involves several steps, including defining the scope of the project, identifying costs and benefits, assigning values to them, and calculating the NPV of the project.

A CBA template for RPA projects should include the following components:

- **Project details**: This section should include the project name, project description, and the expected implementation timeline.

- **Costs**: This section should include all the costs associated with RPA implementation. This can include the cost of RPA software and hardware, implementation costs, and ongoing maintenance costs.

- **Benefits**: This section should include all the benefits of RPA implementation. This can include improved productivity, increased accuracy, reduced errors, and cost savings, among others.

- **Assumptions**: This section should include any assumptions made when calculating the costs and benefits of the project. This can include assumptions about the rate of return, the expected lifespan of the RPA software, and the expected increase in productivity.

- **Financial analysis**: This section should include the financial analysis of the project. This can include the NPV, **internal rate of return (IRR)**, and payback period of the project.

- **Sensitivity analysis**: This section should include a sensitivity analysis of the project. This involves testing the impact of changes in key assumptions on the financial analysis of the project.

- **Conclusion**: This section should include a summary of the key findings of CBA and a recommendation on whether to proceed with the project.

These components can be organized into an Excel template to facilitate the calculation and comparison of costs and benefits. The template should allow for easy input of values and the automatic calculation of financial metrics such as NPV and IRR. It should also be designed to allow for sensitivity analysis, by allowing users to easily change key assumptions and observe the impact on the financial analysis of the project.

CBA is developed when a project starts so that a business can make an educated decision on whether they want to pursue the opportunity and go with automation or not. But then, how do you measure the actual returns after the project is implemented and when an ROI analysis is done?

ROI is a measure of the profitability of an investment relative to its cost. In layman's terms, ROI tells you how much money you'll get back for every dollar you invest. A high ROI means that the investment is likely to be profitable, while a low ROI means that the investment may not be profitable.

ROI is important to businesses because it helps them make informed decisions about which projects to invest in. When considering multiple projects, businesses can use ROI to compare the profitability of each project and select the one that is likely to generate the highest return.

In the context of RPA projects, ROI is important because RPA implementation can be expensive, and businesses need to ensure that the investment is likely to generate a positive return. By calculating the ROI value of an RPA project, businesses can determine whether the benefits of automation outweigh the costs and make an informed decision about whether to proceed with the project.

The difference between CBA and ROI is that CBA focuses on comparing the costs and benefits of a project to determine its financial viability, while ROI focuses specifically on the profitability of an investment. CBA considers all the costs and benefits of the project, not just the financial ones, and provides a more comprehensive analysis of the project's financial viability. ROI, on the other hand, only considers the financial profitability of the investment and does not take into account non-financial benefits or costs. Both CBA and ROI are important tools for businesses to use when evaluating potential investments, including RPA projects.

The formula to calculate ROI is as follows:

ROI = (Net Profit / Cost of Investment) x 100%

Net Profit is the total profit generated by the investment, and *Cost of Investment* is the total cost of the investment.

To calculate the net profit, you need to subtract the total cost of the investment from the total revenue generated by the investment. The net profit can also be calculated as the sum of all the benefits of the investment minus the sum of all the costs.

Once you have calculated the net profit and cost of investment, plug them into the formula to calculate ROI. This is expressed as a percentage and indicates the profitability of the investment. An ROI value greater than 100% means that the investment is profitable, while an ROI value less than 100% means that the investment is not profitable.

We talked about CBA and ROI and how they help businesses determine whether their investment is giving positive returns or not. All this comes under the analytics part of a project. Now, let's talk about some of the topics that fall under reporting. The first one is queues. Reports generated on queues can not only give you statistics on the daily work of your automation but also help you to provide a closer insight into the process. This is also one of the ways to build confidence in your client. Let's see how it's done.

Queue reporting

Queues play a crucial role in RPA by enabling the efficient and automated handling of large volumes of data and tasks. They provide a central location to manage and prioritize work items, helping to ensure that processes are executed in a timely and organized manner.

In addition to their operational benefits, queues can also provide valuable data for analytics. By tracking the status and progress of work items within a queue, businesses can gather insights into process performance, identify bottlenecks and inefficiencies, and optimize their RPA processes.

To use queues for analytics, businesses can generate reports that provide a snapshot of queue performance and identify trends and patterns over time. Some of the reports that can be generated from queues include the following:

- **Queue status reports**: These reports provide a high-level overview of the current status of work items within a queue, including the number of items waiting to be processed, in progress, and completed

- **Queue performance reports**: These reports provide detailed information on how efficiently work items are being processed within a queue, including the average processing time, queue capacity, and queue utilization rate

- **Work item analysis reports**: These reports provide insights into individual work items, including the time it takes to complete each item, the frequency of errors or exceptions, and the resources required to complete each item

To share these reports with customers, businesses can use a variety of methods, including email, online dashboards, or web-based portals. The reports can be customized to meet the specific needs of the customer and can be shared on a regular basis to provide ongoing visibility into process performance and optimization. By using queues for analytics and sharing reports with customers, businesses can improve their RPA processes and provide greater value to their customers. We saw how queuing data can be used for useful insights with the help of reports. In addition, reports can also be generated from other types of data, which is generated and stored during the entire life cycle of the process execution. Let's see how historical data can help to generate meaningful reports, which helps to give valuable insights into the process.

Keeping the history

Keeping a history of process execution in an RPA can be very useful to get insights into the performance of the automation and identify areas for improvement. Here are some specific ways in which it can be helpful:

- **Identifying bottlenecks**: By analyzing the history of process execution, you can identify the steps in the automation process that take the most time or cause the most errors. This can help you pinpoint areas that need to be optimized to improve the overall efficiency of the automation.

- **Debugging errors**: If an error occurs during the execution of an RPA automation, having a history of past executions can help you identify the root cause of the error. By looking at the previous executions of the automation, you may be able to identify patterns or commonalities that can help you identify the source of the problem.

- **Optimizing process design**: By analyzing the history of process execution, you can identify the parts of a process that are executed most frequently or take the most time. This can help you determine whether there are opportunities to optimize the process design to improve efficiency.

- **Evaluating automation effectiveness**: By tracking the history of process execution, you can evaluate the effectiveness of RPA automation over time. This can help you determine whether the automation is achieving the desired outcomes and identify areas for further improvement.

Overall, keeping a history of process execution can be a valuable tool to optimize the performance of RPA automation and ensure that they deliver the desired results. The question you might now have is, how long do you keep the history? You can't keep history forever, as storage cost and your data grows exponentially. There are many ways to consolidate and compress data, so you extract the essence of a large dataset, keep the compressed data, and discard the raw data. However, to do that you need to have a strategy. Let's see how we can achieve this by having a data retention strategy.

Data retention

Data retention policies are critical for any organization to ensure that data is kept for an appropriate length of time and is properly managed. This is especially important for RPA projects, which often involve the processing and storage of large amounts of data. Here are some types of data retention policies that can be applied to RPA projects and how they can help a company get valuable insights:

- **Legal retention**: This type of data retention policy ensures that data is kept for the length of time required by law or regulation. For example, data related to financial transactions may need to be kept for a certain number of years in order to comply with accounting regulations. By adhering to legal retention requirements, companies can avoid potential legal or regulatory issues and ensure compliance with industry standards.

- **Business retention**: This type of data retention policy is based on business needs and ensures that data is kept for as long as it is required to meet operational or strategic goals. For example, data related to customer behavior may be retained for a certain period of time to help a company understand customer preferences and improve marketing strategies. By retaining data for business purposes, companies can gain valuable insights into their operations and make more informed decisions.

- **Disposition retention**: This type of data retention policy specifies when and how data should be deleted or disposed of. This ensures that data is not kept longer than necessary and helps to reduce the risk of data breaches or security incidents. By having a clear plan for data disposition, companies can ensure that they don't hold on to data that is no longer needed and reduce the costs associated with data storage and management.

By implementing data retention policies for RPA projects, companies can ensure that data is properly managed and used to gain valuable insights into their operations. By retaining data for legal, business, or disposition purposes, companies can optimize their RPA processes and gain a competitive advantage in their industry. We saw how data retention and keeping its history helps in collecting valuable insights into the process, and having a data retention policy complements that effort. Once we have a sufficient amount of data, the next step is to put it to use. That is done through analytics. Let's discuss how analytics can be used on data collected for RPA projects. Data can be analyzed using historical or real-time analytics, helping to make more sense of the process of automation.

Analytics

Analytics can complement RPA in several ways, and together, they can provide businesses with powerful insights into their operations and investments. Here are some ways in which analytics can complement RPA and help businesses get insights into their investment and ROI:

- **Monitoring performance**: Analytics can be used to monitor the performance of RPA processes in real time. By collecting and analyzing data on the performance of RPA bots, businesses can identify areas for improvement and optimize their automation processes.

- **Identifying trends and patterns**: Analytics can be used to identify trends and patterns in data collected by RPA processes. For example, businesses can use analytics to track the frequency and types of errors encountered by RPA bots, which can help them identify areas for improvement and optimize their processes.

- **Measuring ROI**: Analytics can be used to measure the ROI value of RPA investments. By collecting and analyzing data on the cost savings and efficiency gains achieved through RPA, businesses can determine the value of their investment and identify areas where further investment may be warranted.

- **Predictive analytics**: Analytics can be used to forecast the future performance of RPA processes. By using predictive analytics to analyze historical data, businesses can anticipate future trends and identify potential issues before they arise, enabling them to make more informed decisions.

Overall, analytics can provide businesses with valuable insights into their RPA investments and help them optimize their automation processes for maximum efficiency and ROI. By combining RPA with analytics, businesses can gain a competitive advantage in their industry and improve their bottom line.

We talked about all types of reporting and how it can help an RPA project to add value and inform businesses to direct them in the right direction. We saw how reports can provide insight into ROI and the effectiveness of automation. In continuation of this effort, there is another aspect called the active reporting of incidents, which brings issues immediately to the concerned parties. Let's talk about real-time alerts and notifications.

Alerts and notification

Alerts and notifications are critical components of any RPA system. They are used to inform stakeholders of important events or issues that require their attention. Here are some best practices to design an effective alert and notification system in RPA:

- **Define clear criteria**: Before designing an alert and notification system, it's important to define clear criteria for when alerts should be triggered. This can include specific events, thresholds, or errors that require attention. Defining clear criteria ensures that alerts are triggered only when necessary, and stakeholders are not overwhelmed with unnecessary notifications.

- **Establish a priority system**: Not all alerts are created equal. Establishing a priority system for alerts ensures that stakeholders know which alerts are most important and require immediate attention. This can help to ensure that critical issues are addressed promptly and that stakeholders are not distracted by less urgent notifications.

- **Design with stakeholders in mind**: When designing an alert and notification system, it's important to consider the needs of stakeholders. Notifications should be delivered in a timely and effective manner, and stakeholders should have the ability to customize the alerts they receive. This helps ensure that stakeholders are informed in a way that works for them and can take appropriate action when necessary.

- **Make it reusable**: Alert and notification systems are reusable components that can be used across multiple RPA projects. By designing a system that is flexible and adaptable, it can be easily integrated into future projects, reducing development time and costs.

To make the alert and notification system reusable, it's important to document the design and implementation process thoroughly, including the criteria and priority system used. This documentation can be used as a guide for future projects, making it easier to implement the system in new contexts.

To summarize, an effective alert and notification system in RPA should be designed with clear criteria, a priority system, stakeholders' needs in mind, and the potential for reuse in future projects. By following these best practices, businesses can ensure that their RPA systems are monitored effectively and that stakeholders are informed of critical events in a timely and effective manner.

We talked about topics such as reporting, data retention, analytics, and notifications, but that's not all – a **solution architect (SA)** also needs to make sure that the process is resilient, and the goal should be to always discover the unknown. Let us do a deeper dive into the topic.

Resilience and discovering the unknowns in RPA projects

For an SA of an RPA project, ensuring resilience is crucial for the successful implementation and long-term sustainability of a solution. Resilience encompasses the ability of the RPA solution to withstand unforeseen challenges, adapt to changing environments, and recover quickly from potential failures.

To achieve resilience, it is essential to proactively identify and address unknown factors that may arise during the implementation process. In this topic, we will explore strategies to ensure resilience in an RPA project and the approaches to uncovering the unknowns.

Building a resilient RPA solution

Resilience is the key to having robust and stable automation. RPA needs this, as there are so many factors that can break the process. Having resilience can help avoid some of those breaking points:

- **Comprehensive requirements gathering**: To develop a resilient RPA solution, thorough requirements gathering is essential. Engage with stakeholders to understand their pain points, expectations, and objectives. It is crucial to identify any hidden complexities, exception scenarios, and dependencies that could impact the solution's resilience. This phase lays the foundation to create a robust architecture.

- **Scalable and flexible architecture**: Design an architecture that supports scalability and flexibility. This involves considering factors such as load balancing, fault tolerance, and the ability to handle increased volumes of data and processes. By designing a modular and extensible architecture, the RPA solution can adapt to future changes, such as new applications or process variations, without significant rework.

- **Error handling and recovery mechanisms**: Incorporate robust error handling and recovery mechanisms within the RPA solution. Implement techniques such as exception handling, logging, and notifications to proactively identify and address potential failures. Design error recovery mechanisms to minimize the impact of errors and enable a system to recover gracefully.

- **Security and compliance**: Ensure that the RPA solution adheres to security and compliance standards. Implement access controls, encryption, and data protection mechanisms to safeguard sensitive information. Regularly monitor and update security measures to address emerging threats and vulnerabilities.

Discovering the unknowns

There is a limit to what you can learn from the team, SME, and experts who work on the manual process. Here are some things that are visible only when a process or automation runs. This is known as discovering the unknown:

- **Continuous stakeholder engagement**: Engage with stakeholders throughout the RPA project to uncover potential unknowns. Regular meetings, workshops, and discussions help to gather valuable insights, identify hidden requirements, and understand evolving business needs. By maintaining an open line of communication, you can address uncertainties in real time and adapt a solution accordingly.

- **Comprehensive process analysis**: Perform a detailed analysis of the existing processes to uncover potential unknowns. Conduct process walk-throughs, interviews, and observations to identify any undocumented or exceptional scenarios. Analyze historical data and logs to understand patterns, anomalies, and potential failure points. This analysis helps reveal hidden complexities and informs the design of a resilient solution.

- **Proof of Concepts (PoCs) and prototyping**: Utilize PoCs and prototypes to uncover potential unknowns early in the implementation process. By building small-scale versions of the RPA solution, you can test its functionality, integration capabilities, and performance. Feedback from stakeholders during the PoC phase can help identify gaps, refine requirements, and address any unforeseen challenges.

- **Continuous testing and quality assurance**: Implement a rigorous testing and quality assurance process to discover unknown issues. Conduct functional, integration, and regression testing to uncover bugs, edge cases, and performance bottlenecks. Utilize automated testing tools and frameworks to ensure comprehensive test coverage. Encourage user acceptance testing to gather feedback from end users and address any usability or functionality concerns.

- **Monitoring and feedback loops**: Identify areas for improvement, address unforeseen challenges, and enhance the resilience of the RPA solution. Regularly analyze monitoring data and incorporate feedback into the development and maintenance processes.

- **Collaboration with experts and peers**: Engage with experts and peers in the field of RPA to leverage their knowledge and experience. Participate in forums, conferences, and communities to learn from others' experiences, best practices, and lessons learned. Collaborating with experts exposes potential unknowns and provides insights into effective approaches to address them.

- **Continuous learning and adaptation**: Recognize that the discovery of unknowns is an ongoing process. Stay updated with industry trends, emerging technologies, and evolving business requirements. Continuously enhance your knowledge and skills to adapt to new challenges and uncover potential unknowns. Foster a culture of continuous learning within the project team, encouraging innovation and creative problem-solving.

Ensuring resilience in an RPA project requires a proactive approach to address potential unknowns. By building a resilient RPA solution through comprehensive requirements gathering, scalable architecture, robust error handling mechanisms, and adherence to security and compliance standards, you establish a strong foundation. Discovering the unknown involves continuous stakeholder engagement, comprehensive process analysis, PoCs, continuous testing, monitoring, and collaboration with experts. By embracing a mindset of continuous learning and adaptation, you can uncover and address unknowns to enhance the resilience of the RPA solution. A resilient RPA solution enables organizations to navigate uncertainties, adapt to changes, and achieve long-term success in their automation initiatives.

So far, we have talked about all the aspects of RPA and automation projects. We have seen how to design, develop, follow best practices, and manage and maintain a successful RPA project. However, what about post-deployment? Although it is not the direct responsibility of the SA to monitor the RPA project, they might get involved in it during the hyper-care period. This is the period of one to two months post-deployment when solution is in production, where the SA and development team monitors the performance and other aspects of the automation. So, how do we monitor, and why is it crucial in the initial stages? Let's discuss this.

As a solution architect overseeing an RPA project, the period after deploying a new solution in production is critical. During this phase, known as hyper-care, close monitoring of the process is crucial to ensure a smooth transition and address any issues that may arise. This book discusses the importance of monitoring in the initial days of a new RPA implementation in production and explores effective monitoring strategies to maximize the success of the solution.

Monitoring the health

Post-deployment monitoring is a must. This is the hyper-care period when the automation is fragile and tends to break and needs tweaking:

- **Early detection of issues**: Monitoring the RPA process in the initial days of production allows for the early detection of issues and potential bottlenecks. Despite thorough testing and quality assurance during the development phase, unforeseen challenges or edge cases can still arise in a live production environment. Monitoring provides real-time visibility into a system's behavior, enabling prompt identification and resolution of any issues, thereby minimizing their impact on operations and end users.

- **Performance optimization**: Monitoring the newly deployed RPA solution helps evaluate its performance and identify opportunities for optimization. By tracking **key performance indicators** (**KPIs**) such as processing times, error rates, and resource utilization, you can gain insights into potential performance bottlenecks or inefficiencies. This information can then be used to fine-tune the solution, optimize processes, and improve overall efficiency.

- **User experience and adoption**: Monitoring an RPA solution during hyper-care allows you to monitor the user experience and adoption rates. By capturing user feedback and monitoring user interactions, you can identify any usability issues, training gaps, or resistance to change. This insight helps you to tailor training programs, user support, and documentation to enhance user adoption and satisfaction, ensuring a successful transition to the new solution.

- **Compliance and risk mitigation**: Monitoring the RPA process is crucial to ensure compliance with regulatory requirements and mitigate potential risks.

Here are some effective monitoring strategies in hyper-care:

- **Real-time monitoring**: Implement a comprehensive real-time monitoring system that captures critical metrics and events from the RPA solution. This includes monitoring system performance, transaction logs, error logs, and exceptions. Real-time monitoring enables immediate detection of issues, allowing quick response and resolution.

- **Dashboard and alerting**: Develop a centralized dashboard that provides a holistic view of the RPA process. The dashboard should display key metrics, performance indicators, and operational status in a visually intuitive manner. Implement alerting mechanisms to notify stakeholders of any critical events or anomalies that require immediate attention. Alerts can be configured for specific thresholds or predefined conditions, ensuring prompt action when necessary.

- **Error and exception tracking**: Implement a robust error and exception tracking mechanism to capture and log errors and exceptions encountered during the RPA process. This allows in-depth analysis and investigation of the root causes, enabling proactive measures to prevent their recurrence. Additionally, it helps prioritize issue resolution based on their impact on business operations.

- **User feedback and support channels**: Establish channels for users to provide feedback, report issues, and seek assistance. This can include dedicated support email addresses, ticketing systems, or user forums. Regularly review and analyze user feedback to identify common pain points or areas of improvement. Provide timely responses and resolutions to user queries to ensure a positive user experience and foster user adoption.

- **Performance analytics and trend analysis (continued)**: Identify areas of improvement, and proactively address potential issues. By analyzing historical performance data, you can detect gradual degradation or emerging trends that may impact a solution's effectiveness. This information enables proactive measures to maintain optimal performance and identify opportunities for further optimization.

- **Continuous improvement and iterative enhancements**: Use the insights gained from monitoring the RPA solution during hyper-care to drive continuous improvement. Regularly review monitoring data, identify areas for enhancement, and prioritize iterative enhancements based on their impact and feasibility. This iterative approach ensures that the solution evolves and adapts to meet changing business needs, optimizing its performance and value over time.

Monitoring during the hyper-care phase is crucial for the successful implementation of a new RPA solution in production. It enables early detection of issues, optimization of performance, assessment of user experience and adoption, and mitigation of compliance and risk-related concerns. By implementing effective monitoring strategies such as real-time monitoring, dashboard, and alerting systems, error and exception tracking, user feedback channels, and performance analytics, SAs can proactively address challenges, ensure a smooth transition, and continuously improve the RPA solution. Monitoring not only helps identify and resolve issues promptly but also provides valuable insights for ongoing optimization and the long-term success of RPA implementation in a production environment.

One thing that I have personally observed is that we forget to keep the RPA platform updated and upgraded: "If it ain't broke, don't fix it." This doesn't apply to platforms and technologies that continuously evolve and need updates and upgrades from time to time. Let's talk about the general principle and how should we plan for the updates and upgrades.

Updates and upgrades

Upgrading an RPA platform requires careful consideration and planning to ensure a safe transition without disrupting the current environment. To build a safe upgrade strategy and maintain business continuity, the following factors should be kept in mind:

- **Review release notes and documentation**: Thoroughly review the release notes and documentation provided by the RPA platform vendor. Understand the new features, enhancements, bug fixes, and any known issues associated with the upgrade. Assess the relevance of these changes to your specific use cases and determine the potential impact on your current environment.

- **Test the upgrade in a sandbox environment**: Create a sandbox or testing environment that closely resembles your production environment. Perform a trial upgrade in this isolated environment to evaluate the compatibility of the new version with your existing processes, applications, and infrastructure. Test critical workflows, integrations, and dependencies to identify any potential issues or conflicts.

- **Assess compatibility with existing components**: Evaluate the compatibility of the upgraded platform with your existing components, such as operating systems, databases, browsers, and other software dependencies. Ensure that all necessary prerequisites are met and that any potential conflicts or incompatibilities are addressed prior to the upgrade. Consult the platform vendor's compatibility matrix and seek their support if required.

- **Backup and rollback plan**: Before proceeding with the upgrade, ensure that a comprehensive backup of your existing environment is performed. This includes backing up configurations, workflows, scripts, and any other relevant artifacts. Develop a rollback plan that outlines the steps to revert to the previous version if any critical issues or unforeseen complications arise during the upgrade.

- **Prioritize non-disruptive upgrade methods**: Consider upgrade methods that minimize disruptions to ongoing operations. Options such as hot upgrades, where a system remains online during the upgrade process, or phased deployments, where the upgrade is rolled out gradually across different environments or regions, can help maintain business continuity. Evaluate the feasibility of these methods and their impact on your specific environment.

- **Plan for downtime and communication**: If a complete system shutdown or downtime is unavoidable during the upgrade, plan it during a low-impact period, such as weekends or non-peak hours. Communicate the scheduled downtime to all stakeholders, including end users, IT teams, and business units. Provide clear instructions on what to expect, the anticipated duration of the downtime, and any alternative workflows or contingency plans in place.

- **Conduct User Acceptance Testing (UAT)**: Involve end users and SMEs in the UAT process to validate the upgraded platform's functionality, usability, and performance. Create test scenarios that encompass critical use cases and real-world workflows. Encourage users to provide feedback, report any issues, and ensure that their requirements and expectations are met post-upgrade.

- **Monitor and address post-upgrade issues**: After the upgrade, closely monitor the performance, stability, and user feedback of the upgraded platform in the production environment. Establish a feedback mechanism for users to report any issues or concerns. Promptly address and prioritize these issues, providing timely updates, patches, or workarounds as necessary to maintain business continuity.

- **Continuous training and support**: Offer training and support to users, administrators, and developers to ensure a smooth transition, and enable them to leverage the new features and functionalities of the upgraded platform. Provide documentation, tutorials, and user guides to facilitate the adoption of the upgraded version. Offer assistance to address any questions or challenges that arise during the transition.

- **Document and update a business continuity plan**: As part of the upgrade process, document any changes or updates made to the business continuity plan. Include details about the upgraded platform, its dependencies, and recovery procedures if there are any unexpected issues or failures. Communicate the updated plan to relevant stakeholders and ensure that it aligns with the new platform version.

By considering these factors and following a well-structured upgrade strategy, you can minimize risks and ensure a safe upgrade of your RPA platform while maintaining business continuity. Here are additional steps to complete the upgrade process:

- **Conduct a pilot upgrade**: Before rolling out the upgrade to the entire production environment, select a representative subset of processes or applications and perform a pilot upgrade. This allows you to validate the upgrade process and assess its impact on a smaller scale. Gather feedback from users and stakeholders involved in the pilot to address any specific issues or concerns before proceeding with the full upgrade.

- **Perform comprehensive testing**: Execute thorough testing after the upgrade to validate the functionality, performance, and stability of the upgraded platform in the production environment. Test critical workflows, integrations, and system interactions to identify any regression issues or unexpected behavior. Use automated testing tools and manual testing techniques to ensure comprehensive test coverage. Address and resolve any issues or defects discovered during this phase.

- **Implement a phased rollout**: Consider implementing a phased rollout approach to manage the upgrade across different departments, teams, or geographies. By gradually deploying the upgraded platform, you can closely monitor its impact, address any issues that arise, and ensure a controlled transition. Define clear criteria for each phase, such as completing successful testing or user training, before proceeding to the next phase.

- **Communicate and train users**: Effective communication is crucial throughout the upgrade process. Notify all relevant stakeholders, including end users, IT teams, and management, about the upcoming upgrade. Provide clear instructions on how the upgrade will impact their workflows and any necessary training or support resources available to assist them. Conduct training sessions or workshops to familiarize users with the new features and functionalities.

- **Monitor post-upgrade performance**: Continuously monitor the performance and stability of the upgraded platform after the rollout. Implement monitoring tools and analytics to track KPIs, system health, and user feedback. Establish a feedback mechanism where users can report any post-upgrade issues or concerns. Proactively address and resolve these issues to ensure a seamless transition and uninterrupted operations.

- **Document lessons learned**: As the upgrade process concludes, document the lessons learned and best practices discovered throughout the upgrade journey. Capture insights on the challenges faced, the successful strategies employed, and areas for improvement. This documentation will serve as a valuable resource for future upgrades, ensuring a more streamlined and efficient process.

- **Post-upgrade support and maintenance**: Continue providing support and maintenance activities after the upgrade. Address any residual issues, provide bug fixes or patches as necessary, and ensure ongoing support for users. Stay updated with the vendor's release cycles, new patches, and updates to maintain a platform's stability, security, and performance in the long term.

By adhering to these steps and incorporating your business continuity plan, you can confidently upgrade your RPA platform while minimizing disruptions and ensuring the continuity of critical business processes. A well-planned and executed upgrade strategy will enable you to leverage new features, improve performance, and optimize the use of your RPA platform to drive enhanced automation and operational efficiency. Let's discuss the final topic, which is also one of the most important – change management. RPA or automation is introducing a change in the way people work. It will change our day-to-day work routine, which will introduce other changes. Change is inevitable; we need to learn how to embrace it. Managing change in a controlled and systematic manner is what change management is all about. Let's see how it can be done seamlessly.

Change management – enabling seamless and effective transitions

Change management plays a crucial role in the world of RPA, as it helps organizations navigate the complexities associated with implementing and scaling RPA initiatives. This topic outlines the importance of change management in RPA and proposes strategies to ensure the seamless handling of changes throughout the RPA life cycle.

The following list shows the importance of change management in RPA:

- **Minimizing disruption**: RPA implementations often involve significant changes to existing processes, systems, and job roles. Change management methodologies provide structured approaches to mitigate the disruption caused by these changes. By effectively managing the transition, organizations can minimize resistance, optimize user adoption, and maintain business continuity during RPA deployments.

- **Stakeholder engagement and buy-in**: Change management fosters stakeholder engagement and buy-in by involving key stakeholders from the early stages of RPA initiatives. Engaging stakeholders, including business users, IT teams, process owners, and management, allows their input, ensures alignment with organizational goals, and creates a sense of ownership and commitment. This collaboration helps overcome resistance, encourages knowledge sharing, and facilitates successful change implementation.

- **User training and support**: Change management facilitates the development and delivery of comprehensive user training programs. By equipping users with the knowledge and skills required to adapt to the new RPA processes, tools, and interfaces, organizations can enhance user confidence, productivity, and acceptance. Effective training and support reduce errors, accelerate the learning curve, and drive successful RPA adoption.

- **Risk mitigation and compliance**: Change management processes provide frameworks to assess and mitigate risks associated with RPA changes. Proper change management ensures adherence to regulatory and compliance requirements, safeguards data integrity and security, and mitigates potential operational risks. By integrating risk management practices into change management processes, organizations can proactively address potential challenges and maintain a controlled environment.

The following are some strategies to seamlessly handle change in RPA:

- **Establish a change management framework**: Develop a comprehensive change management framework tailored specifically for RPA initiatives. This framework should outline the key stages, roles, responsibilities, and communication channels involved in managing changes throughout the RPA life cycle. Define clear processes for change identification, assessment, approval, implementation, and post-change evaluation.

- **Engage stakeholders early**: Involve stakeholders from the outset of RPA initiatives to gain their support, capture their requirements, and address their concerns. Conduct stakeholder analysis to identify key individuals or groups, establish open lines of communication, and foster a collaborative environment. Regularly communicate the purpose, benefits, and progress of RPA initiatives to keep stakeholders informed and engaged.

- **Conduct impact assessments**: Before implementing changes, perform thorough impact assessments to understand the potential effects on processes, systems, users, and the organization as a whole. Identify potential risks, dependencies, and mitigation strategies. Engage SMEs, process owners, and IT teams to gather insights and validate the impact assessment. This helps to prioritize changes and ensure a smooth transition.

- **Develop comprehensive training programs**: Design and deliver comprehensive training programs to equip users with the knowledge and skills required to adapt to RPA-driven changes. Tailor training materials to different user groups, considering their specific roles and responsibilities. Provide hands-on training, job aids, and user documentation to support users in effectively utilizing an RPA solution. Establish mechanisms for ongoing support and address user queries promptly.

- **Communicate and manage expectations**: Effective communication is essential to manage change seamlessly. Establish clear communication channels to disseminate information, address concerns, and manage expectations throughout the RPA journey. Develop communication plans that outline key messages, target audiences, and timing. Emphasize the benefits of RPA and how it aligns with organizational goals and individual interests. Address potential resistance by proactively addressing concerns, providing transparency, and highlighting success stories and early wins.

- **Pilot testing and feedback**: Conduct pilot testing of RPA changes in a controlled environment before full-scale implementation. Gather feedback from users and stakeholders involved in the pilot to identify any issues, refine processes, and validate the effectiveness of the changes. Incorporate feedback and make necessary adjustments to ensure that the changes align with user requirements and expectations.

- **Change documentation and knowledge sharing**: Document all changes made throughout the RPA life cycle, including process modifications, system integrations, and user roles and responsibilities. Maintain an updated repository of documentation, change logs, and standard operating procedures to facilitate knowledge sharing and enable smooth transitions during personnel changes or future upgrades. Encourage collaboration and information exchange among teams involved in RPA to foster continuous learning and improvement.

- **Monitor and evaluate**: Establish mechanisms to monitor and evaluate the impact of changes implemented through RPA. Track KPIs, user feedback, and operational metrics to assess the effectiveness of the changes. Regularly review the outcomes and identify areas for improvement or refinement. Use this feedback loop to drive continuous improvement and iterate on the RPA solution.

- **Change governance and oversight**: Implement change governance mechanisms to ensure adherence to change management processes and policies. Establish a change control board or committee responsible to review and approve proposed changes. This governance structure provides oversight, ensures compliance, and maintains control over the RPA environment. Regularly review and update change management policies and procedures to align with evolving business needs and best practices.

- **Continuous communication and reinforcement**: Change management is an ongoing process. Continuously communicate the value and benefits of RPA to sustain engagement and support. Reinforce the importance of adhering to established change management processes and policies. Encourage a culture of continuous improvement, where feedback, ideas, and lessons learned are actively sought and shared.

To summarize, change management is essential for successful RPA initiatives, as it helps organizations navigate the complexities of implementing and scaling RPA solutions while minimizing disruption. By establishing a robust change management framework, engaging stakeholders, conducting impact assessments, providing comprehensive training, and fostering effective communication, organizations can seamlessly handle changes throughout the RPA life cycle. Embracing change management practices ensures smooth transitions and user acceptance, ultimately driving the realization of benefits and ROI from RPA investments.

Summary

In this chapter, we discussed various aspects of change management in the context of RPA initiatives. We emphasized the importance of change management in ensuring seamless transitions and maintaining business continuity. Some key points covered include the following:

- The significance of change management in minimizing disruption and resistance during RPA implementations
- The role of stakeholder engagement and buy-in in fostering successful change adoption
- The need for comprehensive user training and support to facilitate the transition to new RPA processes and tools
- The importance of risk mitigation and compliance in change management to ensure data security and operational stability
- Strategies for seamless change handling in RPA, such as establishing a change management framework, conducting impact assessments, and promoting effective communication and feedback
- The value of pilot testing, documentation, and ongoing monitoring and evaluation in ensuring the effectiveness of RPA changes
- The need for continuous improvement and reinforcement of change management practices throughout the RPA life cycle

By implementing these strategies and approaches, organizations can navigate the complexities of RPA implementations, optimize user adoption, and realize the full benefits of automation. Effective change management enables organizations to adapt to RPA-driven changes while minimizing disruption and maximizing the value derived from RPA investments.

Questions

1. What are the key benefits of incorporating change management in RPA initiatives?
2. How can stakeholder engagement contribute to successful change implementation in the context of RPA?
3. What are some strategies to mitigate risks and ensure compliance during RPA change management?
4. How can effective communication help manage expectations and overcome resistance during RPA deployments?
5. Why is it important to conduct impact assessments and pilot testing before implementing changes in RPA?

Epilogue

As we reach the end of this book on becoming an SA, I hope you have gained valuable insights and guidance on embarking upon this rewarding career path. The role of an SA is multifaceted and constantly evolving, demanding a unique combination of technical expertise, strategic thinking, and effective communication skills. It is a role that requires adaptability, continuous learning, and a passion for problem-solving.

Throughout this book, we explored the fundamental principles and practices that can help you become a successful SA. From understanding business requirements to designing scalable and secure solutions, we have delved into various aspects of the role. Remember that while technical knowledge is crucial, it is equally important to develop strong interpersonal skills, enabling you to collaborate effectively with diverse teams and stakeholders.

Becoming an SA is not merely about acquiring certifications or mastering specific technologies. It is about embracing a mindset focused on finding innovative solutions to complex problems, while considering factors such as cost, feasibility, and long-term sustainability. It involves staying up to date with emerging trends and technologies, as well as continuously refining your understanding of business needs and industry dynamics.

As you embark on your journey as an SA, remember that every project is an opportunity for growth and learning. Embrace challenges and setbacks as stepping stones toward improvement, and always seek feedback from your peers and clients to refine your skills. Foster a culture of continuous improvement, and strive to develop a holistic understanding of both technical and business domains.

Lastly, don't forget the importance of collaboration and teamwork. SAs rarely work in isolation; they thrive in an environment where they can leverage the knowledge and expertise of others. Build strong relationships with developers, business analysts, project managers, and other stakeholders, as their insights and perspectives can greatly enhance the quality of your solutions.

In conclusion, I encourage you to embark on this exciting journey with passion, curiosity, and a commitment to lifelong learning. As an SA, you have the opportunity to shape the technological landscape, solve complex problems, and make a meaningful impact on organizations and society as a whole. Embrace the challenges, seize the opportunities, and continue to evolve as an SA.

Thank you for accompanying me on this journey to become an SA. I wish you the very best in your endeavors in the role. May you create innovative and impactful solutions that leave a legacy.

Happy architecting!

Index

`Packtpub.com`

Subscribe to our online digital library for full access to over 7,000 books and videos, as well as industry leading tools to help you plan your personal development and advance your career. For more information, please visit our website.

Why subscribe?

- Spend less time learning and more time coding with practical eBooks and Videos from over 4,000 industry professionals

- Improve your learning with Skill Plans built especially for you

- Get a free eBook or video every month

- Fully searchable for easy access to vital information

- Copy and paste, print, and bookmark content

Did you know that Packt offers eBook versions of every book published, with PDF and ePub files available? You can upgrade to the eBook version at `Packtpub.com` and as a print book customer, you are entitled to a discount on the eBook copy. Get in touch with us at `customercare@packtpub.com` for more details.

At `www.Packtpub.com`, you can also read a collection of free technical articles, sign up for a range of free newsletters, and receive exclusive discounts and offers on Packt books and eBooks.

Other Books You May Enjoy

If you enjoyed this book, you may be interested in these other books by Packt:

UiPath Administration and Support Guide

Arun Kumar Asokan

ISBN: 9781803239088

- Explore the core UiPath Platform design and architecture
- Understand UiPath Platform support and administration concepts
- Get to grips with real-world use cases of UiPath support, DevOps, and monitoring
- Understand UiPath maintenance and reporting
- Discover best practices to enable UiPath operations scaling
- Understand the future trends in UiPath platform and support activities

Intelligent Automation with IBM Cloud Pak for Business Automation

Allen Chan, Kevin Trinh, Guilhem Molines, Suzette Samoojh, Stephen Kinder

ISBN: 9781801814775

- Understand key IBM automation technologies and learn how to apply them

- Cover the end-to-end journey of creating an automation solution from concept to deployment

- Understand the features and capabilities of workflow, decisions, RPA, business applications, and document processing with AI

- Analyze your business processes and discover automation opportunities with process mining

- Set up content management solutions that meet business, regulatory, and compliance needs

- Understand deployment environments supported by IBM Cloud Pak for Business Automation

Democratizing RPA with Power Automate Desktop

Peter Krause

ISBN: 9781803245942

- Master RPA with Power Automate Desktop to commence your debut flow
- Grasp all essential product concepts such as UI flow creation and modification, debugging, and error handling
- Use PAD to automate tasks in conjunction with the frequently used systems on your desktop
- Attain proficiency in configuring flows that run unattended to achieve seamless automation
- Discover how to use AI to enrich your flows with insights from different AI models
- Explore how to integrate a flow in a broader cloud context

Packt is searching for authors like you

If you're interested in becoming an author for Packt, please visit `authors.packtpub.com` and apply today. We have worked with thousands of developers and tech professionals, just like you, to help them share their insight with the global tech community. You can make a general application, apply for a specific hot topic that we are recruiting an author for, or submit your own idea.

Share Your Thoughts

Now you've finished *RPA Solution Architect's Handbook*, we'd love to hear your thoughts! Scan the QR code below to go straight to the Amazon review page for this book and share your feedback or leave a review on the site that you purchased it from.

`https://packt.link/r/1803249609`

Your review is important to us and the tech community and will help us make sure we're delivering excellent quality content.

Download a free PDF copy of this book

Thanks for purchasing this book!

Do you like to read on the go but are unable to carry your print books everywhere? Is your eBook purchase not compatible with the device of your choice?

Don't worry, now with every Packt book you get a DRM-free PDF version of that book at no cost.

Read anywhere, any place, on any device. Search, copy, and paste code from your favorite technical books directly into your application.

The perks don't stop there, you can get exclusive access to discounts, newsletters, and great free content in your inbox daily

Follow these simple steps to get the benefits:

1. Scan the QR code or visit the link below

https://packt.link/free-ebook/9781803249605

2. Submit your proof of purchase
3. That's it! We'll send your free PDF and other benefits to your email directly

www.ingramcontent.com/pod-product-compliance
Lightning Source LLC
Chambersburg PA
CBHW062112050326

40690CB00016B/3292